THE PROFESSIONAL HELPER

ABOUT THE AUTHOR

Willie V. Bryan is Professor Emeritus, Health Promotion Sciences, University of Oklahoma Health Sciences Center. Dr. Bryan was an administrator and professor at the University of Oklahoma Health Sciences Center for 32 years. In 1985, he received the President's Committee on Employment of the Handicapped Book Award for *Psychosocial Aspects of Disability,* which he co-authored. Before his services at The University of Oklahoma, he served as a Vocational Rehabilitation counselor for the State of Oklahoma and also served as Director of Rehabilitation and Personnel for Goodwill Industries of Oklahoma City. Dr. Bryan has a master's degree in psychology, with an emphasis on rehabilitation counseling, another master's degree in education, and a doctorate in counseling. He currently teaches courses on cultural diversity, helping relationships, psychosocial aspects of disabilities, nonprofit management, problems of professional helpers, and family counseling for the Colleges of Liberal Studies and Advanced Programs, University of Oklahoma, Norman Campus. Dr. Bryan has received an Outstanding Teaching Award and a Superior Teaching Award from the University of Oklahoma.

Second Edition

THE PROFESSIONAL HELPER

The Fundamentals of Being a Helping Professional

By

WILLIE V. BRYAN, Ed.D.

CHARLES C THOMAS • PUBLISHER, LTD.
Springfield • Illinois • U.S.A.

Published and Distributed Throughout the World by

CHARLES C THOMAS • PUBLISHER, LTD.
2600 South First Street
Springfield, Illinois 62704

©2015 by CHARLES C THOMAS • PUBLISHER, LTD.

ISBN 978-0-398-09085-2 (Paper)
ISBN 978-0-398-09086-9 (Ebook)

First Edition, 2009
Second Edition, 2015

Library of Congress Catalog Card Number: 2015022593

With THOMAS BOOKS *careful attention is given to all details of manufacturing
and design. It is the Publisher's desire to present books that are satisfactory as to their
physical qualities and artistic possibilities and appropriate for their particular use.*
THOMAS BOOKS *will be true to those laws of quality that assure a good name
and good will.*

Printed in the United States of America
CR-R-3

Library of Congress Cataloging-in-Publication Data

Bryan, Willie V.
 The professional helper : the fundamentals of being a helping profession-
al / by Willie V. Bryan, ED.D. -- Second Edition.
   pages cm
 Revised edition of the author's The professional helper, 2009.
 Includes bibliographical references and indexes.
 ISBN 978-0-398-09085-2 (pbk.) -- ISBN 978-0-398-09086-9 (ebook)
 1. Counseling. 2. Social service. 3. Human services. I. Title
 BF636.6.B79 2015
 158.3--dc23
                                                    2015022593

This book is dedicated to the many students I have taught and will teach; they keep me motivated.

PREFACE

The first edition of *The Professional Helper* discussed characteristics of an effective helper which included understanding self as well as understanding various components of a client's life that can have impacts upon the helping professional's ability to be successful in assisting the client. In the second edition, I have added information with regard to some of the major issues the United States has encountered, and to some degree successfully overcome with the involvement of the helping professional. Additionally, this second edition projects into the future of the United States' human relations with regard to some of the issues the nation will encounter and need the assistance of helping professionals.

The second edition of *The Professional Helper* is divided into three parts. Part I covers personal skills that a helper should possess. Additionally, Part I discusses some of the understandings one must have in order to be an effective helper.

Part II of the second edition discusses some of the human relations evolutions the United States has gone through and the impact these have had on American society. Stated in other terms, the United States has attempted, and in many situations, has been successful in making progress toward being a more inclusive nation. Considerable credit for the improvement in human relationships can be credited to helping professionals' advocacy for more equal opportunities and fairness in the American society. Additionally, Part II discusses future evolutions that are needed, and the role helping professionals can play in achieving success in making the United States a more inclusive nation.

Part III of the second edition provides information with regard to psychological theories of several individual and family therapies. This information is provided to help professional helpers understand several theories and therapies that if understood and utilized will increase their chances of being successful in assisting clients better understand their issues thus leading to acceptable resolution to those issues. Additionally, the discussions of the theories are provided to assist the helpers to develop their own professional approaches to helping clients.

W.V.B.

CONTENTS

THE PROFESSIONAL HELPER

Part I

ESSENTIAL UNDERSTANDING FOR HELPING PROFESSIONALS

Chapter 1

THE PROFESSIONAL HELPER

Chapter Outline
- Introduction
- Kinds of Helping Relationships
- Characteristics of an Effective Helper
  - Effective Communicator
  - Effective Listener
  - Integrity
  - Ethical
  - Motivator
  - Compassionate
  - Self-Awareness and Self-Confidence
  - Patient
  - Available
  - Awareness of Cultural Differences
  - Possesses Understanding of Human Behavior
  - Possesses Understanding of Resources
  - Possesses Understanding of Family Dynamics
- Summary
  - References

Chapter Objectives
- Provide a basic understanding of various kinds of helping relationships
- Provide a basic understanding of the characteristics an effective helper must possess

INTRODUCTION

One of the oldest human acts is helping or assisting other beings. Helping in the early stages of human existence was perhaps a purely selfish act–selfish in that it was a means of survival. Each individual within the group needed the help and support of the other members to meet their daily needs. Over the centuries, helping has remained a selfish act and at the same time has evolved into a benevolent act of assisting others with regard to functioning in sometimes complicated social environments. The act of helping also has remained selfish in that virtually all helping, unless the helping is a forced act, still answers some psychological human needs, such as recognition, feelings of being needed, and meets some spiritual and/or social responsibilities, and the list could continue. Despite the self-serving aspect of helping, the act of assisting others remains essential to the survival of the human race. Without feelings of concern and compassion for the needs of other humans, one can easily understand that the world would have little, if any, order. There is no doubt that imbedded within the human spirit is the desire to survive; along with this need is the desire to share our lives with like-minded individuals. Given this connection of the human spirits, helping others to meet their survival needs becomes one of the basic human building blocks of an orderly society.

In this book, the terms *helper* and *counselor* are used interchangeably. Also, the term *helper* refers to numerous other helpers, such as social workers, case managers, and rehabilitation specialists, to mention only three. Likewise, the terms *helpee*, *client*, and *patient* are also used interchangeably.

As previously stated, helping is as old as human existence; everyone needs help, and, to some extent, everyone provides assistance to others. Therefore, there are various forms of helping, including informal and formal, as well as nonprofessional and professional. What has primarily been discussed in this text is professional helping.

As professional helpers, we have to be cognizant of the importance of our work and the impact our work can have on the lives of those, whom for whatever reason, engage us as helpers. Some helpees go to professional helpers because their situations, from their viewpoint, have gone beyond their abilities to control. They may have sought the advice of family and friends, but find that the situation has not significantly improved. They may have engaged in a variety of activities attempting to eliminate the worry involved in their life situation, but have not received the desired relief. Generally speaking, they are emotionally hurting and/or experiencing emotional stress and are expecting some relief. The point being made is that when helpees come to a professional helper, whether as self-referrals or otherwise, they need help.

As patients or clients seek help from a medical or legal professional, they look to him or her as professionals qualified to meet their needs. These types of expectations are no less true when a helpee seeks, or is referred to a professional helper. Therefore, it is incumbent on the professional helper to be prepared to meet the reasonable expectations of the helpee or those who have referred the person. This does not mean that the professional helper has to be a miracle worker and be able to solve any and all types of problems that helpees present. Obviously, this is unrealistic. However, the helper must be prepared to provide the best professional and ethical services possible. Consequently, this means that, as a professional helper, you must prepare yourself first by understanding yourself—understanding your emotions, your motivations, your attitudes and prejudices, and your attitudes about various life situations that helpees bring to the helping relationship. Second, as a helping professional, you must have a sound understanding of human behavior—to be more specific, you must have an understanding of the various ways that human behavior is motivated. Third, you must have some theoretical understanding of how to conduct the helping relationship from the standpoint of process, establishment of goals and objectives, and implementation of the same. Finally, incorporated in all of the steps and process has to be adherence to ethical standards that protect the rights of the helpee.

The helper must have prepared him or herself for this most important profession because a great deal is at stake. The results of most professional helping relationships go beyond easing or eliminating the emotional stress of the helpee—in many cases, the results impact family relationships and the ability to adequately interact with friends, coworkers, and other acquaintances. Certainly, the impacts go far beyond the immediate moments.

The helping professional has to view him or herself as one who is helping the helpee meet his or her potentials as a human being, thus being able to make positive contributions to the society in which he or she lives. There can be no more noble cause than this.

KINDS OF HELPING RELATIONSHIPS

Following the theme of an orderly society, we frequently classify helping as informal or formal. Informal implies a nonprofessional, nontherapeutic relationship, although this definition is not totally accurate. An act of helping one's friend rearrange furniture in her home, although not a professional helping relationship, can be therapeutic from the standpoint of helping relieve some of the friend's stress of putting some order to her immediate surroundings. Okun (2002) identifies informal helping relationships as help occurring when the helping relationship is secondary to another relationship. Professor Okun continues her explanation of helping relationships by explaining that "formal helping situations are ones in which the helper/helpee roles are stated or implied by positions or contact and the specific reason for contact is known to be for the provision of some kind of help" (p. 30).

In an effort to further dissect the helping relationship, we can view the relationship from the perspective of whether it is a professional helping relationship or a nonprofessional relationship. A professional helping relationship is one in which a person is academically trained in the sciences of understanding human behavior, understanding one's own motivations and psychological needs, as well as trained in the arts of effective communication and managing various complexities of human interaction, such as stress management and other personality disorders to mention only two. One could further dissect the helping relationship by identifying paraprofessionals and nonprofessional relationships. Paraprofessionals are generally considered as persons who have a lesser degree of training than professional helpers. Although they may not have the academic degrees, professional credentials, and/or the intensity of training as the professional helper, skillful paraprofessionals make significant contributions to the field of helping. Identifying the helper from the perspective of whether they are professional, paraprofessional, or nonprofessional is risky, in that there are several variables to consider when evaluating the type of service being performed. Offered as examples, if one views the service from the standpoint of academic credentials, the professional helper may have the academics but lack intensity and depth of training. Conversely, the person may not have the academic credentials but possess life experiences as well as years of practical experience in dealing with certain types of situations. Former substance abusers who become substance abuse counselors come to mind with regard to this example.

Although some texts attempt to classify helpers by certain professions and/or academic and license/certification (and they have the right to make those distinctions) this text is more concerned with identifying the qualities, both personal and professional, that the helper should have to be an effective helper. Stated in other terms, I am more concerned with identifying and discussing some of the fundamental characteristics, qualities, and understandings that a helper must possess to help his or her clients effectively deal with life situations.

CHARACTERISTICS OF AN EFFECTIVE HELPER

The anatomy of a helping relationship is a simple one: the person or persons seeking or needing help, the person or persons attempting to provide help, and the situation or situations that bring the helpee and helper together. Although the makeup of a helping relationship is relatively simple, the human interaction within the helping process can be anything but simple. Chapter 3 discusses the importance of the helper understanding him or herself, and Chapter 4 discusses the helper understanding human behavior. Within this chapter, there is discussion of some qualities a helper must possess to be effective in the process of being a helper.

Brammer and MacDonald (2003) have pointed out that "the personal qualities of helpers are significant for positive growth of helpee as are the methods they use" (p. 26). They continue by stating that an effective helper has self-perceptions and traits distinct from non-helpers, such as identification with people rather than things, adequate capacity to cope with problems rather than lack of problem-solving ability, and more self-revelation and willingness to be themselves than self-concealing.

Professional competency and personal integrity are undeniable traits that a helper must have to be effective as a professional helper;

these are traits the ensure the psychological and emotional well-being
of the helpee. The best training that one may receive from competent
counseling training programs, social work programs, and case management programs, to mention only three helping professional training programs, does not guarantee competent professionals. The professional helper must be dedicated to assisting the client resolve his or
her problems. There are two points of which to take note from the previous statement: The helper must be **dedicated**, and the helper must
assist in helping solve the client's problem(s). With regard to dedication, one might think that no one goes into a helping profession if he
or she is not committed to being a force for positive change. I acknowledge that most helpers enter into the profession for the correct
reasons; however, under pressure such as workload, criticism from superiors, and/or public officials and sometimes the general public, as
well as resistance from clients, professionalism and integrity may temporarily take a back seat to convenience.

Unless the helper is working in a private practice, control over her
working environment may be difficult. One must remember the vast
majority of professional helpers work within environments other than
private practice. When the previously mentioned situations occur, and
they will, the professional helper must maintain his resolve of maintaining an attitude that promotes doing what is best for his client(s).
Some may comment that this is an easier statement to make than a
promise to fulfill. This quite often is true; however, through complete,
careful, and accurate documentation of case files, most criticism can
be appropriately handled. Confidentiality of clients' records may ham-
per full disclosure of information to the public and some public officials; however, the helper's superiors will be able to understand actions taken or not taken. As far as public criticism, although certainly
not enjoyable, sometimes criticism goes with the territory of being a
professional helper.

With regard to the second point of assisting in problem solutions, it
is tempting and quite often a good feeling to think that as the helper
you solved a problem for a helpee. However, the helper should not be
the problem solver; rather, she should be in the position of assisting
the clients with finding and implementing solutions to their problems.
The professional helper should be a teacher, a mentor, a motivator,
and a guide to assisting the helpee find solutions to his or her life situations. As is discussed later in this book, most clients have within

themselves the answers to most, if not all, of their life situations. Quite often what they need is someone to assist them in sifting through and evaluating the various possible responses to the situation. In some cases, clients are so overwhelmed by the situation they are unable to think clearly enough to recognize possible solutions that are literally in front of them. In other cases, clients may be fearful of venturing into uncharted territory, fearing they will make mistakes and/or make matters worse.

Effective Communicator

Communication is a key ingredient that will help determine whether the helping relationship is a success or failure. Virtually all aspects of the helping relationship depends on communication between the helper and the helpee. Although the previous statement is an expression of the obvious, the real fact is that we tend to overlook the various ways we communicate. Quite often we think of communication as being verbal interaction; however, according to researchers such as Birdwhistell (1970) and Mehrabian and Wiener (1967), as much as 80% of our communication is nonverbal. Therefore, much of our interaction in a helping relationship involves such actions as body posture and facial expressions, or lack thereof, to mention only two.

It is essential that the professional helper master the art of effectively communicating nonverbally as well as verbally. Also, the helper must be equally skilled at understanding the client's verbal and nonverbal communication.

With regard to effective communication, it is one thing to recognize various forms of communication; however, understanding and being comfortable with various expressions of communication is another concern. For example, understanding and being comfortable with clients' silence is important. Some helpers begin to feel discomfort when a client becomes silent. Some helpers tend to feel that every moment within the helping relationship should be filled with conversation, and unfortunately when there is silence they interject words to fill the perceived void. Experienced helpers who are comfortable with silence and recognize the possible benefit of this silence will allow a reasonable period of time to pass and, if the silence continues, may remind the client that he or she has ceased talking and inquire what the helpee thinks his or her silence means. Stated in other terms, the helper should recognize that silence in the session has meaning; therefore, rushing in with his, the helper's, conversation may relieve the client of having to explain what is or is not causing the silence. It is important that the helper recognize silence as another form of communication.

Effective Listener

When I was in graduate school, my professors and some of the textbooks on counseling and interviewing emphasized listening with the third ear. The point was to listen for meaning more than the actual words that were being emitted. Stated in other terms, the authors and professors were saying to listen for hidden meaning–meanings that transcended the spoken words. Although I knew the pearls of wisdom these professionals were imparting to we aspiring helping professionals were important, as a beginning counselor I did not realize the difficulty involved in carrying through with this advice. Beginning helping professionals often experience difficulty with regard to maintaining attention to what is being said while attempting to observe body language, listen for underlying meanings, take notes mentally or physically, think of the next appropriate response, as well as attempt to demonstrate to the helpee a serious degree of being fully present while she is discussing her immediate concerns. Without questions, being effective with regard to listening to all aspects of the client's conversation is a difficult balancing act, but nonetheless an essential one. The helper can fake some aspects of being a good listener and perhaps fool the helpee into believing that he is being fully attentive while she, the helpee, is talking; however, in so doing, the helper is cheating the helpee with regard to being able to provide the most appropriate assistance he can provide. It is debatable whether the helper is being unethical, but there is no question with regard to the fact that the helper is cheating himself with respect to growing as a professional helper.

Given the complexities of being an effective listener, a relevant question is: "How does one become an effective listener? There are no easy answers to this question. Experienced professional helpers will acknowledge that, as they look back over their careers, they cannot identify at which point they began to feel comfortable with listening with the third ear. Stated more succinctly, they have difficulty identifying at which point they began to incorporate the many aspects of effective listening. The best answer that I and other experienced professional helpers can give is that with dedication to improving one's listening skills and considerable practice, one will achieve positive results as a skilled listener.

Although it is difficult to precisely define how and when one **becomes an effective listener**, the following are some suggestions that will help:

1. Ask questions. Listening does not always mean being silent. By asking for clarification with regard to things the helpee is saying, one will get a clearer understanding of what one is hearing. Considerable information can be lost by assuming understanding of what is being said. Seeking clarification aids the helper with regard to listening to underlying meanings of the messages being verbally expressed. Also asking questions demonstrates to the helpee that the helper is interested and attentive to what is being said, thus the flow of information may increase.

2. Observe body language. Notice the level of comfort the client exhibits as he speaks. Being uncomfortable in a helping setting is a natural reaction for the helpee; however, careful observation of the level of discomfort as the helpee speaks can provide clues with regard to significant or sensitive information. To be more specific, by recognizing when the helpee's discomfort level goes beyond the normal or baseline discomfort, an astute helper can identify when the conversation of the helpee ventures into sensitive territory.

3. Listen for logic in the helpee's conversation. It is normal for clients to become nervous and forget facts as well as get confused in discussing some issues. However, being confused and illogical are often two different acts. When clients began to leave out relevant facts and the information being presented does not tie together, or does not make sense, this is often an indication that the client is more than confused. Quite often this means that the client, for a variety of possible reasons, is trying to avoid discussing significant issues. Carefully listening to the client's conversation will aid in making this observation.

4. Listen to the client's tone of voice. Change in the tone of voice often means that the client has significant emotional attachment to what is being discussed. This should be a signal to the helper that additional attention should be given to the topic. Because this indicates an increase in the emotional level, the helper should be careful with regard to exploring the issues. This doesn't mean *not* to explore the issues; rather, it means to carefully process information or lack thereof.

5. Listen to determine whether the helpee takes any responsibility for her actions. As human beings, we are not responsible for others' behavior. However, we are responsible for our own behavior, thus the helper should listen to determine whether the helpee takes responsibility or blames others for the situation. It may be true that others have significant responsibility for some or all of the issues being discussed; however, blaming others, generally speaking, does not solve problems. Taking responsibility for one's own actions goes a long way toward resolutions to significant life issues. Taking responsibility for one's behavior, as previously stated, is important; however, the helper also has to be aware of some client's tendencies to become martyrs and take responsibility for others' behavior. Just as avoiding responsibility for one's own behavior meets some psychological need, the helper must realize that assuming responsibility for others' actions also meets a psychological need. Therefore, in the case of the martyr, it is important to understand why he is assuming undeserved responsibility and help him understand what he is doing and why.

6. Listen to the client's responses to your questions. How the client responds to questions can provide considerable information with regard to how willing the client is to put forth efforts to solve the issues. If a helper consistently hears the helpee refer to others as the ones to deal with the issues, this should be a flag alerting him to the fact that he must work with the client to accept her share of the responsibilities in solving the problems.

Integrity

One may be tempted to think that listing integrity as a characteristic of an effective helper is too simplistic, thus promoting the following questions: Don't all helping professionals have the best interests of their clients as their number one priority when engaging in the helping process? Don't most, if not all, helping professionals enter this profession with the purest of thoughts? My answer to these rhetorical questions is, for the majority of helping professionals, a resounding yes! However, one must look at the nature of the business in which we function. Clients come to us with personal issues, some emotionally charged and others that may seem to be much less sensitive (regardless of what we consider the sensitivity level, the issue generally is significantly important to the client). The helper may be professional. However, first he is human, and as humans we are curious and quite often nosy. Curiosity is a good trait for a helper, but problems occur with regard to how we use the information. To be more specific, how we use the information outside the helping setting is the issue. Sharing this information with family members is inappropriate, but it is sometimes done. Also interesting and spicy client information should never become conversation pieces at cocktail parties and other social settings.

The helping professional should keep his professional life separate from his personal life. Helpees do not come to a helper expecting to be ridiculed because of the nature of their problems, nor do they enter the helping relationship to have their problems and issues discussed by the helper to family and friends. The professional helper must have the best interests of the helpee as his primary concern at all times.

Ethical

Most national helping organizations have ethical standards and ethical codes of conduct to which they insist their members adhere. Brammer and MacDonald (2003) have pointed out that helpers' ethical behavior is guided by community standards and practices, moral expectations based on cultural patterns or religious beliefs, and local, state, and federal laws. Ethical standards provide the professional helper with guidelines to follow as he assists his clients. Some of the areas covered by ethical standards for helping professionals are guidelines with regard to: (a) issues of multiple relationships, (b) informing helpers of their rights, (c) physical and/or sexual contact, (d) confidentiality, (e) helper competence and limitations, and (f) nondiscrimination. There are other areas that address ethical standards; therefore, professional helpers should consult the agency and/or organization for which they work for a list of those ethical standards. Additionally, professional helpers should consult professional organizations for ethical standards by which they expect their members to govern themselves.

Motivator

To be an effective helper, one must be a motivator, and part of being a motivator means being motivated to help others. Professional helpers may become motivated to help for a variety of reasons. Some are motivated for humanitarian reasons, wanting to improve the lives of others and diminish distress and suffering. Others may be motivated for the previously mentioned reasons and also are motivated to help to meet some of his internal needs, such as recognition from peers, family, and community. Whatever the reasons, to be effective and have maximum positive impact, the helper must exhibit an internal and external passion for assisting others to deal with their life situations.

Compassionate

Being compassionate means the helper is open, honest, and understanding with regard to the helpee's issues and life situations. Being compassionate also means that the helper can work with the helpee and not be overly judgmental. Stated in other terms, the helper is able to be empathic with the client's problems. This does not mean that the helper has to condone and/or agree with the client's behavior. However, empathy allows the helper to get as close to the client's emotional level as possible, thus creating a bond of trust that will aid in information sharing and discovery of solutions to the life situations being encountered.

Being compassionate also means being caring but maintaining a professional emotional distance. As a professional helper, one should not become too emotionally involved with client's issues. Objectivity of opinions and dispensation of information become compromised when one becomes too emotionally involved. Additionally, one risks crossing ethical lines by becoming emotionally involved.

Self-Awareness and Self-Confidence

To be an effective helper, one must have a high level of self-awareness and self-confidence, as well as a good understanding of her strengths, weaknesses, prejudices, and things about which she feels strongly, either pro or con. Self-awareness assists the helper in understanding her idiosyncratic views and actions. This understanding makes taking responsibility for her beliefs and actions much easier, hopefully not allowing the helper to deny and/or overlook her limitations. Confidence in one's abilities helps the helper to project a sense of leadership to the helpee, as well as display feelings of comfort in assisting the client. Self-confidence helps the helper establish strong boundaries within the helping relationship that assist in developing and maintaining the professional distance necessary for an ethical and effective helping relationship. If the helper is confident in his professional and personal relationship skills, she will not slip into the habit of trying to always please the client, especially when sensitive discussion occurs and there is a need for direct and forthright opinions to be expressed.

An additional component of self-confidence is to love oneself. Professional helpers must care deeply about themselves—their abilities as both an ordinary human being and as a professional who has chosen as his profession to be a helper. To be effective at helping and caring for others and their problems, one must care passionately about oneself and have a good prospective with regard to his life situations. The professional helper must be content with whom he is before he can make someone else content. This fact is important because, without personal contentment, focusing on someone else's life issues becomes difficult. Stated in other terms, if the helper is going through his own problems, he may have difficulty giving his undivided attention to his client's problems. Granted, this can be easier said than done because, although we are professional helpers, we are human beings first. Considering this reality, we will have personal problems, and unfortunately some will occur during the process of helping a client. Professional helpers must learn to separate their personal lives from their professional lives; when this appears not to be possible, helpers must move away from the helping relationship and refer the helpee to someone else.

Patient

The professional helper must be patient and allow the client the psychological space to think through his life issues and the options available to him. As a professional helper, it may be tempting to provide too much help, especially in the area of developing options to apply to pressing problems. Sometimes the saying of "not being able to see the forest for the trees" is applicable when working with clients. What may seem obvious to the helper may not appear on the client's mental radar. As a professional helper, one must remember the helping relationship is not about you as the helper but about the client learning to develop appropriate methods of reaching insight into his life issues. The helping relationship is as much about empowering the helpee with regard to developing skills to solve future problems as it is about solving current problems. Therefore, the helper must be patient and allow the client to explore and, in the process, develop methods of solving problems that will not only resolve the current issues but can be used in helping solve future problems.

Available

Almost everyone who has to be seen by a physician more than once has experienced the frustration of delays in obtaining an appointment. Clients who need to have an appointment with a professional helper at a time or times other than regularly scheduled appoints should be able to see their helper within a reasonable period of time. Just as physicians make concerted efforts to see patients who have emergencies in a timely fashion, the professional helper should also make a similar effort. Having made this declaration, I must point out that availability can be a double-edged sword, in that the helper can be too available–too available in the sense that the client becomes dependent on the helper to resolve all of his personal issues, many of which could be handled by the client if he would venture away from his comfort zone, the professional helper, and do some personal problem solving. The professional helper has to know his client and the client's problem-solving skills as well as his emotional state to determine when the helpee needs help. There is no formula anyone can provide with regard to the helper making the decision of when to intercede; therefore, the situation becomes a judgment call.

Awareness of Cultural Differences

The professional helper must realize that for most situations there is a variety of ways to perceive those situations; therefore, in many situations, there are an equal number of solutions to the situation. Thus, the helper's view of the situation and subsequent ideas of how to solve the problem may not be the Holy Grail for which the client is seeking. There may be numerous acceptable solutions to a situation, and the solution or solutions acceptable to the client may be impacted by her cultural views. Therefore, it is imperative that the professional helper become sensitive to cultural differences. It is impossible to know all things with regard to all cultural issues, but it is possible to be sensitive enough to allow for different ideas and patterns of thoughts other than your own. The following insightful comments by Drennan (2007) provide an eloquent explanation of the importance of being sensitive to cultural differences:

> An effective helper must be tolerant, knowledgeable, and equipped to assist individuals outside their own ethnic group. Each client should be regarded as an individual with a distinct history, social, and familial environment that may or may not be related to the client's reason for requesting help. Therefore, a helper must not assume a universal broad-spectrum approach, but rather must adapt her helping methods to reflect the specific needs of each autonomous individual. It is essential that a helper listen and be attentive to a client's non-verbal behavior to identify problems; a dilemma that would normally be of no consequence in one culture might be considered a crisis in another.

More discussion of cultural awareness is provided in **Chapter 5** (this volume).

Possesses Understanding of Human Behavior

To be successful in most life ventures, it is imperative that one has a well-thought-out plan of action. Similarly, to be an effective professional helper, one must have a basic helping plan of action supported by a theory or concepts of what motivates human behavior. Recognizing inappropriate behavior is not sufficient to ensure a successful helping relationship. The professional helper must have a concept of what motivates inappropriate behavior as well as an understanding what causes humans to react in the variety of ways we react.

As is discussed in Chapters 12 and 13 (this volume), prominent psychological theorists put forth their views on motivating factors that influence human behavior, and they use their theories of human behavior to guide their goals for therapy and the techniques of therapy to impact clients' behavior. Each of the theorists discussed in the previously mentioned chapter, as well as others not mentioned, have differing views with regard to what motivates human behavior, and each to varying degrees is successful. This means that there is not one answer to the question of what motivates human behavior but several, perhaps many, answers to this important question.

For the professional helper to be effective, she must study human behavior through observations and readings and hopefully be mentored by an experienced helper in order to develop a theory or concept of human behavior with which she is comfortable in applying to working with clients. Hopefully, over a period of time, she will develop her own beliefs with regard to human behavior and through application refine her theory so that it is her approach to helping, not a copy of a prominent theorist and/or mentor. Once her theory is sufficiently developed, she will hopefully be able to develop effective goals and techniques that are extensions of her theory.

A detailed discussion of **understanding human behavior** is provided in Chapter 4 (this volume). The previous discussion was designed to emphasize the necessity of professional helpers developing their own theory of human behavior if they want to be effective.

Possesses Understanding of Resources

Knowledge of appropriate resources is one of the most important things a professional helper can possess, especially if he is a social worker, case manager, or community organizer, to mention only three. Most helpees come to a professional helper with specific needs and expectations. Many of those needs relate to community and other resources. Knowledge of resources and being able to connect the helpee with the appropriate agency or persons to supply those resources can be one of the most helpful things the helper can do for his clients. As discussed in Chapter 8 (this volume), rarely does the helper have knowledge of the variety of resources available in a large community; however, it is imperative that the helper develop a file of resources and keep the file updated. Additionally, as much as possible, keep in touch with resources so you are on a first-name basis with the potential helpers. See Chapter 8 for more information with regard to **understanding resources**.

Possesses Understanding of Family Dynamics

Most, if not all, issues with which a helpee needs professional assistance do not occur in a vacuum; they occur as a result of interactions with others and, generally speaking, will have an impact on other people. In many cases, those who are impacted are family members. Therefore, it is important that professional helpers have an understanding of family dynamics. With the following comments, Benokraitis (1996) adequately describes the important role the family plays in family members' lives: "The family remains a critical primary group that provides its members with love, understanding, security, acceptance, and companionship through intimate, long-term, face-to-face interaction. The family is also expected to support its member in times of psychological crises and emotional stress" (p. 6).

Given the significant roles the family and its members play in times of stress and other factors that cause disequilibrium in one's life, being aware of how to utilize the family as a resource can be of critical importance. Similarly, in some cases, because of family dynamics, it may be imperative to minimize family influence and impact. Certainly, knowing when and how to intervene is also important.

Being aware of how families communicate, such as who communicates with whom and under what conditions the communication occurs, is vitally important. Equally important is knowledge of the family structure and how this structure impacts the relationships of the various family members, including the helpee who is in need of your professional assistance. These and other issues of family dynamics are discussed in detail in Chapter 13 (this volume).

SUMMARY

In summary, the previously mentioned characteristics are essential qualities that a helper must possess to be effective. Additionally, these characteristics help make the helper a professional, regardless of whether the helper has no college degrees or has a doctoral degree.

Chapter Review Questions

1. Name three (3) characteristics of an effective helper discussed in this chapter and explain how these characteristics help make the professional helper become more effective.
2. What does listening with the third ear mean?
3. Why is understanding a helpee's nonverbal communication important in a helping relationship?
4. Why is listening for logic in a helpee's conversation important?
5. What are ethics and how do ethical standards impact a helping relationship profession?

Mental Exercise

1. List ethical standards by which you believe a helping professional should conduct his or her professional practice.
2. List at least five reasons that you think you will make an effective helper.
3. List at least five weaknesses you will need to improve to make you an effective helper.
4. List reasons that you want to or do not want to become a professional helper.

References

Benokraitis, N. V. (1996). *Marriage and families: Changes, choices and constraints.* Upper Saddle River, NJ: Prentice-Hall.

Birdwhistell, R. L. (1970). *Kinesics and content.* Philadelphia: University of Pennsylvania Press.

Brammer, L., & MacDonald, G. (2003). *The helping relationship: Process and skills* (8th ed.). Boston. Allyn & Bacon.

Drennan, A. (2007). Unpublished paper, University of Oklahoma.

Mehrabian, A., & Wiener, M. (1967). Decoding inconsistent messages. *Journal of Personality and Social Psychology, 6,* 109–114.

Okun, B. F. (2002). *Effective helping: Interviewing and counseling techniques* (6th ed.). Florence, KY: Brooks/Cole.

Suggested Readings

Carkhuff, R. (1983). *The art of helping* (5th ed.). Amherst, MA: Human Resources Development Press.

Loewenberg, F. M., Dolgoff, R., & Harrington, D. (2000). *Ethical decisions for social work practice* (6th ed.). Itasca, IL: F. E. Peacock Publisher.

Chapter 2

THE HELPING RELATIONSHIP

Chapter Outline
- Introduction
- Processes of the Helping Relationship
  - Establishing a Relationship
  - Establishing Rapport
  - Mutual Trust and Respect
  - Securing Helpee's Confidence
  - Confidentiality
  - The Initial Session/Meeting
- Identifying Issues
- Establishing Goals
- Implementing Solutions
  - Exploration
  - Empowerment
- Termination of the Helping Relationship
- Follow-up
- Summary
  - References

Chapter Objectives
- Provide information regarding steps a helper must take toward developing a helping relationship
- Provide an understanding of ways to establish an effective helping relationship

INTRODUCTION

There are a variety of goals that are specific to each helping setting. What I discuss is the overall goal for any helping relationship, which is assisting the helpee with regard to learning how to solve problems. It is my firm belief that unless the client has severe limited intellectual functioning and/or is psychotic to the point that his thinking and reasoning are detached from reality, he has the ability to develop and implement appropriate solutions to his problems. Stated in other terms, most everyone has the capability to solve their psychological problems. If this is a true fact, then appropriate questions are: Why is there a need for a professional helper? What is the professional helper's role in problem solutions? The answer to both questions is that the major role for the helping professional is to help empower the helpee with the courage, resolve, insight, and willingness to explore options and implement appropriate solutions to the situations of concern. It may be tempting and personally psychologically fulfilling for the helper to introduce and implement solutions to the client's problems; however, the helper must always remember the helping relationship is not about him, but rather it is about the well-being of the helpee. As is discussed in the chapter on understanding human behavior, some clients prefer to let the helper "do all the work" with regard to the problem-solving part of the helping process. Likewise, the helper may feel a great deal of self-satisfaction in "solving" the problems. Regardless of how much psychological pleasure the helper receives from this act, she must remember that she is not doing the client any lasting favors by taking over his role in finding solutions to his life situations. The client gains little lasting personal growth when the helper takes charge of his issues and implements solutions.

I acknowledge that there are a number of helping situations that require increased helper involvement. In some instances, such as case managers and social workers assisting clients with complex issues that require expertise or other capabilities the clients do not have, it is understandable that the professional helper will take more of an aggressive role in seeking solutions to clients' issues. Even in those situations, the helper should involve the helpee in making decisions that are within his capabilities. An example of this point can be found in the disability rehabilitation field where the helpee is a quadriplegic and is in need of housing assistance. It may be quite apparent that from a physical standpoint the helpee will not be able to handle the physical parts of moving furniture, clothing and so on. However, he is capable of making decisions with regard to where he would like to live and how he would like his living accommodations arranged. The point being made is that the professional helper should look for ways to include the helpee in decision making and any other areas where he is capable of providing input, whether that input is physical or mental.

In most professional helping relationships, the act or art of helping begins before you physically see the helpee. The preliminary process begins when you receive a referral and agree to become the person's helper, if this choice is yours to make, if not, when the person is assigned as your client. In the process of preparing to work with the client or clients there are some things that should be done to prepare yourself to be as effective as you can be. I call this process analyzing the forthcoming helping relationship. In general terms this means receiving and reviewing background information that will help you make some decisions as to the directions you will take the helping relationship. This author recognizes there are a variety of ways you the helper receives background information, and also realizes that the quality of the information you receive varies; therefore this will determine how well and in-depth you are able to proceed with your analysis. Preparation is a major key to success. The following are some suggested things one should do to prepare for applying the processes of the helping relationship.

As previously stated, there are numerous types of helping relationships, ranging from friends helping friends to professional counseling therapy sessions. Also as previously stated, the emphasis of this text relates to professional helping relationships; however, regardless of the emphasis of the helping relationship there are some components that apply to most helping relationships; therefore some of what is discussed with regard to analysis of a helping relationship will apply to friend helping friend as well as professional helper assisting a client.

The underlying goal of most, if not all, helping relationships is to assist someone achieve a goal, whether that goal is to assist a friend with tidying a room or assisting a married couple with understanding why they are unhappy with their marriage and the options they may have to resolve their unhappiness. Certainly there are significant different roles in a helping relationship depending upon what is expected of the helping relationship. Likewise, depending upon the helping setting as well as goals of the helping relationship there are certain steps that this author has found useful and effective in helping clients solve their problems. Note that I have said helping clients solve their problems. This author strongly believe that unless a person or persons has serious mental and/or emotional problems which prohibits him from implementing rational thinking, then everyone has the potential and capability to understand, and with competent assistance solve his problem or problems. The professional helper is on the scene to help guide the person to understanding the problem(s), understanding his/her options and applying those options in ways that remove the problem rather than increase the problem.

The preamble to effectively analyzing the helping relationship is to make the clients aware that it is your firm belief that there are answers to their problems and they have the answers, and it is your goal to get them to the point that they understand they are the masters of their fate. Some may title this first step as establishing rapport with the client(s). To some extent this is true in that establishing rapport is designed to make the clients feel comfortable with you as the helper and believe that you have their best interest at heart and will do nothing to harm them psychologically. Whereas informing and hopefully making them believe that you as the helper will do no harm certainly is designed to both make the clients comfortable with you as their helper and also believe you are capable to assist them in dealing with their situations. However, believing in themselves to the point they feel empowered and capable, with assistance, to solve their problems is different than having the clients feeling comfortable with you and believing that you are capable of helping them.

Lack of belief in self, generally speaking, is a major part of clients' inability to move forward with implementing solutions to their problems. Stated in other terms, often the problems have existed for quite some time and attempts to solve the problems, or in many cases, lack of sufficient attempts have caused the problem to not only continue to be a problem but has been the result of the problem escalating. The following steps which this author calls analysis of a helping relationship is designed to help guide the professional helper in working with individual clients as well as families.

PROCESSES OF THE HELPING RELATIONSHIP

The helping relationship, like most professional human interactions, has structure, and this structure is called the process. The helping relationship process consists of stages through which the relationship hopefully progresses. The successful helping relationship goes through six distinct stages: **Establishing a Relationship, Identifying Issues, Establishing Goals, Implementing Solutions to Issues, Termination,** and **Follow-up.**

Establishing a Relationship

For a professional helping relationship to be successful, the relationship requires strangers to develop a dialog based on understanding each other, trusting each other, and respecting each other. The relationship does not require that these strangers always agree with each other, but they must understand each other's' motives, trust that each other will be truthful and fair, and respect each other's' viewpoints even if they are different. Most human relations will not survive unless there is trust among those involved. This fact is no less true for the professional helping relationship, especially the client's ability to trust the helper. With the following comments, Brammer and MacDonald (2003) emphasize the importance of trust, particularly the helpee being able to trust the helper:

> A crucial relationship dimension is that of trust-distrust. Helpees are willing generally to accept help from people they trust. For trust to develop, helpees must have confidence in their helpers and must be able to believe what they say. Certain specific helper behaviors, such as clear motives for helping, create trust. The motives of the helper must be apparent and attractive to the helpee, and they must not be a cover for helper efforts to control, manipulate, or punish. (p. 51)

Most helpees want to trust their helper, especially if they are truly interested in changing their behavior. Helpees who are sincere in wanting to change their behavior will enter the relationship with both hope and reservations. They are tired of hurting and want to remove nagging issues of their daily lives; however, along with this desire is a fear of the unknown. In this case, the helper represents the unknown.

It is not a small task to open one's personal history book to a stranger and allow the helper to be privy to many of his weakness, shameful thoughts, and unvarnished actions. Unless the helpee has previously been in a professional helping relationship, he probably does not know what to expect. Add to this fear the many myths surrounding some helping professions such as the profession of counseling and the reservation of being in a psychological helping environment may escalate to proportions of panic.

Given the numerous concerns the helpee may have, it is incumbent that the helper establish a comfort level within which the helpee is able to interact. This comfort level is often called establishing rapport.

Establishing Rapport

Reluctance, embarrassment, anger, frustration, and feelings of helplessness are only some of the feelings a helpee may be experiencing as he enters the helping arena. For many helpees, admitting to themselves that life's events have progressed past their abilities to control them is difficult, thus insult is added to injury when they have to ask for or are required to seek professional help. In fact, it may be perceived, by the helpees, that they are surrendering control of their lives to others. Add a stranger who is summoned to help, and this mixture of simmering emotions begins to boil over.

Considering the previously mentioned scenario, the professional helper may step into a situation where there is a need for help, but there is reluctance on the part of the helpee to accept help, especially from a stranger who may ask him to reveal innermost thoughts and feelings that probably have been kept private and possibly not been shared with his close friends and family members. Under these circumstances, it is imperative that the professional helper establish an environment that will not only allow the individual to share his feelings but will also encourage him to do so.

The question is: How does the helping professional establish rapport? The answer is that there are many ways to establish rapport, and the helper has to develop his own method of setting helpees at ease. Although each helper's approach will differ by varying degrees, the variables that must be part of any rapport establishment approach are honesty and sincerity. As a helper, one may be able to fool the helpee initially with false sincerity and dishonesty with regard to desire to help; however, in the continuing process of the helping relationship, true feelings and attitudes will surface, and most likely, at that point, the helping relationship is seriously in jeopardy of becoming a failure. More discussion with regard to establishing rapport is provided in this chapter in the **Initial Session/Meeting section**.

Mutual Trust and Respect

Reference has been made to how difficult it is for some to submit themselves to the helping process. In light of this, the helping professional should be aware that some resistance, reservation, and reluctance may be apparent in early meetings. One may allow a stranger into the home on a first meeting; however, one generally does not tell his and/or his family's secrets to the stranger. Some of these secrets are only released after a trusting relationship has been developed. Likewise, it is reasonable to consider that helpees entering the helping relationship forum are not going to disclose secrets until they feel that they can trust and respect the helper enough to accept her advice.

The helping professional should not view the helpees as being bad or good, but as persons who are experiencing difficulties. The efforts of the helper should be directed toward assisting the helpee with solutions to problems and utilizing more appropriate behavior rather than trying to assess blame. Although the professional helper may recognize that the helpee has engaged in inappropriate behavior, she, the helpee, must also be recognized as a person who is capable of correcting her mistakes. The helper cannot afford to expend energies blaming the helpee or a gap between the helper and helpee will be established. The helper's sense of righteousness, if expressed either verbally or nonverbally, may cause the helpee to withdraw from the helping relationship or feel guilty and lose confidence in his abilities to help himself, which will be needed to affect change. For these reasons, Carl Rogers, the founder of person-centered therapy, reminds us that an effective helper expresses unconditional regard for helpees. This means a willingness to accept helpees as they are and not withholding acceptance until they become what is thought they should be. This acceptance does not mean that the professional helper condones what the helpees are doing or have done but accepts their behavior as part of their current existence and recognizes that they have within themselves the power to change their behavior to the direction of being more productive.

Securing Helpee's Confidence

As difficult as it may be for some helpees to submit themselves to the helping process, it becomes important for the helper to ensure that the helpees feel that the helper is capable of helping. Most certainly, formal training that leads to degrees and certificates is a foundation on which the professional helper builds skills; however, the application of professional skills, generally speaking, is accepted after confidence has been established with the helpee. The helpee's decision to initially believe in the helper involves much more than the helper's credentials. Professionalism of the office staff and the physical setting of the office, décor, and comfort are factors influencing confidence. In contrast, an office lavished with original artwork and leather furnishing will not sustain confidence if the helper is incompetent.

Studies such as the one by Chaikin, Derliega, and Miller (1976) reveal that the conditions of the office have an effect on client self-disclosure. Clients are more inclined to believe in a helper who looks successful. An office that is well manicured and shows some attention has been paid to the comfort and convenience of its helpee gives that impression. Additionally, a well-trained, professional acting clerical staff adds to the prestige of the professional helper. Imagine walking into an office where the secretary is talking on the telephone or working on the computer and barely acknowledges the helpee's presence. Next, on entering the helper's interoffice, there is a battered desk with books and papers scattered around, a mixture of furniture ranging from prehistoric to early out of space, no pictures on the wall, tattered carpet, and so on. This setting is not conducive to establishing confidence in the helper. Relevant to this discussion, consider the following comments by noted counselor educator and author Arbuckel (1970): "The immediate impression that the client receives when he opens the counselor's door is going to affect him. He should see a reasonably comfortable office with such things as curtains on the windows, pictures on the walls, comfortable chairs, and some evidence of a library and the professional competence of the counselor" (p. 159).

Helpees develop many ideas and perceptions about the professional helper's abilities, from both personal appearance and the immediate surroundings. If the initial impression of the helper is negative and the helper does not work to correct the negativity, most likely the helping process is doomed.

Confidentiality

A final step in establishing a helping relationship is ensuring confidentiality, which is one of the cornerstones of the helping relationship. One of the hallmarks of the helping process that makes it different than ordinary conversation is ensuring that what is said in the relationship is not topic of discussion for social conversation or fuel for frivolous gossip.

As previously stated, often helpees are entrusting the helper with personal information that in one sense is causing the helpee to "expose his soul to the helper." Once this type of information is entrusted to the professional helper, there must be a skillful management of information, and most certainly not the least of responsibilities is to maintain confidentiality. Quite often helpees will test the professional helper by releasing bits of less sensitive information to see what type of steward of this information the helper will be. The helpees will pay particular attention to staff members associated with the helper to determine whether they can detect any leaks of information to them.

Another important point with regard to confidentiality is that the helper must know his limitations with regard to keeping information confidential, and it is imperative that he share this information with his helpees. Depending on the type of helper, as well as local, state, and federal laws, certain information such as child abuse and certain types of threats must be disclosed to certain officials, such as courts of law, and law enforcement officers. Additionally, all helping professionals must be aware of whether they have privileged communication and if so the limitations of the privileged communication. As previously stated, the helper must be knowledgeable of his limitations with regard to maintaining confidentiality.

The Initial Session/Meeting

The initial session with the helpee is perhaps the most important session the helper will have with the helpee because this meeting establishes the tone of the relationship and helps establish the foundation for future helping relationship meetings. As previously stated, helping techniques may vary according to the professional preferences of the helper. My approach to establishing rapport in the initial session is to begin by introducing myself, giving some information with regard to my personal and professional background. I try not to overwhelm the helpee with my background by providing too much information. My belief with regard to the initial meeting is that the helpee will only retain a small amount of information. The reason for this usually is attributed to the helpee being nervous and anxious with regard to what he thinks will transpire during the session. Following my personal introduction, I ask the helpee to tell me about himself, such as where he is from and what he does to relax. I have found that most people feel comfortable talking about themselves, especially discussing things that are of interest to them. Additionally, I have found that most people are comfortable talking about themselves because that is something about which they have a great deal of knowledge. It should be noted that I ask them nonthreatening questions. After spending a few minutes getting the helpee to talk about himself, it is easier to move into the questions regarding issues the helpee is encountering.

Another point that should be made with regard to establishing rapport is the fact that the initial rapport that is established does not always last through the entire helping relationship. It has been my experience that as the helper and helpee move through various significant issues, rapport and trust often have to be refreshed. The helpee may have developed a level of comfort to discuss problem number one; however, problem number two may be a new and different issue, and it may be more emotionally intense than the previous problem. A helper should be aware that it is not uncommon for helpees to initially present certain issues to test whether the helper can be trusted and/or to see the helper's reactions to his position with regard to the issue. Issue number two is a new issue and may be more central to the overall concerns of the helpee; therefore, the helper must be cognizant of this and realize that rapport has to be reinforced.

Returning to the purposes of the initial session, most counselor educators and professional helping educators would agree with Auvenshing and Noffsinger (1984) that the functions of the initial helping session are to: (a) mark the starting point in the helping process; (b) ascertain the client's reasons for coming; (c) relate the client's needs to counselor and agency resources; (d) gather information for intake, evaluation, routing, and referral purposes; (e) serve as a period of mutual testing between helper and helpee regarding compatibility; and (f) initiate the helping relationship. All of the previously mentioned functions are important and essential to developing a successful helping relationship. However, the additional point of the professional helper clarifying his role in the helping process also should be made. Too frequently the professional helper makes the critical **"mistake of assumption"** by assuming that the helpee knows why he is in the helping process and that he understands the helper's role. It is of paramount importance that the professional helper be cognizant that helpees come to the helping relationship from a variety of sources as well as possessing an equal or greater number of ideas of why they are encountering this process.

Clients may be self-referred, agency referred, and/or court ordered, just to mention three possible ways helpees find themselves being involved in the helping process. The helping professional should be cognizant of the fact that the helpee's knowledge of what is to occur in the helping relationship will vary. Some may have previous experience in a helping relationship, whereas others may have no experience or knowledge of the process. Likewise, the helping professional should be aware that referring agencies will also have varying degrees of knowledge of the helping relationship to which they are referring the helpee.

With regard to referring sources, some helpees are only told that the helping relationship will benefit them. One can imagine the apprehension that the person being referred may have with only the previously mentioned information. For example, a helpee who has never been involved in counseling being referred for counseling and being told only that counseling will help her probably will not develop much excitement with the prospects of being in counseling sessions. Many ideas of what counseling is like will flood the helpee's mind, perhaps based on her perception of what might occur. One only has to reflect for a short time about the many perceptions floating around in society about counseling and other forms of psychological help. A few of the wrong perceptions of the helping process that may be occupying the helpee's mental attention are: "Counselors, psychologists, and psychiatrists play with your mind," "Those people check to see if you are crazy," and "They have you take a bunch of tests to see if you are crazy." Other types of helping professionals and their work, such as social workers and case managers, engender equally distorted perceptions of their helping relationship, such as they are only interested in reducing or eliminating my public assistance check, and they are only interested in snooping into my personal life. Given the possible apprehension and torrent of ideas about the helping process, clarification of the role of the helper is essential to establish an environment conducive for the helping process to be successful.

The professional helper should not assume that his helpee knows anything about what is going to occur. It is better to provide too much information than not enough. During the initial session, when the professional helper attempts to establish rapport, among other things, the first order of business should be a thorough explanation of: (a) professional background, (b) how sessions are conducted, (c) ground rules of the session, (d) identifying issues, and (e) establishment of goals.

Professional background—whether the helpee asks for help or is referred for help, the person likes to think he is being placed in competent hands. Regardless of any reservations the helpee may have about possible solutions to his problems, deep within there is hope that this will be the solution to whatever issues exist. An ideal situation will have the helpee investigating, in advance, the background of the professional helper. Admittedly, this is an optimistic view in that too often the helpee assumes the helper to be competent and does not do much, if any, research with regard to the helper's background. It, therefore, becomes the responsibility of the helper to inform the helpee of her credentials and areas of expertise. The professional helper should not assume that helpees know what initials such as EdD, PhD, or MSW signify. Furthermore, explanation of the initials does not necessarily impart knowledge of one's competence. The professional helper should supply helpees with information about his formal educational background, including that which is specific to the professional helping technique (such as workshops, seminar, and so on that she has attended), which relates to her professional competency. Additionally, if the helper has had considerable experience working in certain areas and/or with specific clients, she should present this information to the helpee.

Every helper has to start at some time. Therefore, if she is relatively new in her profession, she should emphasize the extent of her professional training. If the helper has in the course of study trained under the direction of an experienced helper, this should also be emphasized.

The explanation of formal education and practical experience should be brief and concise, taking special precautions not to bombard the helpee with extensive details of education and experience that the helpee will not understand. Brief statements such as "I earned my masters or doctoral degree at X University majoring in X and have continued my education by attending workshops, seminars, etc., also I have been in this line of helping for X number of years," should be sufficient. In addition to these brief statements, the helper should let the helpee know that questions he may have will be answered with respect to professional background. As simple as this process is, it remains a source of concern that some professional helpers continue to assume that either the helpee knows his professional background or is not concerned with regard to the background or, even worse, some become offended when the helpee inquires about professional background, feeling that the helpee is questioning his competency.

Explain how the helping relationship is conducted: here, I am referring to the techniques used in conducting the sessions. As previously stated, helpees have varying degrees of familiarity with the helping process; television, movies, and the Internet to mention only three, have implanted various ideas in the minds of people of what comprises the helping process. To clarify the helping process, the helper must explain his methods of conducting or implementing his brand of helping.

Thus far in this text, I have mentioned counseling, social work, and case management as examples of helping professionals. However, there are numerous other worthy examples of helping professionals and relationships; therefore, it is impossible to identify all the helping relationship techniques. It is sufficient to state that whatever methods the professional helper uses to implement his helping, this should be carefully explained to the helpee.

Rules for the helping relationship must be established. The term rules may, at first glance, appear to be too harsh a word, signifying excessive controls for some types of helping relationships. Perhaps a less controlling word could be used for some types of helping; however, the point being made is that there has to be structure to any helping relationship.

With regard to the helping relationship of counseling and social work, within the first session, the professional helper should have firmly established ground rules by which the helping sessions will be conducted. Rules such as starting on time, length of sessions, how to cancel a session, how to handle emergencies, and how to conduct oneself during the sessions (i.e., if more than one person is engaged in the sessions, such as family counseling, marital counseling, or group counseling, to mention only three types of counseling, no verbal abuse) are examples of procedures the professional helper should have firmly outlined prior to the initial meeting.

Although the exact starting time may not be established until the initial session, it should be emphasized that the sessions will last for a set period of time and will end on time. Certainly these rules should be discussed with the helpee(s) to allow input. The rookie professional helper will discover what the veteran helper already knows: Helpees appreciate reasonable boundaries, although at times one may question this because the helpees may disregard and venture beyond the boundaries. At these occurrences, the professional helper must reemphasize the rules, pointing out that to a great degree the success of the relationship depends on all concerned functioning within the agreed boundaries.

As previously implied, other types of professional helping may not require as extensive structure as counseling and psychotherapy; however, appropriate structure is the cement that holds together any helping relationship. Case management will be used to illustrate a helping relationship that will require some of the structure previously discussed for counseling but not all of the rules discussed. In case management, where the helper is assisting with various appointments, rules such as being on time for appointments and being courteous with regard to canceling appointments are only two examples of establishing structure in nonpsychological counseling settings. To summarize rules and structure, it is sufficient to state that not having them simply invites disorganization in the helping process, which will doom the relationship to failure.

Identifying Issues

This stage requires the helper to assist the helpee in identifying some life issues that have a major influence on his life. It should be noted that I have said *some* of the life issues because in a helping relationship there are often several issues, and some if not all are related to the current situation of the client. The helping relationship can be doomed for failure if too broad of a scope is taken. Stated in more succinct terms, if too many issues are attempted to be solved, the result may be that none is adequately handled. Therefore, it is the helper's responsibility to assist the helpee with regard to exploring the various issues currently impacting his life and further assist with identifying those issues that appear to be having the most significant impacts and have a reasonable opportunity to be managed within the time frame and structure of the helping relationship.

At first glance, the idea of assisting the helpee with identification of relevant issues may seem to be an easy task. However, as we consider some of the dynamics of why the person is in the helping relationship arena, a clearer picture of some of the obstacles that may have to be overcome to identify the relevant life issues impacting the helpee's life comes into focus. There are a number of reasons that the helpee may be in the helping relationship arena. The helpee may be court ordered, thus the dynamics of being seen by a professional helper most often will take on a different meaning than if the helpee was self-referred. The helpee may object to being seen by a professional helper and reject the belief of others that he is in need of professional help. I think that one can see that assisting with identifying relevant issues may be made more difficult by the manner in which the helpee becomes a potential participant in the helping process.

Under more ideal referral circumstances, such as self-referral, identifying issues is not always easy. The helpee may be flooded with issues, all of which have some degree of concern to him. Helping the helpee sort through these issues becomes the number one priority. Other self-referral helpees may be well aware of the major issues that need to be confronted; however, because of reluctance to share crucial information, the helpee holds back, thus making the exploration of issues more difficult.

Establishing Goals

Once relevant issues have been identified, the establishment of goals to deal with the issues become of paramount importance. Goals become the action plans that hopefully will either remove the issues or help make them less problematic. Similarly identification of significant issues to be addressed should be guided by the concerns of the client and as much as possible should have major input of the client. Authors such as Okun (2002) and Egan (1994) agree that goals set in the helping relationship should be those of the client, not the goals of the counselor. However, having made this statement, Okun issues the following warning:

> The helping relationship must focus on areas of concern to the helpee, not on concerns that the helper thinks the helpee ought to work on. This necessity may become a serious issue in some organizational settings where a conflict may exist between organizational policies, which you as the helper may represent, and the needs of the helpee. For example, if you are working in a correctional institution and are sent an inmate who is causing some disruption and is seen as a troublemaker who must be changed, you may find that you and this inmate have different objectives. Yours may be, of institutional necessity, to help the inmate conform to the system, whereas the inmate's objectives may be to disrupt and get whatever attention results from the disruption. (pp. 213–214)

Differences in objective often occur in other human services settings, such as department of human services and public schools, to mention only two. As Okun (2002) points out, no one can tell you what to do in a similar situation. However, I point out that this is where you as the helper "earn your stripes" as a professional as you work with the client to assist her in understanding that it is in her best interest to conform to legal and "just" organizational objectives. Furthermore, the helper will have to convince the client to establish goals that will offer the best chances of success.

The establishment of goals should be a joint effort between the helpee and the professional helper. It is certain that in many helping situations, the professional helper is inviting failure if he dictates the goals to the helpee because the goals become the professional helper's goals, not the helpee's goals. Some helpees may attempt to abdicate their responsibility in deciding which goals are the most important for the helping relationship. When this happens, the helper will be wise to work with the helpee in the process of decision making. Assisting the helpee in developing confidence in his decision-making abilities will benefit the helpee in making future life decisions.

Goals should serve as directional signs for both the helpee and the professional helper. Goals can be the cement that bonds the helping process together. Both short- and long-term goals should be established. The short-term goals should be formulated so their accomplishment will serve as motivation and lead to the attainment of the long-term goals. In this manner, meeting short-term goals will have served as motivation that drives the helpee toward the conquest of the long-term goals. At this point in the discussion of establishing goals, I present a few simple rules in establishing both short- and long-term goals.

1. Goals should be stated in clear and specific terms. To identify a goal such as "The individual will be better able to deal with personal problems" is too general and does not mean much. Being specific with regard to which problem(s) or the kind of problems the helpee will be better able to handle is much more meaningful and adds direction to the helping process. An example of a specific goal could be for a person with a learning disability to, within 2 weeks, identify a tutor to assist with specific reading skills.

2. Goals should be stated in measurable terms. Granted, it is much easier to establish measurable goals when dealing with a quantifiable product than it is when assisting with interpersonal relationships. However, goals that relate to interpersonal relationships, which are carefully conceived, can be measured. Goals such as spending specific amounts of time with a particular family member or the family in general can be measured. Again, these goals have to be specific, such as identifying a specific amount of time and/or particular activities.

3. Goals should be realistic. One should take into consideration the helpee's resources when establishing goals. It is senseless to assist the helpee formulate goals the helpee will not be able to attain for lack of adequate resources (i.e., time, money, and educational background, to mention only three needed resources).

4. Helpees must have input in the establishment of goals. As previously stated, the establishment of goals is primarily for the benefit of the helpee. Helpees should be discouraged from turning over their responsibilities for providing solutions to their problems to the helper. This is a major reason that the helper should encourage the helpee to take ownership of his issues as well as the possible solutions to those issues.

Once in the helping process, too frequently helpees look to the professional helper to solve their problems. Some falsely believe the reason that they are participating in the helping process is to turn over the problem portion of their lives to the professional helper. Although it may be flattering to the professional helper, to be considered that powerful is not productive. Establishment of realistic, understandable, specific, and achievable goals can best be accomplished with full participation of the helpee.

Implementing Solutions

Exploration

In most cases, there will be more than one possible resolution to issues confronting the helpee. A critical component of the helping process is the helper working with the helpee to explore the various possibilities for relief and resolution of the confronting situation. *Exploration* is another term for fact finding—determining what can offer the best resolution to the problem(s). As is discussed in Chapter 12 (this volume), some psychological theories promote the idea that the client has the answers to her problems, and it is the responsibility of the counselor to utilize techniques that encourage clients to bring to the forefront of their minds information that they already possess. Sometimes the client can be so consumed by the issue or issues confronting her, she has difficulties recognizing solutions. Perhaps this is where the phrase "can't see the forest for the trees" originated.

Regardless of the psychological theory the helper uses to assist the client, he has to assist the client in a search for solutions. The client must be actively involved in this search; if not, the final solution will not be the client's solution but the counselor's solution. If the solution is not one the client has had the majority of input in developing, she will not have been empowered, and the ultimate goal of all professional helping relationships should be the empowerment of the helpee.

Once the exploration stage has produced results that the helpee and the helper believe has the potential of providing relief to the helpee, the next stage of implementing the results of the exploration occurs. It should be noted that, in the process of implementing the solutions, it may be necessary to revisit the exploration stage if the desired results do not occur. If this happens, neither the helpee nor the helper should feel that there has been a failure. There are a number of variables that might cause a potentially good solution to not be a good fit. Variables such as timing of implementation and unexpected impact on others are only two of several possibilities.

Returning to the implementation of solution(s), testing the impact of the solutions is necessary to make a determination of whether they are appropriate. In the process of testing, two events may occur: One is what I call the **eureka effect**, which occurs when the helpee begins to understand her situation better and what is causing the discomfort associated with the situation. Often what occurs with an increased understanding of the situation is the feeling that "at last I know what is bothering me; therefore I can now handle the situation." Along with the light bulb coming on and illuminating the situation may be the belief that there is no longer a need for assistance. The problem with this belief is the fact of the understanding (or thinking that one understands) does not guarantee a solution. Therefore, the helper should explore with the helpee the possibility of testing the solution to determine the degree to which the helpee understands. The second problem is the **resistant to change**. From a psychological standpoint, we become accepting of routines even if those routines create some discomfort and are emotionally unhealthy. Requests for change often creates additional discomfort and uncertainty, and when faced with living with the familiar or venturing into the unknown, too often we choose the familiar. Offered as an example is obesity that is caused by the lack of willpower to curb overeating rather than obesity resulting from genetics. Although we know that overeating and eating certain foods cause us to gain weight and is not healthy for us, we too frequently choose to continue this unhealthy lifestyle rather than change our eating habits. It appears that sometimes the unwillingness to change is stronger than being rational and doing those things that are most productive for our well-being.

The point being made is that making the decision to change one's behavior is often a difficult process. One responsibility of the professional helper is to assist the helpee with regard to feeling comfortable with making decisions to change behavior and believe in his ability to live with those changes. When the helpee makes decisions to change and experiences the positive results of those changes, he will become confident in his ability to make appropriate life decisions; as a result of this self-confidence, the helper will have helped empower the helpee.

Empowerment

By being a teacher and consultant to the helpee, the helper assists the helpee with regard to: identifying problematic issues, setting goals to attack the issues, exploring or testing the relevance of the defined solutions, and implementing those solutions that appear to have reasonable chances of managing the defined issues. The helper becomes a consultant to the helpee as they progress through each of the stages; in this process, the helper is teaching the helpee to have confidence in herself and to believe in her abilities to solve life problems. The success of managing the issues will give the helpee the skills, techniques, and confidence to manage future life issues. With each successful management of issues, the helpee becomes more independent with regard to managing her life. The helper is successful when the helpee does not have to be dependent on him to help manage her problems.

Termination of the Helping Relationship

As previously discussed, the helping relationship is not about satisfying the ego of the helper. Rather it is about assisting the helpee solve or manage issues that are impacting his or her current life situations, as well as developing the skills and self-confidence to handle future issues. Therefore, a major part of the helping relationship and the ultimate goal of the relationship are to reach a successful conclusion. Consequently, the professional helper has to prepare himself and the helpee for the formal ending of the relationship.

With regard to termination, *preparation* is the key word. Planning for termination should begin well before the ending date of the relationship. In cases where either insurance or agency policy limits the number of helping contacts, the planning for termination begins with the first meeting when the helper informs the helpee of the limitations of the helping relationships. Part of the helper's plan of action should include a timetable for resolution of the helpee's issues, and the timetable should be discussed with the helpee. In this type of situation, a relevant question is what happens if the helpee's issues have not been resolved at the end of the proscribed time limit? The answer is this: If the helper cannot find ways to continue working with the helpee, the helper should research referral resources that will be compatible with the helpee's needs. It is always a good idea for the helper, in this type of situation, to plan in advance for the possibility of running out of time, which will help lessen the chance of leaving the helpee without closure to his issues.

In an ideal situation where there will be reasonable time to devote to helping bring the helpee's issues to successful or at least reasonable closure, the helper should introduce the fact that at some point the helping relationship will end. Certainly, the helpee knows that the helping relationship will eventually end; however, she probably will not know how and when the relationship will end. Therefore, the helper should explain his process of terminating a helping relationship. This discussion should occur early in the relationship—if not the first meeting, then certainly no later than the second meeting.

The mechanics of termination should include phasing in termination. Each session should begin with an overview of progress that has been made in previous sessions of the relationship, and each session should end with both an evaluation of the session and a discussion of what is to occur at the next session. Certainly, events may change what actually occurs at the next session; however, it is better to have a plan for the next session than to wait for events to dictate what will happen. Returning to the phasing-in process of termination, as the helper and helpee discuss progress that has been made, when there is an agreement that significant progress has been made, the helper should begin the discussion of phasing-in the termination. An example of how this could occur follows: If the helping session has been occurring once a week, it could be changed to 2-week intervals; if progress continues, the session could be changed to 3-week intervals; and so on until the relationship reaches the point that the helpee and helper feel that the helpee can function without the helping sessions. Another advantage of changing the intervals of the helping relationship relates to the facts that in some cases helpees begin to depend on the helping relationship and is reluctant to end the relationship. Changing the intervals also helps break the dependency that may have occurred. Additionally, as the helpee devotes more time and effort to working on issues without the helper, the helpee gains self-confidence.

Other procedures of termination are providing the helpee with information about how to access the helper if needed once the helping relationship has been terminated and providing the helpee with other resources that can be utilized. The idea of providing the helpee with a method of contacting the helpee has to be carefully handled because the helper does not want the helpee to become dependent on him and the helping relationship. However, the helper does not want the helpee to feel abandoned. Providing other resources can help avoid both the helpee becoming dependent on the helper and feelings of being abandoned.

Follow-up

The final process of the helping relations is checking on the well-being and hopefully the progress that the helpee is making since termination. I cannot give a time frame for the follow-up and how many times to follow up because each helping relationship is different, thus having different needs for follow-up. As the professional, you can make that judgment call.

If the helpee is making sufficient progress, there may not be a need for additional follow-up beyond the first and/or second follow-up. In a situation where the helpee is not making sufficient progress, the helper can recommend providing additional help and/or referring the helpee to other helpers and resources.

SUMMARY

In summary, as with most endeavors, a well-designed and executed plan increases the chances of the plan being successful. Likewise, a professional helping relationship has stages through which it progresses. If each stage is well planned and executed, there is a good chance that the helping relationship will succeed.

Chapter Review Questions

1. What are the six stages of a successful helping relationship discussed in this chapter?
2. What are some of the things a professional helper must do with the helpee in the initial meeting session?

3. How should goals be established in a helping relationship?
4. What are some of the steps a helper should take with regard to terminating a helping relationship?
5. Why is follow-up important in a helping relationship?

REFERENCES

Arbuckel, D. S. (1970). Counseling: Philosophy, theory and practice (2nd ed.). Boston: Allyn & Bacon. In Bryan, W. V. (1996). *In search of freedom.* Springfield, IL: Charles C Thomas, Publisher.

Auvenshing, C. D., & Noffsinger, A. R. (1984). *Counseling: An introduction for the health and human service.* Baltimore: University Park Press.

Brammer, L., & MacDonald, G. (2003). *The helping relationship: Process and skills* (8th ed.). Boston: Allyn & Bacon.

Chaikin, A. L., Derliega, V. J., & Miller, S. J. (1976). Effects of room environment on self-disclosure in a counseling analogue. *Journal of Counseling Psychology, 23* (5), 479–481.

Egan, G. (1994). *The skilled helper: A problem management approach to helping* (5th ed.). Pacific Grove, CA: Brooks/Cole.

Okun, B. F. (2002). *Effective helping: Interviewing and counseling techniques* (6th ed.). Pacific Grove, CA: Brooks/Cole.

Suggested Readings

Carkhuff, R., et al. (1981). *The skills of helping.* Amherst, MA: Human Resources Development Press.

Combs, A. W. (1994). *Helping relationships: Basic concepts for the helping professions* (4th ed.). Boston: Allyn & Bacon.

Corcoran, J. (2005). *Building strengths and skills.* Oxford: Oxford University Press. Hutchins, D. E., & Cole, C. C. (1986). *Helping relationships and strategies.* Monterey, CA: Brooks/Cole.

Long, V. O. (1996). *Communication skills in helping relationships: A framework for facilitating personal growth.* Pacific Grove, CA: Brooks/Cole.

Pope, K. S., & Vasquez, M. J. T. (2007). *Ethics in psychotherapy and counseling: A practical guide* (3rd ed.). San Francisco: Jossey-Bass.

Chapter 3

UNDERSTANDING SELF

Chapter Outline
• Introduction
• Self-Understanding
• Reasons We Are Prejudiced
• Understanding One's Values
  • What are Your Beliefs with Regard to the Nature of Humans?
• Views of Human Development
  • Role Culture Plays in Human Behavior
• Summary
• References

Chapter Objectives
• Encourage helper to conduct self-exploration of personal views

INTRODUCTION

In the rush to become a helping professional, we often overlook the need to understand ourselves as human beings. To be more specific, we learn theory, techniques, and process, but we too often forget to recognize that we are humans before we are professionals. We also often fail to take into account the fact that we have feelings, opinions, beliefs, and prejudices that come into play as we work with our clients. Furthermore, we fail to examine these various components that make us who we are.

This examination is necessary to determine how components of our personality impact the ways we interact with the people who come to us for help. Once we have learned techniques and theories, read text-books, and been told by professors and professionals working in the helping field and other people we respect that we can do a great deal of good with the training we have received, we act as if this information transforms us into superhumans who have a shield that protects us for exposing and projecting our attitudes, opinions, beliefs, and prejudices onto our clients. However, experienced, seasoned, and sensitive professional helpers know that they have to be aware of the previously mentioned human emotions and also be aware of the impact and role these emotions play with regard to their impact on us as a professional helper.

Therefore, it is imperative that the helper conduct a self-examination of beliefs, feelings, and attitudes. The following are some of the "self-understandings" that a helping professional should consider: type of clients with whom one would find difficult to help, understanding one's emotions, understanding one's limitations, understanding one's motivations to become a helping professional, understanding one's prejudices, and understanding one's values and worldviews.

The following section provides some advice with regard to the previously mentioned self-understandings.

SELF-UNDERSTANDING

Types of clients with whom you may have difficulty assisting: Helping professionals do not live in sterile environments; therefore, we are not immune to having prejudices, biases, and negative opinions. Stated in other terms, helping professionals are part of a society and cultures and are both affected by and contribute to the norms of their environments. Although we may wish to think that we are open-minded enough to accept and understand that clients have faults and be nonjudgmental about the same, the reality is that helping professionals are not superhumans who enter into the helping areas with a blank and forgiving mind with regard to social and societal issues of the day. We bring to the helping venue our own beliefs and biases with regard to past and current events. Most helping professionals attempt to be as nonjudgmental and accepting as possible; however, there is no way that one can switch on and off one's viewpoints of life events as if they were attached to an electrical outlet.

Being part of communities and being exposed to various forms of media that distribute worldwide information, it is virtually impossible for helping professionals not to develop opinions with regard to events affecting their environment. Therefore, it is imperative that the helping professional examine his beliefs and opinions and be honest with himself with regard to the types of life situations clients may bring to him with which he would have difficulties assisting the client to overcome.

Most of our beliefs and opinions are influenced by our family relationships, friends, peers, and close associates. As we prepare to enter the helping profession field, we should take a thorough inventory of many of our beliefs and opinions, which may come into play as we work with clients. We should examine these views not so much with the idea of changing them (in some cases, this may be the appropriate decision), but with thoughts of how will these views impact working with helpees. Issues related to race, ethnicity, sexual preference, and issues of abuse (such as child, sexual, spousal, and elderly) are but a few of the issues of which the aspiring helping professional should examine himself.

A relevant question at this point is: After examination, what should be done with regard to the results? The answer to this question is complicated, and in some cases there is no easy answer. There are several possibilities: (a) specialize in an area of helping that does not require you to have contact with the type of client for which you feel you cannot have positive regard. This is a somewhat simplistic answer that contains a reality that many, if not most, helping professionals will not have. The majority of helping professionals will be employed by agencies and organizations that require the professional to work with any that become their clients. Certainly, there are agencies and organizations that specialize and accept certain types of client; therefore if the helping professional is fortunate enough to have the appropriate training and is hired to work in this kind of agency, this will be the optimal answer to the previously mentioned question. If this is not a realistic solution, consider items b through d. (b) Referral of clients to other helping professionals who are emotionally capable of dealing with that client's issues is another possibility, if that option is available within the work setting. (c) Engage yourself in psychological counseling with a qualified helping professional to work with you on dealing with your inabilities and/or unwillingness to work with certain types of clients.

Specifically, work with the professional on identifying why you have difficulties working with certain types of clients, and work with the professional with regard to separating your personal feeling from your professional work. (d) Explore with your supervisor the possibility of having another helping professional assist you in your work with the helpee.

Understand your emotions: In addition to possessing certain professional skills, working with clients requires being patient enough to allow the clients to express themselves verbally, nonverbally, and emotionally. Additionally, professional patience on the part of the professional helper is required in the face of helpee resistance, helpee manipulation, and possible helpee anger, to mention only three of the myriad of possible helpee behaviors. In the helper–helpee relationship, the professional helper must always remember that she is in the power position with regard to this relationship; therefore, she must be in control of her emotions. Being a professional helper does not make one immune to having and displaying negative emotions toward the helpee. To establish and maintain a productive professional relationship, the helper must understand her emotions and keep them in check, quite often in some difficult times. Thus, the professional helper must not only know what triggers negative emotions within her, but should take a personal emotional survey check before each session with a helpee. Events at home, at work, with colleagues, and with other helpees can affect the professional's emotional outlook at a given moment, and things within a session that would not normally negatively affect her may unexpectedly come to the forefront. Therefore, as previously stated, an emotional check before each session is important.

Understanding your culture(s): With regard to being an effective helper, considerable discussion is often given to understanding cultural differences, as is also the case in this text. However, to be an effective helper, it is also imperative that the helper understand his views with regard to his own cultures. Most individuals place considerable pride in their cultures; however, this is not true for all people and all aspects of their cultures. In past years, some ethnic/racial minorities/cultures were devalued by the dominant culture, and the ethnic/racial minorities whose cultures were being devalued sometimes bought into the unfair and inaccurate criticism of lifestyle, intelligence, and work ethic, to mention only three. As a result of this and other cultural criticisms, as previously stated, some ethnic/racial minorities developed negative and inferiority feeling with regard to their cultural heritage and composition. Fortunately, most ethnic/racial minorities have made in-depth personal evaluations of their cultural heritages and have developed overdue pride in their cultures. Additionally, to be fair to dominant cultures, they have begun to value culture differences and see the value of these various cultural attributes and thus, to a great degree, have discontinued the devaluation of other cultures.

Despite the increase in cultural pride by ethnic/racial and other cultural groups, no one's culture is perfect, thus there are aspects of one's culture in which one may not have as much pride as other aspects of the cultural makeup. Therefore, the professional helper, regardless of whether he is from an ethnic/racial minority group or from the dominant cultural group, should conduct a cultural inventory examining those aspects of his culture of which he is proud and those aspects of which he has less pride. At this point, the question the reader may be having is what does this have to do with being an effective helper? The answers are: (a) the views one has with regard to her cultural makeup will have an impact on her personality, and (b) the views one has with regard to one's concepts of her cultures can and often will be reflected on helpees who are from similar cultural backgrounds. Offered as an example of the second point, perhaps one of the concepts of the helpee's culture is that there are a significant number of persons within that culture living on public assistance or significant numbers are substance abusers. Also let's say that the professional helper accepts this criticism as truth, feels ashamed of this allegation, and has worked hard via education and employment to distance himself from being associated with this cultural concept. His acceptance and possible dislike of this cultural concept may be reflected in his attitude toward helpees from his culture who represent one or both of the previously mentioned criticisms. The point being made is that the helper must have a good understanding of his cultural makeup and how his likes and dislikes of his culture impacts his beliefs, attitudes, and behaviors.

Understand your limitation: Given that the helper is in the power position and viewed as an authority, with regard to the helping relationship, frequently the helpee may expect much more than the professional helper is professionally and emotionally able to deliver. Similarly, the helping professional may feel he should have all the right answers to the helpee's questions. Additionally, the helper may allow his ego to push himself into dealing with issues of which he has little, if any, knowledge and expertise. The professional helper should always be aware of his limitations and be honest with himself and his clients in this regard.

Understanding your motivation for becoming a helping professional: It cannot be repeated enough that professional helpers are humans, and being a professional is one aspect of our total self. Given this obvious fact, this means that we have life goals—things that we want to accomplish in life that will help make a statement to society that we have contributed something to our community, state, nation, and perhaps the world.

Professional helpers should ask themselves several questions: Where does becoming a professional helper fit into my life goals? What has motivated me to become a professional helper? What rewards do I expect as a result of being a professional helper? Professional helpers should enjoy being of assistance to others; however, helping goes beyond enjoyment—helping fulfills some needs within us. Additional relevant questions should be: Am I engaging in this line of professional work for recognition from others? Am I doing this with the dream of becoming famous and making huge sums of money? Am I doing this because I am curious about other people's lives and obtain enjoyment hearing other's concerns? All of these questions relate to the master question of how does being a helping professional fit into our life goals? Another question that should be given consideration is: Is this my life ambition or is this a step leading to my ultimate goal? A mortal sin will not have been perpetrated on the world if becoming a professional helper is one step of several that will hopefully lead to other goals, as long as clients are not used as stepping platforms.

Understand one's prejudices: Most people prefer to think of themselves as being open minded and not harboring prejudices toward or against other people. However, the truth is that all humans have some prejudices. The reality questions are: To what degree do we have our prejudices? How do these prejudices impact our relationships with others?

The act of prejudging a person or a group of people is the foundation for developing a bias for or against the individual or group. There are many reasons that we are prejudice. However, we can condense many of the reasons into three broad categories: ethnocentrism, lack of significant intergroup contact, and preferences for categorization.

REASONS WE ARE PREJUDICED

Ethnocentrism: Ethnocentrism is a belief that one's culture is superior to all other cultures. In understanding ethnocentrism as it relates to the helping professions, one must view cultures from a broader prospective than race and ethnicity. Culture also can mean class, lower class, middle and upper class, educated class versus less educated class, and the distinctions could continue. The point being made is that in many, if not most, helping relationships, there is a cultural difference between the helper and the helpee, and the power difference, generally speaking, favors the helper. Consciously or subconsciously, viewing clients as not equal to you as the helper is a form of ethnocentrism.

Perhaps without realizing what is happening, the helper may react to the helpee in a superior manner. Unfortunately, action such as emphasizing perceived weaknesses of helpees can create a feeling of superiority on the part of the helper. From a conscious psychological standpoint, most helpers do not think of themselves as being superior to their helpees; however, actions such as highlighting a helpee's weakness to coworkers and immediate family members, as well as speaking in a derogatory manner to clients, betray the hidden or underlying feelings of the helper.

Lack of significant intergroup contacts: One of the ways we minimize prejudiced thoughts and actions is to get to know our clients. By becoming familiar with their wants, needs, beliefs, and values, we quickly learn that regardless of social status and perceived differences, we are more alike than different. The lack of contact with persons who appear to be different is often a major reason for the development and perpetuation of stereotypes and prejudices, as well as other misperceptions.

In the following comments, Spicer (1989) emphasizes the negative influence of the lack of contact with persons of cultures different from our own:

Throughout the world many people tend to value their way of life and reject other lifestyles. Our sense of belonging and social harmony can be disrupted when we encounter other cultures and we often seek to maintain our equilibrium by viewing these other people as inferior and even dangerous. Because our prejudices are largely unconscious these negative stereotypes can persist and, without our knowing it, have an impact on our interaction with other people. (p. 2)

It is imperative that we as helping professionals become aware of preconceived beliefs of people whom we consider to be different from us and recognize the impact these beliefs are having on our interacting with our clients.

Preference for categorization: Preference for categorization is the third major reason that we exhibit prejudice toward some people. As a society grows, the need to be organized becomes increasingly important. Thus, one way of establishing and maintaining order is to categorize various parts so that needs can be sufficiently identified and the appropriate goods and services can be provided. Consequently, it is difficult to envision an orderly society without using various forms of categorization. Classifying provides a quick and convenient way of identification. As most things in life, there are good and bad qualities to categorization; the good quality is that categorization provides a quick means of identification. However, the negative side is that, in some instances with regard to identification, labels are attached, and unfortunately sometimes those labels are less than complimentary and/or provide an inaccurate description of an individual or group of individuals. Once applied, these labels stick, and generations after generations suffer the consequences.

Unfortunately, after generations of these prejudiced labels have been perpetuated, they become accepted as truth. Forgotten is the fact that these labels were based on our need to categorize people and the assigning of attributes without having sufficient intergroup contact.

UNDERSTANDING ONE'S VALUES

Personal Theory: In most instances, human actions are not random acts that occur without foundation for their existence. Stated in other terms, our actions are based on some beliefs and circumstances that we have experienced. The circumstances that propel our actions may not be readily available to our conscious recollection at the time of our actions. Likewise, the beliefs that support our manner and way of reacting also may not be at the forefront of our memory as some of our actions are launched. Despite the lack of immediate understanding of why we feel and/or act in certain ways, there are reasons for those actions. The relevance of this to professional helpers is the fact that we have certain beliefs and attitudes about human nature that impact the manner in which we think of human action. Thus, these thoughts and beliefs affect the way we work with clients, albeit many times subconsciously.

The American Heritage Dictionary of the English Language, third edition (1992) defines *theory* as "a belief that guides action or assists comprehension or judgment." Each helping professional has personal beliefs that help guide her assistance provided to a client. These beliefs may not be conscious, they may not be organized, and they may not be published as part of her professional resume. However, these beliefs exist, and they perform a major role in how the helper views and interacts with clients. They should be a major consideration of the professional helper as she selects a professional theory or theories to work with clients.

One should note that I have introduced two types of theories: personal and professional. Professional theory is the theory or theories that the helping professional uses to help him understand human actions and assist in helping the client help himself, whereas personal theory is one's personal views with regard to human nature and how human nature is displayed in the environment. As previously mentioned, the helper's personal theory will impact the professional theory or theories she chooses to help guide her counseling therapy or other forms of helping. Given that, for most of us, our personal theory is not well organized and often is in our subconscious. The following discussion is an attempt to guide the helper with regard to organizing his thoughts and bring to the forefront of his mind his thoughts of human nature, thus developing an organized personal theory.

One of the keys to understanding oneself is to understand one's view of human nature (i.e., understanding what causes people to do and react in the manners they do). What we think of people and what we think of how we as humans are wired, has an impact on how we will react to them from both personal and professional standpoints. In

this part of the chapter, I present a number of topics that should pro-
voke thought on the part of the reader with regard to how you view
human nature. By doing this, it is hoped that the reader will better understand his or her personal philosophy of human dynamics and how
this belief impacts the helper's ways and methods of dealing with people. As previously stated, it is this author's contention that, whether we
realize the fact, we have components of a theory of human nature and
human dynamics, although these components are generally not well
organized and often are in our subconscious. These theories are developed from interacting with family, friends, significant others, people we like and trust, people we dislike, as well as people we hold in
high esteem and people for whom we have little regard. Stated in
other terms, the components of our theories are developed from our
life experiences and the interpretation we place on life events that we
experience in this life journey.

The benefit of the reader giving in-depth thought to the following
topics will be that, as the helper she or he will be better able to select
and/or develop a theory or theories and better understand the reasoning for selecting the theory. The following topics are: (a) belief with
regard to the nature of humans, (b) view of human development, (c)
role that past behavior plays with regard to human development, (d)
basic goals of humans, (e) normal and abnormal human personality
development, (f) amount of control individuals have over their lives,
and (g) impact of culture.

At the end of this chapter, the reader is encouraged to list on a sheet
of paper each of the seven previously identified topics and begin to answer them. These seven topics as stated are listed as questions at the
end of this chapter. After completing the reading of this chapter, please
go to the **mental exercise section** at the end of the chapter and answer the questions.

As you gain more experience in working with helpees, you should
review your answers and add to or delete some of the responses. You
should be aware that with experience your views of human nature will
change; therefore, your answers to the seven previously mentioned
topics will probably change over time. In fact, most theorists modify
their theories and experiences as additional scientific information,
with regard to human behavior, becomes available.

I have provided some discussion with regard to each topic to clarify and emphasize the importance of the topic, not to influence your

decision with regard to the topic. The answer to each of the seven topic questions should be your opinion.

The answers to these topics are personal and individual, and the topics are presented to start you on your journey of discovering your personal theory of human nature. My views of human nature in this exercise are irrelevant; only your opinions are relevant!

What are Your Beliefs with Regard to the Nature of Humans?

Do individuals have innate drives to do good? Are individuals innately evil and do they have to be guided toward appropriate behavior? Do individuals strive to create a balance between good and evil in their lives? Are humans innately selfish—primarily concerned with their own survival? As helping professionals examine their beliefs with regard to the nature of humans, all of these, and more, questions of the psychological makeup of human beings should be considered. The helping professional's opinion with regard to the previously mentioned questions strikes at the heart of how the helper will judge the actions of the helpee, the reasons for his actions, and the extent of the assistance the helpee will need to help resolve his life situation(s).

In our daily lives, our beliefs with regard to human nature help guide the way we interact with others. This statement implies that our beliefs are born from our experiences. By understanding our views, we have a chance to modify, strengthen, and/or eliminate unwanted and inappropriate views.

The author has presented the previously mentioned questions to hundreds of students, and the majority initially state that as humans we are neither innately good nor evil. Rather we are born with a blank slate, and societal and environmental factors are the major contributors of our psychological makeup. Perhaps the reason that many indicate this as their belief is because, without having given in-depth thought to the question, this is a safe position to take. In contemporary American society, initially few people want to think that there may be a sinister side to our personality. Additionally, we do not like to think of ourselves as being selfish. However, as students are pressed to give more than surface thought to these questions, they begin to point out that persons reared in loving homes sometimes do deplorable things. Likewise, there are numerous examples of children reared in deplorable conditions devoting their lives to selfless causes attempting to help others, sometimes helping at risk to their own safety.

As helping professionals, we must examine our beliefs with regard to basic human nature. If our belief is that the human nature is basically good, the helper will look for the good within the client and work with the client to bring forth the good within him. If the helper thinks that human nature is innately selfish, he will work with the client to show how self-centered actions are standing in the way of the client becoming a happier and more complete individual. Whatever the helper's basic views of human nature are, he will think of incidents to reinforce this belief. Granted, this thought process may be subconscious, nevertheless it will occur.

As humans, we tend to look for evidence to reinforce and support our beliefs. Therefore, it is imperative that the professional helper be aware of what his beliefs are. Understanding the forces that are impacting his life will help the professional helper develop empathy in working with a client. Empathy will occur because the helper will have a deeper understanding of why he has certain feeling with regard to the client's issues and will also have a much clearer understanding of why he as the helper is concentrating on certain issues in the client's life.

As an example of how one's personal beliefs impact views of human behavior, Sigmund Freud's beliefs regarding human nature, in part, resulted in the development of psychoanalytic therapy. Freud believed that the basic emotional composition of humans is to seek pleasure and attempt to avoid pain. He believed that to avoid pain and increase our chances of experiencing pleasure, we are inclined to be selfish. Stated in other terms, we will do things that cause us to feel good, and sometimes this pleasure may come at the expense of others' well-being; therefore, we must keep check on our motives for action and be attuned to the need to be considerate of others' feelings and well-being as we attempt to meet our needs.

What does this have to do with helping professionals' need to understand their beliefs with regard to the psychological composition of human nature, especially as one considers that this is a belief and perhaps not reality? The answer to this question revolves around the fact that one's beliefs with regard to human nature will impact how one interacts with clients. If the helping professional thinks that, as humans, we are endowed with intentions of doing good to and for others, born with the desires to be selfless; putting others' well-being before our own survival, this pattern of beliefs will impact the manner in which we conduct the helping relationship (i.e., it will impact the standpoint of the types of questions asked, the depth of inquiries into personal feelings, and the directions in which we attempt to assist the client with regard to finding solutions to his life situations). Likewise, if the helping professional believes the natural tendency of humans is to be selfish–thinking of our own welfare and meeting our own needs–this will both subconsciously and consciously impact the nature of his interaction with the client.

VIEWS OF HUMAN DEVELOPMENT

Is human development based on the forces of nature or is development based on how one is reared? A third possibility is a combination of nature and nurture. If this is the belief, one has to think about under which circumstances do nature and nurture come into play and the impact.

Unless the helping professional believes that life is predetermined, she has to consider that human behavior is motivated by force or forces of the environment. If this is the case, the helping professional must think about the forces that are impacting the client's life. Additionally, she must consider to what extent these forces are having an impact on the client's life. Simply taking the position that human behavior is predicated on both forces of nature and personal family environment is not enough to effectively assess and assist the client. The professional must look at the types of forces and the client's interpretation of the impact and relevance of these forces on his life.

The importance of the helping professional's understanding of her views of how human behavior is developed will determine how she approaches the variables that are involved in creating the client's life situation. To be effective, the helping professional must have some theoretical foundation on which she develops her approaches to helping clients. Examining and understanding her views with regard to how natural forces that may have been beyond the control of the client has directed his life, as well as understanding personal family forces, which to some extent may have also been beyond his control, are affecting his life are crucial to effectively assisting with alternative ways of living with and/or handling the client's life situation.

Role past behavior play with regard to human development: In looking at humans and their behaviors, the professional helper must realize the obvious–that behavior does not appear from thin air and does not occur without some reasoning behind the acts and actions. The theory that helps serve as a guide to a professional helper as she assists clients must take into consideration from where the motivation for the behavior comes and the importance of that information in the helping process. The helper cannot deny that the helpee has a past and included in that past are actions that have caused reactions. Acknowledging that past behavior obviously exists and has had an impact on the helpee's life does not mean that the helper has to believe that the most important factors motivating the client's behavior is predicated on previous experiences. Likewise, the helper does not have to deny that past behavior has not had significant impacts on the client's current behavior. However, the professional helper must acknowledge that the client's past is real and determine whether a successful outcome depends on dealing with that behavior and, if so, to what extent and if no, why? Additionally, the professional helper must deal with her assessment of how the client has and is currently dealing with his past. The professional helper may decide that the past is having an impact, but the resolutions to the client's problems are not dependent on dealing with the past. If the helper chooses to delve into the client's past and possibly uncover suppressed information, she must be aware that considerable skill may be required to deal with this type of information. A good rule of thumb with regard to suppressed information is that the information is in that state for a specific reason, and it is often too emotionally difficult for the client to handle, thus uncovering this information may expand the client's problems. This is not to say that suppressed information should not be handled. In fact, in some cases, it may be necessary to look into some of the locked closets. What is being implied is that caution must be taken when dealing with suppressed information, and the helper must be well trained to be effective and not create more problems.

Basic goals of humans: Incorporating this question into one's theory is necessary and quite difficult to answer. There is no one set of specific goals to which all humans subscribe. In dealing with this question, the professional helper must draw on his own beliefs with regard to basic goals of humans. With rare exceptions, most humans seek safety, survival, and happiness in their lives. However, how we as humans attempt to attain these goals becomes a major factor in our reaction to daily life. Understanding the how of obtaining basic goals is a key component of the helper's development of his theory. More discussion with regard to this subject is found in **Chapter 4** (this volume).

Normal and abnormal human development: *Not all life problems that clients bring to a helping relationship setting involve abnormal behavior.* Likewise, not all behavior presented is normal behavior. It is difficult to understand how a helper can consider himself a professional if he does not have some views with regard to what constitutes normal behavior and what represents abnormal behavior. To make these determinations, the helper has to be aware of the surroundings, or environment in which the actions are taking place. Provided as an example, in some tropical and/or hot climates, being seen in public with little or in some cases, no clothing may be considered as normal or acceptable behavior, whereas in Western society as well as most other societies, this would be considered abnormal behavior. Another example is that in some cultures, spanking (not beating) a child is normal behavior, and in others in the same country, this behavior is viewed as inappropriate and subject to legal penalties. The point being made is that the professional must be aware of what is considered normal and acceptable and what is considered abnormal and in what context the judgments are being made.

Certainly, behaviors that are blatant violations of prevailing local, state, and/or federal laws, such as physical child abuse or elder abuse, are easily identified as abnormal behavior. However, in some instances, behavior becomes a judgment call with regard to whether it is normal or abnormal behavior. Some people are reared in environments where certain behavior is judged by the masses as unacceptable. However, the same behavior is condoned by the person's family, friends, and peers. This is not meant to mean that such behavior is to be condoned by the helper. However, an understanding of why the behavior is occurring should add some directions to the development of the helping relationship. Therefore, the helper's view of what is normal behavior and what is abnormal behavior will have an important bearing on how he views helpees' behaviors. Thus, this will impact this part of his theory regarding human behavior.

Controls individuals have over their lives: I speak of control, not in the context of the amount of freedom one has within a given society. Rather, I refer to the amount of free will one has with regard to deciding the direction of her life. Stated succinctly, what are your beliefs with regard to the degree of control clients have with regard to directing their lives? Is life already scripted and we have little or no choices in regard to the direction our lives take? If our choices are already scripted, what role does the helping professional play? If this is the belief, then the helping professional may believe that his role in life is scripted and the decisions he makes as a helper are predetermined. Again, if this is the belief, this brings up an interesting point. Is the helper basically free from any responsibility with regard to the solutions he helps the client implement? Therefore, the helper may believe that he should do the best and most appropriate things he can for his clients, and because the outcome is already ordained, he and the client could not have made any other choices. Another interesting question is this: If things don't go well in the helping relationship, should the helper examine what went wrong to avoid making those choices again?

Continuing with the question of how much control one has over life situations, the helper should determine whether he believes that each person has limited controls over life situations. If this is the case, the helper must determine: How much control do individuals have and under which conditions individuals can exert these controls? Finally, do individuals have free will to make any decision he or she desires?

The answers to the previously presented questions will have a major impact on how the helper interacts with his clients. Additionally, the helper's views with regard to the questions will impact the professional theory or theories he will feel comfortable adopting.

Role Culture Plays in Human Behavior

Few, if any, dispute the fact that one's worldviews are impacted by one's cultures. Therefore, two of the questions to which a professional helper should attempt to seek an answer are: To what extent do cultures impact? How do the impacts influence the helpee's behavior? Because we are aware that everyone has culture and that each individual will experience his culture in an individual way, the helper should, as much as possible, determine how the helpee is influenced by his cultural stimulations. If the professional helper does not do this, he will be guilty of one or both of the following misjudgments: (a) judging the helpee on stereotypical views of culture subscribed to a group of people, such as "all people act that way," or (b) the helper will judge all people based on the cultures with which he has developed his worldviews. Either one can and probably will be unproductive for the helping relationship.

SUMMARY

In summary, it is imperative that the professional helper develop a personal theory with regard to human behavior. Answering the seven previously mentioned topics will aid in the development of the personal theory. The reader is encouraged to both modify the seven topics and develop additional topics with regard to human behavior.

Chapter Review Questions

1. Why is it important for a helping professional to understand his or her emotions?
2. Why is it important for a helping professional to understand his or her limitations?
3. What does the term *ethnocentrism* mean?
4. In your opinion, is it important for a helping professional to examine his or her motives for becoming a helping professional? Explain your opinion.

Mental Exercise

1. What are your beliefs with regard to the nature of humans?
2. What are your views of human development?
3. What role or roles do past behaviors play with regard to human development?
4. What are the basic goals of humans?
5. What is normal and abnormal human personality development?
6. How much control do individuals have over their lives?
7. What is the impact of culture on human behavior?

8. List several types of clients/helpees with which you feel you would have difficulties helping and discuss why.
9. List any type of client/helpee which you would refuse service, if you had that option in your work site or practice.
10. List some of your motives for wanting to become a professional helper, if being a professional helper is one of your goals.
11. If you are a professional helper or your plans are to become a professional helper, what do you expect to gain from being in this profession?
12. List five strengths that you have that you think will or could help you be an effective professional helper.
13. List five weaknesses that you have that you think would be a liability for you as a professional helper, and how could you correct those liabilities?

References

Spicer, J. (1989). *Counseling ethnic minorities.* Center City, MN: Hazelden.
The American Heritage Dictionary of the English Language (3rd ed.). (1992). Boston: Houghton Mifflin.

Suggested Readings

Alisan, L. (2007). *Exploring identity: Concepts and methods.* New York: Palgrave Macmillan.
Aronson L. (2008). *Interviewing clients across cultures: A practitioner's guide.* New York: Guilford Press.
Baldwin, M. W. (Ed.). (2005). *Interpersonal cognition.* New York: Guilford Press. Cohen, A. P. (1994). *Self-consciousness and alternative anthropology of identity.* New York: Routledge.
Macrae N., et al. (Ed.). (1996). *Stereotypes and stereotyping.* New York: Guilford Press.

Chapter 4

UNDERSTANDING HUMAN BEHAVIOR

Chapter Outline
- Introduction
- Theorists' Views
  - Sigmund Freud and Psychoanalysis
  - Alfred Adler and Adlerian Therapy
  - Carl Rogers and Person-Centered Therapy
  - Fredrick (Fritz) Perls and Laura Perls and Gestalt Therapy
- Existential Theorists
  - Abraham Maslow
- Behavioral Theorists
- My Views of Behavior
- Assessing Behavior
- Identifying Major Issues
- Identifying Cultural Factors
- Identifying Acculturation Issues
- Identifying Crisis Meeting Resources
- Determine Definition of the Issue
- Summary
  - References

Chapter Objectives
- Present Some Theorists' Views of Human Behavior
- Present a Method of Assessing Human Behavior

INTRODUCTION

For a professional helper, understanding oneself is crucial to understanding and managing one's motivations, as well as providing an understanding of one's feelings with regard to assisting with helpers' issues and life situations. Similarly, understanding one's views of human behavior, for a helping professional, is critical with regard to determining helpees' motivations for reacting as they may act.

Understanding human behavior is one of the keys to being successful as a professional helper. It is through the observation of behavior, or in some way becoming aware of the helpee's behavior and one's interpretation of this behavior, that significant judgments are made, which often determine the direction that the helping relationship will go. As we think of human behavior, initially our thoughts of behavior seem to be clear: behavior is good or bad, appropriate or inappropriate. However, as helping professionals we must be aware that behavior is not as definitive as that simplistic explanation. With regard to developing a better understanding, one must examine human behavior from many angles, such as what is motivating the behavior, what are the prevailing social norms that influence the behavior, what is the person's perception of his behavior, and what are some of the other factors that are influencing the behavior? These and many other issues with regard to understanding human behavior are addressed in this chapter. However, first we look at some prominent theorists' views of human nature.

THEORISTS' VIEWS

Sigmund Freud and Psychoanalysis

As psychological theorists developed their therapies, one of the major components with which they engaged time and effort was to enunciate their understanding of human behavior. As has been stated several times in previous chapters, concepts of human behavior are critical to the development of a helping relationship therapy. It is almost impossible to assist a helpee with an effective helping plan without having some concepts of why the helpee behaves the way he does.

Psychological therapy would be much simpler if there was one, or perhaps two, correct ways to view and understand human behavior. The reality is that there are many ways to view human behavior and many of the views have some degree of validity. Some of the varieties of viewing human behavior are evident in the concepts that some of the leading psychological therapist have used in developing their psychological approaches to helping.

Arguably, the most influential theorist of the twentieth and thus far twenty-first centuries is Sigmund Freud. The reason I contend he is the most influential is not because he is the most accurate or the most popular, but because his views have influenced most modern psychological theories and therapies. In some cases, other therapists and theorists have used various components of his theories and therapies to develop their therapies, whereas in other cases some therapists have disagreed significantly with Freud and developed their therapies in opposition to his precepts. Either way, Freud, directly or indirectly, has influenced most modern-day therapies.

With regard to Freud and human behavior, in his development of psychoanalytical therapy, Freud contends that human behavior is predicated on information that is stored in the subconscious mind. Freud contends that material stored in our unconscious memory influences our current behavior. Therefore, to understand current behavior, one needs to have an understanding of what is stored away from our conscious memory and to have an understanding of why that information is not readily available to our immediate recall. Some may view human behavior in this context as predeterministic behavior–the person has little or no control over its release because the person is reacting to information and feelings that have been stored away in the subconscious. The reality is that the person does have control. Perhaps the subconscious does have some control over the thoughts and feelings the person has; however, the release of the energy, in the form of reaction, can be controlled by the person. By thinking before acting, the person can control and direct the release of energy. Assisting the client to think before acting can be a major goal of the helping professional in working with clients with regard to controlling behavior.

Freud seems to be implying that the irrational forces, unconscious motivations, and biological and instinctual drives determine our behavior. Freud's concept of the unconscious influencing current behavior, from a psychoanalytical therapeutic standpoint, can be considered as holding the key to understanding problematic behavior. This understanding is developed because Freud discussed the fact that one of the reasons we store information in our subconscious is that the information is too troublesome to psychologically handle; thus, to protect our mental state, we, in a sense, forget the action or significant portions of the action. Also, in understanding Freud's concept of the unconscious, one must remember that the basic element of psychoanalytical theory is that as humans our basic instinct is to prevent pain and increase pleasure; therefore, hurtful information or memories are relegated to the unconscious to avoid pain. Thus, from a psychoanalytical theory standpoint, a goal with regard to assisting a client is to bring the unconscious to the conscious level so the client will understand why she behaves in certain ways. An additional goal is to strengthen the client's ego so that her behavior coincides with reality.

A compact summary of psychoanalytical view of human behavior is: (a) human behavior is driven by instinctual urges, (b) the unconscious repressed material provides a major influence on current behavior, and (c) defense mechanisms are developed to compensate for the repressed material and to avoid psychological pain. Psychological theorists may disagree with Freud with regard to the importance of the unconscious; however, most do not disagree with the concept that the unconscious exists and does influence behavior. Therefore, a major contribution that Freud made to psychological theories and the understanding of behavior has been the fact that he brought to awareness the fact that the unconscious exists and has an impact on behavior. Where other psychological theorists disagree with Freud is the extent that the professional helper should devote to working with the client regarding understanding information held in the unconscious.

Alfred Adler and Adlerian Therapy

In contrast to Freud's concentration on the unconscious as holding the key to why we behave the way we do, a former colleague of Freud, Alfred Adler, developed his individual psychology or Adlerian therapy as almost the opposite of Freud's contentions. Adler did not believe that the professional helper had to concentrate on the unconscious to understand the motivation for human behavior. Adler contended that at an early age, around six (6) years, we begin to think about what we would like to be in life. Adler says that we begin to develop a concept of our **ideal self**, and in this process we begin to realize that we are not where we should be with regard to being that ideal self. He called this feeling or realization a state of **inferiority**. In this case, inferiority does not mean we are less than other, but we are not what we should be. It is at this point that we begin to work toward our ideal self and, to use an Adlerian phrase, try to reach a state of **superiority**. Again, the term *superiority* does not imply what we normally think of when we hear the word; in Adlerian terms, it means being the best we can be.

As we begin to develop our long-range life goals, to move from the state of inferiority toward the state of superiority, we begin to develop our patterns of behavior that lead toward these life goals. Therefore, based on Adlerian theory, our behavior is predicated on two things: our environment or social setting and our perception of that setting. Adler's theory views human behavior as having a linear progression moving from the previously mentioned state of inferiority toward a state of superiority. In this progression, all behavior should be considered from a social context. Adler believed that humans strive to be part of a social order. Thus, their behavior should be judged from the social environment within which the person is involved and the contribution or lack thereof that the person makes to that social environment.

Adler posits that behavior is influenced by events. He further promoted the idea that behavior occurs in a social context. Therefore, for the helper to more accurately understand a person's behavior, the helper must become aware of the helpee's perception or phenomenological perspective. Adlerian theory concentrates on three areas of motivation: (a) people are motivated by their setting of goals, (b) people are motivated by the way they deal with the tasks they face in life, and (c) people are motivated by their social interests. Thus, as a person makes positive contributions to his social environment, the behavior is considered normal or appropriate. Conversely, negative contributions to the social environment means the person is not living up to his potential of positively contributing to the society in which he lives.

Adlerian theory of human behavior differs significantly from the Freudian theory, in that Adlerian theory promotes the idea that behavior is rooted in a conscious awareness as opposed to the Freudian view of behavior being unconsciously motivated. Adler believed that it is our present perceptions that form our reality and influence our behavior, not past experiences. As previously stated, Adlerian theorists posit that behavior is to be viewed in a social context. To be more specific, they believe the individuals who express social interest usually focus their social inclinations toward positive and healthy activities. Socially active, mentally healthy people show an interest in activities that benefit society. Individuals who have poor mental health are more likely to be selfish and direct their interaction in ways that primarily benefit themselves. According to Adler, our success and happiness are directly correlated to social connectedness. Individuals who lack social connection are often discouraged and can lead unproductive lives (Corey, 2005).

From the Adlerian prospective, to assist those clients who have lost their social connection, and thus are in need of a psychological helping relationship, the professional helper must work with the client to reeducate him back on a healthy and socially connected pathway. During reeducation, the helper will assist the client to better understand his ideal self, reeducating the client to his original goals. According to Corey (2005) and Bitter (2007), individuals with social interests strive toward healthy and socially useful aspects of life, whereas neurosis, psychosis, and criminal behavior can be understood as a retreat from these tasks.

Carl Rogers and Person-Centered Therapy

Person-centered therapy, which was developed by psychologist Carl Rogers, has at least six basic concepts that he believed were central to human development: (1) The client is fundamentally the center of his world; (2) because a client is the center of his world, his perception is reality and therefore to what the individual will react; (3) a client's behavioral goals are to meet her needs as she perceives them; (4) portions of a client's perceptions are then incorporated into oneself; (5) one's perceptual field and interaction with the environment combine to develop the self; and (6) human beings behave in ways that are consistent with their personal concept of self.

Although Carl Rogers, through his person-centered therapy, does not specifically address what constitutes normal or abnormal behavior, one can deduce some concepts of human behavior from the basic philosophy of the theory. Person-centered therapy belongs to the humanistic school of psychological thought and, as such, believes in the growth potential of humans. In this case, growth potential means the ability to understand one's life situation and, within the appropriate setting, to find appropriate solutions to one's problems.

What does the previous information tell us about Carl Rogers' unspoken beliefs with regard to human behavior? One, we have the ability to recognize appropriate or correct behavior versus inappropriate behavior. Two, we are part of a social environment, thus we have the ability to understand the social norms of our environment. Three, although we may be the center of our own world, we have the ability to recognize that we must interact in socially acceptable ways. Four, because we have the ability to recognize the previously mentioned social norms, we have the ability to correct maladaptive behavior and conform to prevailing societal standards.

One important concept of person-centered therapy that relates to behavior is the idea that as humans we react to our perception of reality. This perception of reality is what helps determine our behavior in a given situation. However, unless the person has severely impaired cognitive abilities, she knows right from wrong, appropriate from inappropriate behavior. Therefore, one of the goals of person-centered therapy is to assist the helpee by establishing a therapeutic environment conductive to correcting her perceptions.

A key to person-centered therapy is that the professional helper does not have to tell the person what is the correct behavior or course of action; as previously stated, she has the ability to find the right course of action. Again, the role of the professional helper is to help establish the right therapeutic environment for the client to correct her perceptions.

Fredrick (Fritz) Perls and Laura Perls and Gestalt Therapy

Gestalt therapy, which was developed in the 1940s by Fredrick (Fritz) Perls and his wife Laura, is also part of the humanistic school of psychotherapy. The Perls, through their gestalt therapy, differ from Sigmund Freud and psychoanalytical therapy in that they concentrate on the present rather than placing an emphasis on past events and the unconscious. This therapy also differs from its fellow humanistic therapy stablemate, Adlerian therapy, from the standpoint of its emphasis on present behavior rather than the future, which is a component of Adlerian therapy, although Adlerian therapy can be interpreted as being both present and future oriented.

The key word in gestalt therapy is **awareness** of how one is feeling and perceiving events at that particular moment in time; therefore, gestalt therapy is a present–rather than a past–or future-oriented therapy. Gestalt therapist emphasizes that understanding behavior in the present moment is key to understanding "why a person behaves as he does." Focusing on the past can be a way to avoid coming to terms with the present (Corey, 2005, p. 195). Although gestalt is present oriented, some therapists recognize that past events or perceptions of past events do affect current perceptions, and they call this **unfinished business**. Remaining true to the foundation philosophy of present orientation, the therapist assists the client in working through these feelings by having him concentrate on how this situation is making him feel in the here and now. Therefore, the helpee's phenomenological viewpoint is critical to understanding the motivation of human behavior.

Existential Theorists

There is no one person who developed existentialism; the philosophy of existentialism has existed since humans developed reasoning abilities. As is discussed, the philosophy of existentialism is an integral part of many psychological therapies, particularly humanistic therapies.

Existentialism is a philosophy more than it is a therapy. The essence of existentialism is that as humans we are in a constant state of change and evolving. Additionally, we have the capability to have the ultimate control of our lives. The ultimate control of our lives is how we think about our self and our life situations. Existentialism teaches us that as human beings we will have suffering in our lives; however, the important control is how we deal with life events; how we, within our mind, think about and handle these events. Existentialism teaches us not only about suffering, but about all aspects of our lives, and again how we think and react to whatever events, at least from a cerebral standpoint, determine our behavior. Thus, this is our ultimate life control.

Therefore, how existentialism contributions to our understanding of human behavior relate to our perception of events and how this perception impacts our life situation. Stated in other terms, as humans we have the ultimate control of our lives, which is how we perceive our life situations, and this perception or feelings with regard to our situations determine our behavior. A paraphrasing of the nineteenth century European-born philosopher Friedrich Nietzche may best illustrate existentialism and human behavior: "If one has the why to live he can withstand almost any how."

From a psychological therapeutic standpoint, existentialism is considered as part of the humanistic school. It is my opinion that humanism should be part of what should be considered the existentialism school. Stated another way, because existentialism philosophy is part of each humanistic therapy, it appears that existentialism is the underpinning of these therapies. Therefore, instead of the humanistic school of psychological thought therapies, such as Adlerian, person-centered, gestalt, and so on, they should be part of the existentialism psychological school of thought.

No human being invented, founded, or constructed existentialism. It is, in my opinion, part of the human spirit. The philosophy of existentialism has existed ever since humans began to think about their worlds and their lives beyond self-preservation. For thousands of years, humans have contemplated their existence and what their lives mean. Corey (2005) captures the essence of existentialism with the following words: "Being a person implies that we are discovering and making sense of our existence" (p. 136). The philosophy of existentialism can be found in the teaching of all major religions that promote peace, love, self-sacrifice, and making choices.

Three basic principles characterize existentialism's view of human behavior: (a) humans have choices, (b) humans are responsible for their behavior, and (c) humans have the freedom to change. There are two basic roles the helping professional should assume with regard to existentialism philosophy and human behavior when working with a client who is experiencing life situations and is seeking professional help: (1) work with the client to help him understand where he is not living a fully authentic life and is not utilizing his options with regard to making appropriate life choices, and (2) assist the client in taking responsibility for his behavior and not blaming others for his life situations. The professional helper may have to point out to the client that others may have contributed to his life situations and may have limited his choices. However, choices do remain, and using those options may mean some hardship and/or suffering. Nevertheless, that is part of life, and he will be stronger for having taken control of his life.

Abraham Maslow

Doctor Maslow's humanistic approach to human motivation posits that human behavior is predicated on satisfying needs. In this regard, he put forth his famous hierarchy of needs, where he proposed that as humans we have certain needs that occur in a progression fashion that must be met. Stated in other terms, there are basic or lower level needs that must be met before higher level needs can be met; therefore, our behavior is based on meeting the required needs. The needs and their levels of importance to humans are as follows. The lowest and most basic needs that motivate human behavior are physiological needs: food and other life-sustaining elements, shelter, and at least minimum levels of comfort. The second-level needs, according to Maslow's hierarchy of needs, are safety and security. Although this level appears to be a straightforward set of needs, one also must remember safety and security are relative to one's life situation and environment. The third level—love and belonging needs—indicates that once Levels 1 and 2 have been met, our behavior is motivated by trying to seek the companionship of friends, coworkers, and other acquaintances, as well as develop close and devoted relationships with family. Additionally, at this level, our behavior seeks intimate and loving relationships with sweethearts. The fourth level is self-esteem needs, where our behavior motivation relates to receiving the respect of others and self-respect. The highest human need that impacts our behavior is self-actualization, which means we are attempting to fulfill our human potentials. Other theorists have referred to this as meeting our fullest potential and being fully authentic.

Behavioral Theorists

The foundation for behavior therapy is classical conditioning and operant conditioning. Russian physiologist Ivan Pavlov is considered to be the first to demonstrate classical conditioning. Pavlov demonstrated that when an unconditioned stimulus such as food produces an unconditioned response such as salivation and is associated with a conditioned stimulus such as the ring of a bell, if the paring is repeated often enough, the conditioned stimulus alone will produce the unconditioned response. This established the relationship of stimulus and response (behavior).

B. F. Skinner expanded the knowledge of behavior with the concept of operant conditioning. Skinner postulated that behavior that is positively reinforced will be repeated; conversely, behavior that is punished or ignored will be eliminated. Skinner's contribution established the concept that the quality and/or type of reaction to the stimulus determines what will happen to the behavior.

Other behaviorists, such as Arnold Lazarus, Albert Bandura, Albert Ellis, Aaron Beck, Joseph Wolpe, and others, have made significant contributions to the understanding of human behavior. Aaron Beck introduced principles of learning theory to behavioral therapy, which has led to the development of cognitive behavior therapy. Albert Bandura also has made significant contributions to the concept of what affects human behavior; he also utilized principles of learning theory to help explain how behavior is changed. According to Corey (2005), Bandura posited that "behavior is influenced by stimulus events, by external reinforcement and by cognitive mediation experiences" (p. 230). Albert Ellis introduced the concept of human's irrational thinking as a major factor affecting how humans behave, thus creating rational emotive behavior therapy.

As one may observe, the original function of behaviorism (classical and operant conditioning) treated human behavior as significantly devoid of the influence of the process of thought (Bryan, 2007). However, with the previously mentioned contributions—of introducing, cognition, and learning theory to behavior therapy—human behavior therapy has shifted, now recognizing that we have the capability to impact our environment, which in turn will have significant impacts on our behavior.

My Views of Behavior

All behavior has purpose: To be an effective helping professional, one has to become adept at observing and making assessments with regard to the helpee's behavior. Regardless of whether you believe that behavior is a result of attempts to satisfy instinctual urges or the result of our ego attempting to control those instinctual urges, or perhaps some other view (such as behavior is reacting to perceptions of social and/or environmental events), you have to recognize that all behavior has purpose. It is a necessary requirement that you develop a reasonable and logical understanding of the client's behavior. In his

theoretical foundation of individual psychology, Alfred Adler emphasized that behavior is purposeful, goal directed, and conscious. Too
often as helping professionals, we become aware of clients' behaviors
and make judgments, such as the behavior is good or bad, appropriate, or inappropriate, rational or irrational. These types of judgments
may be necessary; however, they do not answer the major questions
that must be answered: What is motivating this behavior? Why is this
behavior occurring? What is the purpose of this behavior? Without
reasonable answers to these and other questions with regard to the
purpose of the behavior, the helper basically is groping in psychological darkness trying to understand the helpee and his life situation.
Also without an understanding of the purpose of the behavior, many
times the solutions that the helper and helpee develop become at best
temporary because, without knowing the purpose of the behavior and
more specifically which needs are being met by the behavior, the behavior and problems it creates will reoccur.

Behavior is learned: With the exception of the instinctual urges of
an infant to meet primal survival needs, most other behavior is
learned. Behavior is learned from significant others. In this case, significant others mean more than family, close friends, and peers and
persons for whom one has considerable respect. Significant others can
mean persons with whom one does not have a relationship, but the
person has acquired status that one would like to have. This status can
be, from a societal standpoint, either positive or negative. To be more
specific, the status could be having considerable material possessions,
such as occupational position, money, cars, clothing, and jewelry that
have been obtained through dubious and/or illegal means. The helpee
may not admire the person but have some admiration for his accomplishments and possessions; thus, this person's behavior may serve as
motivation for the helpee.

The professional should review the helpee's past to discover what
the client learned, how the facts were learned, and under which conditions they were learned to understand what is considered, in his, the
helpee's, mind as acceptable and unacceptable behavior. Additionally,
the helper should determine what the consequences or benefits of the
behavior are, and finally the helper should determine which changes
the helpee would like to have occur with regard to the behavior.

Human behavior is affected by perception: One of the most
common beliefs of humanistic therapies is that our beliefs and atti-

tudes of our surroundings affect the way we behave. Our perceptions are our realities. The fact that one's perception is inaccurate does not change the behavior; what does impact change in the behavior is a new perception, hopefully a more accurate one. A significant concept of cognitive behavior therapy is that our thoughts impact our behavior; thus, cognitive behavioral therapists help clients develop goals and work with the client to change perceptions, therefore changing behavior.

Behavior is affected by social norms and environmental factors: All societies establish both formal and informal rules by which its inhabitants are expected to conform. Likewise, to be considered good citizens, most people conform to the rules established by its society; therefore, their behaviors are influenced by these formally stated or implied rules of conduct. Some people, however, choose not to conform, and their behavior is often judged to be abnormal or maladaptive. In some cases, this is a correct and appropriate evaluation, but in some instances, societal rules are unfair and/or applied unequally, thus defiant behavior, although against societal standards, is warranted. Regardless of compliance or noncompliance, the social norms and environmental factors impact human behavior.

To be effective, the helping professional must be aware of the social norms and environmental factors that surround the helpee. Understanding social norms is more than having an understanding of the federal, state, and local laws. The understanding must extend to community and family standards. The helper also must develop and understand the client's perceptions of these various formal and informal standards of conducts and understand the benefits and disadvantages of conformity or nonconformity.

Behavior is a relationship between cognitive processes and environmental factors: Similar to the discussion regarding behavior being affected by environmental factors and social norms, one's behavior is a response to how the individual conceptualizes his surroundings. This means that most behavior is not spontaneous and instinctual. Most behavior is a product of some thought, albeit sometimes hurried and perhaps irrational, being given to the rewards and possible punishment of the act. This also means that most behavior changes as a result of one's surroundings. To elaborate, most people will assess their immediate environment to determine the rewards or punishment of behavior within that environment; consequently, behavior is adjusted based on the perceptions of the immediate environment.

As is indicated by the various views of theorists with regard to what motivates human behavior, there are a number of thoughts concerning what and how human behavior is motivated. It is imperative that the professional helper develop his theory of human behavior. Additionally, the professional helper must formulate ideas with regard to assessing behavior.

ASSESSING BEHAVIOR

An important part of understanding human behavior and effectively helping a helpee is to be able to make assessments of the person's motives, reactions, actions, and feelings with regard to her life situations. The helper should not think that his initial assessment is chiseled in stone; the reality is that as the helper and helpee move through the helping process and the helpee becomes more comfortable with the helper, new information is released by the helpee and thus additional feelings of the helpee are revealed. Therefore, the initial assessment must be revised. Because the initial assessment may not be totally accurate, it should not be an inhibiting factor in making needed assessments. There are two types of assessments that must be made. One assessment is assessing the motivations for the current behavior. The second type of assessment relates to assessing the variables that are impacting the life situation(s) being encountered by the helpee, as well as resources that the helpee currently possesses which can be used to help resolve the life situation(s).

With regard to assessing factors motivating behavior, the helper must determine the following: (a) What has the helpee learned with regard to the consequences of his behavior? (b) What is normal behavior in the helpee's environment, and what is abnormal behavior in the helpee's environment? If the helpee is engaging in abnormal behavior, what is the basis for this behavior?

Assessing the helpee's concept of the consequences of his behavior, as previously stated, is important because if the helpee has either been rewarded for his behavior or not received any significant negative consequences of the behavior, there have been few to no incentives to change the behavior, assuming the behavior is inappropriate. The knowledge obtained from this assessment will give the helpee a window into the mindset of the helpee. The helper's assessment of what is considered normal and abnormal behavior within the helpee's environment is critical. The helper will make a mistake of significant magnitude if he judges the helpee's perception of right and wrong, normal and abnormal behavior based on his, the helper's, standard. Even making a judgment based on prevailing societal standards is not sufficient to determine the helpee's perception of what is normal or abnormal within his personal life. The helpee may have been reared within a family, either nuclear or extended, that either promotes or condones some behavior that is in opposition to societal standards. Offered as examples, a helpee may have been reared in a family environment where excessive alcohol consumption and/or use of illegal substances are accepted. The helpee will recognize that this type of behavior is not condoned by the general society; however, this type of behavior is both accepted and condoned within his immediate environment. Other scenarios could be developed, however, I think the point has been made.

With regard to assessing life situation variables, some of the initial assessment items should be: (a) identifying major issues facing the helpee; (b) identifying any cultural, ethnic, and/or racial issues impacting behavior; (c) determining whether there are any acculturation issues to be considered; (d) identifying family dynamics; (e) identifying the person and/or family crisis meeting resources; and (f) identifying the persons and/or family's definition of the issues.

Ponterotto and his associates (1995) provide an appropriate summary of the importance of assessment with the following comments, although referencing the helping profession of counseling can apply to many, if not all, helping professions:

> Successful counseling requires an accurate assessment of the client's concerns, which includes an in-depth understanding of the factors that influence the client's experience, perception, and presentation of her or his problems. Furthermore, comprehensive assessment entails viewing the client as a unique individual, as a social unit within a family and as a member of a cultural group. (p. 357)

Identifying Major Issues

When working with a client, as much as possible, the client should be the one who determines the life issues that he feels are the most relevant, at that time, and the ones that should be the first to receive attention. Although this is the ideal, the helper should develop ideas with regard to significant issues affecting the helpee's life. The issues developed from discussion and observation with the helpee should be used by the helper to help guide the helpee and his development of goals for the helping relationship.

Identifying Cultural Factors

The helping professions have begun to recognize that racial, ethnic, and gender issues can have a significant impact on the behavior of clients. As discussed in **Chapter 5** (this volume), clients' cultures have a tremendous impact on how they view their life situations. The client's perception of how fair or unfair society is to him and others, which he considers to be similar to himself, impacts his view of many aspects of his world. Clients who believe they are oppressed or have been oppressed quite often will have a significantly different view of society than someone who has been privileged to have been dealt with fairly by society. Euro-American culture has been the dominant culture in America for several hundred years, and its domination has been so encompassing that virtually all other cultures have either been suppressed, assimilated, or eliminated. Critics of the domination of Euro-American standards would argue that other cultures have had to conform to the Euro-American culture's standards or risk being significantly diminished. Euro-American culture has been the benchmark by which most everything in America is judged (Bryan, 2007). To the extent that cultural groups feel displaced from the mainstream society, their feelings of loyalty to the norms of the society may equally be displaced.

When one speaks of cultural diversity, often issues of discrimination of various groups become part of the discussion. Most of the time, issues of racial and ethnic discrimination take center stage; however, women of all ethnic and racial groups arguably have been the recipient of discrimination as much as, if not more than, some other ethnic and racial groups. When female clients are seen by a male helper, they may feel they are not going to be taken as seriously as a male client and that their issues are going to be minimized.

The United States attempts to keep political issues and government separate from religion and many religious issues. However, from a personal standpoint, for those persons who participate in or adhere to some organized religion, their faith means a great deal to their everyday life. In fact, for some their religious faith has more relevance to them than perhaps any other cultural component of their lives. Considering the importance that religious faith plays in some client's lives, the helping professional must develop an understanding of the impact that religion may have on the client and his or her life issues. In fact, the helper may find that the client's religious faith may serve as a valuable resource in resolution of some of the client's life issues.

Identifying Acculturation Issues

Related to ethnic/racial considerations is level of acculturation. This can be of particular concern when working with clients who were not born and reared in the United States or lived a significant number of their formative years in a foreign country. As previously stated, everyone and their behavior to some extent are impacted by the environment in which they have lived. Customs, traditions, and belief systems supported by the social environment play a role in determining how clients behave. Persons coming from such environments relocating to the United States generally have two major choices: They can isolate themselves with others who share the same or similar cultural traits or they can immerse themselves into American ways of thinking and acting. With regard to the latter, some immigrants choose to involve themselves into American ways of living and also attempt to maintain some of their original homeland cultural ways. When this occurs, the parts of American ways they adopt is called acculturation. Helping professionals working with immigrants must be aware of their client's level of acculturation. Important questions to be considered are: (a) What are the behavioral values the client(s) are holding onto from their original homeland? (b) How do these differ from the local social values? (c) How much of the local values do the client(s) understand and accept as appropriate behavior?

Helping professionals assisting families that are immigrants or if some of its members are immigrants, must be cognizant of the fact that within the family there may be several levels of acculturations. Some immigrant families, based on tradition and/or economic survival, may have several generations living within the same household. Therefore, there may be some in the family who are totally traditional home country with regard to their cultures; also within the same household may be members who were exposed to both the original country's traditions and American ways of life. Additionally, some families will have a third level of acculturation of children who were either born or reared during their formative years in the United States. This type of family can present unique situations for the professional helper. The helper must determine the various levels of acculturation that exist within the household; also he must determine whether the various levels of acculturation are presenting any conflict with regard to the issue(s) being discussed, and finally he must assist with solutions that firmly address the issue(s) and respect the other levels of acculturation.

Identifying Crisis Meeting Resources

Once we settle into routines, we become comfortable with them and/or accept them as part of our lives. Once these routines have become embedded into our daily existence, too often we become reluctant to change. The point being made is that for most people change is difficult; therefore, the fewer new things that the professional helper has to introduce into the person's life, the less chance of rejection occurring. Given this fact, the helper must work with the client to determine the resources she has to use in dealing with the life issue. In many instances, the old proverb that one cannot see the forest for the trees is appropriate when working with some clients. Helpees may become very engrossed in what they consider problems; this level of involvement often creates in their minds feelings of hopelessness, and, consequently, they may overlook possible solutions to the problems. Stated in other terms, because of this feeling of being overwhelmed by the situation, clients often overlook resources with which they have to apply to the situation. Wise helpers will first look to the client for resources he has and encourage the client to use them.

Determine Definition of the Issue

The helper must determine how the client defines the problem(s). Does he view the problem as the worst thing that could have happened to him or does he view the problem as indeed a problem, but he has faced problems before and he will have to work at resolving these issues? Determining how the client defines the problem(s) will give the helper clues to the client's frame of mind and will also provide the helper with information about how to assist the client.

The helper must not fall into the trap of assuming how the client will react to a situation. Also the helper must not compare this client's situation with other similar situations and evaluate the current client's response to previous clients' responses. There are numerous factors that make each situation unique. It is sufficient to say that the helper does not have to mentally run through a list of variables such as race, ethnicity, gender, and socioeconomic status to remind him of differences to consider. He simply has to remind himself that each client is a unique individual.

SUMMARY

In summary, as previously stated, understanding human behavior is an essential requirement for a helping professional to be successful in assisting a helpee. Several theorists' perceptions of what motivates human behavior have been provided to give the helper a glimpse of how they evaluate their helpee's behavior. The point being made is that there is no one right answer to understanding the motivations of human behavior; rather, there are numerous ways of viewing human behavior. The helper is encouraged to borrow from any of the theorists discussed, as well as those not discussed, and add to his or her perceptions and beliefs with regard to human behavior. It is certainly acceptable for the helper to utilize theorists' perceptions as his or her basis for handling behavioral issues until he or she has enough practical and professional experience to develop a theory of human behavior that is unique to his or her perceptions.

Also, the professional helper must learn to assess behavior. Understanding what motivates human behavior is important. Likewise, being able to assess a helpee's current situation in which the behavior is occurring is equally important.

Chapter Review Questions

1. What were some of Sigmund Freud's views with regard to what motivates human behavior?
2. What were some of Alfred Adler's views with regard to what motivates human behavior?
3. What were some of Fredrick and Laura Perls' views with regard to what motivates human behavior?
4. What were some of Carl Rogers' views with regard to what motivates human behavior?
5. What were some of the existentialists' views with regard to what motivates human behavior?
6. What were some of B. F. Skinners' views with regard to what motivates human behavior?
7. What were some of Albert Ellis' views with regard to what motivates human behavior?

Mental Exercise

1. Describe your views with regard to what motivates human behavior.

REFERENCES

Bitter, J. R. (2007, Spring). Ansbacher memorial address: Am I an Adlerian? *Journal of Individual Psychology, 63* (1), 1–31.

Bryan, W. V. (2007). *Multicultural aspects of disabilities* (2nd ed.). Springfield, IL: Charles C Thomas Publisher.

Corey, G. (2005). *Theory and practice of counseling and psychotherapy* (7th ed.). Monterey, CA: Brooks/Cole.

Ponterotto, J. G., Casas, J. M., Suzuki, L. A., & Alexander, C. M. (Eds.). (1995). *Handbook of multicultural counseling.* Thousand Oaks, CA: Sage.

Suggested Readings

Blumberg, M. S. (2005). *Basic instinct: The genesis of behavior.* New York: Thunder Mouth Press.

Crook, L., Chagnon, N., & Iorns, W. (Eds.). (2000). *Adaptation and human behavior: An anthropological perspective.* New York: Aldine deGruyter.

Edgeton, R. B. (2005). *The balance of human kindness and cruelty: Why we are the way we are.* Lewiston, NY: Edwin Mellen Press.

Greene, R. R. (Ed.). (2008). *Human behavior: Theory and social work practice* (3rd ed.). New Brunswick, NJ: Aldine Transaction.

Hall, J. C., & Bowie, S. L. (Eds.). (2007). *African American behavior in the social environment: New perspectives.* New York: Haworth Press.

Kainz, H. P. (2008). *The philosophy of human nature.* Chicago. IL: Open Court.

Robbins, S. P., Chatterjee, P., & Canda, E. R. (1998). *Contemporary human behavior theory: A critical perspective for social work.* Boston: Allyn & Bacon.

Smith, J. L. (2000). *The psychology of action.* New York: St. Martin's Press.

Van Wormer, K., Besthorn, F. H., & Keefe, T. (Eds.). (2007a). *Human behavior and the social environment: Macro level: Groups, communities, and organizations.* Oxford: Oxford University Press.

Van Wormer, K., Besthorn, F. H., & Keefe, T. (Eds.). (2007b). *Human behavior and the social environment: Micro level: Individuals and families.* Oxford: Oxford University Press.

Chapter 5

UNDERSTANDING CULTURAL DIFFERENCES

Chapter Outline
• Introduction
• What Is Culture?
• The Case Against the Melting Pot Theory
• Understanding Ethnic/Racial Groups' Histories
• Understanding the Helpee's Concepts of Normal and Abnormal Behavior
• Becoming Culturally Sensitive
• Understanding Acculturation
• Understanding Situational Control
• Summary
• References

Chapter Objectives
• Present information with regard to understanding cultural differences
• Present ways of becoming culturally sensitive

INTRODUCTION

For many years, the United States was identified as the melting pot of the world. This designation implied that the United States welcomed people from different parts of the world, and once they became part of the fabric of the country, they, along with other freedom-loving immigrants, melded together to make a united group of people from diverse backgrounds. In theory, this was an ideal way of integrating human beings into a social salad bowl mixture. However, in reality, this may have happened in a limited way, but not to the extent many social planners would have liked. Despite the United States not truly becoming the melting pot of this planet, arguably the United States has the most diverse population on this planet. Because of the diversity, there is a need for an understanding of the needs of the various diverse populations that comprise the United States.

From a psychological helping profession standpoint, there is a disconnection between what exists and what should exist. To be more specific, the reality in America is that the various ethnic/racial groups that comprise the country never truly melted into one American culture. However, for many years, from a psychological helping relationship standpoint, we have treated these diverse groups as if they had formed one culture. Our helping theories have been developed based on one standard–Euro-American male–and our helping techniques have been developed and applied likewise. This perhaps would be realistic if all groups had similar experiences as Euro-American males and were treated on an equal basis as Euro-American males.

In this chapter, I discuss some historical information of which professional helpers should be aware with regard to ethnic/racial minorities. This information provides the helper with a foundation for understanding some actions, reactions, and beliefs that impact ethnic/racial minorities' behavior. Additionally, this chapter provides tips on how to become culturally sensitive, thus assisting professional helpers to become better able to work with diverse populations.

WHAT IS CULTURE?

There are numerous definitions of *culture*. How culture is defined depends on the person and/or profession that is putting forth the definition. For example, anthropologists define culture as part of the environment that humans have made, including artifacts as well as laws and myths that were or have been established. Sociologists may use some of the anthropological definitions and also place a strong emphasis on the social environment established by humans. The point being made is that there is not one all-inclusive definition of culture that is accepted by all professions.

Although there is no single definition accepted by all professions, there are common points that one can observe in most all definitions and they are: (a) Culture is a group orientation; (b) culture is learned behavior, attitudes, beliefs, and values, not inherited; and (c) culture is learned via socialization rather than through a formal teaching process. Given these common characteristics of culture, I have stated the following as a definition of culture: "Culture is commonly held characteristics such as attitudes, beliefs, values, customs and patterns of behavior possessed by a group of people, which have been learned and reinforced through a socialization process" (Bryan, 2007, p. 8).

As helping professionals, it is nice to have a succinct definition of culture. However, the helper must have more than a definition; she also must have a deeper understanding of what constitutes culture and how this understanding impacts the helping process. The following are some important facts with regard to culture.

Humans create culture–culture is not inherited but is developed through a socialization process. Therefore, the premise that by classifying persons into ethnic, racial, and religious groups (to mention only three groups) and stating that persons within these groups have the same culture we can explain their existence is false. By clustering people together based on perceived shared characteristics, too often we have believed that we are able to categorize their outward behavior and their inner emotions. Again this assumption is false, and the following facts make these beliefs untrue: Culture is influenced by proximity, culture is not restricted by race or ethnicity, and culture is mobile. To be more specific, regardless of ethnicity or racial background, the local social and environmental atmosphere have an influence on the person's cultural development. Certainly, racial or ethnic factors do impact one's cultural development; however, local culture, in which the person is involved, will have a profound impact on one's cultural development.

It is a mistake to classify people by their racial and/or ethnic background and stereotypically attribute patterns of behavior to those groups and judge all by those stereotyped attributes. The problem with this behavior can be illustrated by the fact that this type of thinking and behavior clusters all American Indians into one group and judges them accordingly. This does not take into consideration that in the United States there are several hundred different tribes of American Indians who have many common characteristics and also have as many, if not more, distinct customs, beliefs, and traditions.

Additionally, the other ethnic/racial groups' cultural development is impacted more by their local environment than the artificial classification of race or ethnicity. If a person, regardless of race/ethnicity, physically moves from one location to another, he takes with him many aspects of his current culture. However, over time, being influenced by the new cultural environment, he will gradually adopt the new prevailing cultures. Therefore, culture is both mobile and significantly impacted by the local environment.

Each group develops its own culture: Each individual is part of many cultures, and if she intends to be accepted by those cultures, she incorporates many of that group's cultural values. If the group's values are contrary to the person's values, hopefully she removes herself from the group and associates with a group that has values, beliefs, and attitudes that are congruent with her cultural beliefs. Therefore, the helping professional must not merely look at the person's ethnic/racial classification and from that observation think he has an understanding of the client's culture. The helper must take into consideration the local environment in which the person lives and conducts his daily life activities to get a clearer picture of cultural influences.

THE CASE AGAINST THE MELTING POT THEORY

The statement that the United States is a land of immigrants has been made numerous times, and to a great extent the statement is correct. Because the United States for many years has been viewed by many as a land of unlimited opportunities, many persons from other countries have come to the United States to improve their life situations. As a result of the immigration, in the previous centuries, of various ethnic/racial groups and cultures to the United States joining the existing diverse population, someone put forth the concept that the United States would become the "human melting pot" of the world. The belief was that the United States would extract the best characteristics of the various immigrant groups and, through combining these desirable traits and characteristics, a new and unique American would emerge. One can question whether there was ever a serious attempt at blending various cultures into one, especially when we view the efforts put forth to remove cultural attributes of the native people of the United States.

The idea of the human melting pot has been accepted and believed by many persons, including many professional helpers. The melting pot theory was a noble idea that never completely materialized. The theory was a simplistic and unrealistic approach to human behavior. The idea of the United States being a human melting pot, in this author's opinion, was doomed from the idea's inception. One reason for the failure of the melting pot theory was the fact that the dominant culture of the United States did not view these immigrants or native people as equal to themselves, thus they found little value in the cultures to be contributed to the melting pot. In effect, the dominant culture's view of the melting pot was for the immigrants and native people to give up their cultural traits and embrace the traits of the dominant culture. A second reason for the failure of the melting pot theory cannot be attributed to the dominant culture. The fact is that many of the immigrants and native people did not want to give up their cultural views and traits. With regard to immigrants, some migrated to the United States to earn their fortunes and return to their native countries and improve the lives of their love ones and themselves, therefore they did not envision any need or desire to part with their native cultural traits. Some of these immigrants did return to their native lands, thus there was little need to try to blend into this proposed unique American melting pot. Other immigrants who decided to remain in the United States were comfortable with their ways of living their lives; to continue to do so in the new land, which they were to call home, they band ed together with others who had the same or similar cultural views, thus extinguishing the fires that could have begun the process of melding together various ethnic/racial groups. The following comments by Atkinson, Morten, and Sue (1993) seem to support this contention: "Many members of racial/ethnic groups find the cultural assimilation philosophy objectionable because it calls for relinquishing their traditional racial/ethnic values and norms in favor of those of the dominant culture" (p. 10).

As previously stated, the melting pot theory was doomed from its inception and was never a good idea. The reason it was not a good idea is that diversity of ideas, diversity of ways of accomplishing tasks, and diversity of dynamics of living are enormous positives for any country. Therefore, the helping professional should maintain an open mind with regard to cultural differences. The helping professional should not develop within his or her mind a model cultural mold into which the helpee should fit. Each helpee should be treated as an individual, not tethered to an idealistic view of human behavior.

Because many helping professionals have bought into the melting pot theory, there often is the belief that all helpees, regardless of their ethnic or racial backgrounds, should think similarly. To further complicate the helping process, the helpers often, perhaps subconsciously, react to these culturally different clients as if they think and react as the dominant culture does. This type of thinking, on the part of the professional helper, creates problems in being an effective helper. First, the helper is ignoring the unique cultural background and traits the client has as a result of his unique life situation. Second, by not being aware of cultural differences, the helper is likely to make erroneous judgments based on inaccurate interpretations.

UNDERSTANDING ETHNIC/RACIAL GROUPS' HISTORIES

Another reason the melting pot theory never materialized is the fact that most, if not all, ethnic/racial groups treasure their heritage. Some may not value their heritage as much as they would like because it is not filled with happy nostalgic memories; however, despite the devaluation of their background, they maintain a firm grip on their heritage because it is part of who they are. Their heritage, which is filled with joy and pain, happy moments, as well as devastatingly sad events, is cherished because all of these events help define who they are. These mixtures of life moments help frame their views of themselves, as well as help shape their outlooks with regard to their futures. An example of these points can be seen within many African Americans. No one can view the actions and events of slavery and segregation as joyful events in their histories and lives; however, many take pride in the fact that their ancestors survived the bleakness of those periods in their histories. The pride is often based on the fact that only strong people of mind and body could have lived through those times; therefore, they are descendants of strong people, which makes them strong. One can review the history of any ethnic/racial group within America and find struggles that the group has experienced, and they view these encounters as validations of themselves and their cultures as representing strong people.

The helping professional must become acquainted with the client's cultural background of oppression and his feelings with regard to this background. Pedersen, Draguns, Lonner, and Trimble (1996) make their feelings known with regard to understanding cultural background with the following comment: "It would be difficult if not impossible for a counselor to have a high level of empathy without first being sensitive to the client's cultural context and background" (p. ix). The helper must maintain an open mind with regard to the client's attitudes toward this type of history. To be more specific, the professional helper must not view the helpee as "hanging onto the past" or view the helpee as using the past as a crutch to justify behavior. It is true that some clients will use past deplorable actions inflicted on their ancestors as a justification to be angry and lash out at society. Although this does occasionally happen, the fact is that the majority of ethnic/racial minority individuals choose to remember what has happened in the past but use this knowledge to motivate themselves to become positive achievers. Therefore, it is imperative that the professional helper working with ethnic/racial minority persons understand as best as he or she can the feelings and emotions that may be associated with historical oppression.

The professional helper must realize that there is no one way that ethnic/racial individuals and groups handle discrimination and oppression. For example, one can become aware of how some Japanese Americans, African Americans, and American Indians have historically dealt with discrimination and oppression. After the Imperial Government of Japan attacked Pearl Harbor, the U.S. government placed more than 100,000 Japanese Americans in camps. The U.S. government was afraid that some of the Japanese Americans were spies or would become spies for the Japanese government. The injustice of this act was revealed when none of these persons was found to be guilty of the suspicion that led to their detainment. Relating this discrimination to the topic of how some individuals and groups of individuals react to oppression, many of the Japanese Americans who were detained refused to talk, after their release, about the experience, even to their children. Their children sensed their parents' hurt and humiliation but rarely received firsthand information with regard to the oppression. In contrast, many African Americans and American Indians have passed down from generation to generation the knowledge of oppressions they and their ancestors have experienced (e.g.,

African Americans endured slavery and segregation, whereas American Indians suffered forced relocation, loss of land, and attempts at stripping them of their ancestral customs and cultures).

With regard to ethnic/racial groups, how historical oppressive information has been passed from generation to generation impacts the recipients' beliefs regarding their place in society and their opportunities for a successful and happy life within society. A point that is being made is that the professional helper cannot assume that because some oppression is in the past and did not directly happen to the helpee that the oppression does not impact his present feelings and emotions.

UNDERSTANDING THE HELPEE'S CONCEPTS OF NORMAL AND ABNORMAL BEHAVIOR

Whether one agrees or disagrees, from a legal perspective, laws define what acceptable behavior is, thus it is relatively easy to define what behavior a given society will legally accept. However, from a social standpoint, what is considered normal and abnormal behavior is much more difficult to determine. The reason for the difficulty is the fact that the concept of normal and abnormal is often defined by one's perception of events and situations. Most humanistic therapies emphasize that each person's perception of events represent that person's reality. Therefore, different people may view the same event in much different ways. Consequently, there is more than one reality.

The perception of events is based on several factors: how one was reared, perceived values gleaned from one's immediate environment, behaviors that have been reinforced or discouraged, and what is viewed as acceptable in one's immediate environment and/or sanctioned by one's significant others, to mention only four factors. A helping professional should not make the mistake of judging a client's view of what is normal or abnormal behavior based on the helper's perception. Nor should she judge the client's perception or the dominant culture's perception. This is not saying that the client's perception is correct and all other perceptions are wrong. However, what is being proposed is a repeat of what has been previously stated–that one's perception represents one's reality. Therefore, the helper must work with the helpee from that standpoint. The helper should do the following:

(a) attempt to understand why the helpee's views differ from the majority of societal views, (b) determine what is influencing these views, (c) determine the ramification of the helpee holding these views, and (d) determine what will be the impact if the helpee changes his or her views. Let us examine the four previously mentioned points.

Examining the culturally different client's views: First, examining the client's viewpoint will reveal considerable information that will be helpful in helping the client. Information that may be gained could reveal whether the helpee is antisocial and is rebelling against authority and rules. Another piece of information that may be gained is whether the helpee's perceptions are based on unclear understanding of societal expectations, or perhaps the helpee is not trying to be antisocial but simply feels societal values are unfair.

What is influencing the culturally different client's views? This second point is related to the previous point but is referring to what is influencing the helpee's views. The helper's inquiry into this point can determine whether peer pressure is having a significant influence on the person being helped. The helper will be able to determine whether the behavior represents an attempt by the helpee to maintain connections with his immediate support group(s). Certainly if the behavior is illegal or immoral, peer pressure or attempting to maintain favor with one's support groups does not justify the behavior; however, the examination by the helper will provide information that will help determine the directions the helping process must go.

Determine the ramification of culturally different views: Stated in other term, what are the consequences of the person maintaining his views? This question becomes somewhat of a double-edged sword. The answer on one side relates to the societal and/or legal consequences, if any, of continuing with the behavior. On the other side is this question: By changing the behavior, what are the personal/social consequences? Does the person being helped lose status among his peers by changing behavior? Does the person suffer personal losses by changing behavior? One rule of thumb this author has lived by in attempting to help clients is to "never take away from a client something of value unless I help that client gain something of equal or greater value." This does not mean that if a client is doing something illegal and gaining substantial monetary resources from the illegal activity that I have to help him replace that monetary loss with something legal of equal monetary value. What this does mean is that I, as the helper, should help the client to understand what the legal and long-range consequences are if he continues with his current behavior, and also help him realize the long-term advantages of staying within societal rules.

The impact of the culturally different client changing his or her behavior: Before the professional helper attempts to help the helpee change behavior, the helper must first have an understanding of how and why the behavior exists. Is the behavior the result of irrational thinking? Is the behavior the result of influence from significant others? These are two of the questions for which the professional helper must seek an answer. In most cases, the behavior will be the result of a combination of factors. The answer to the two previously mentioned questions and other questions designed to ascertain the motivation of the behavior will help guide the efforts to modify the helpee's behavior.

The benefit of obtaining answers to the questions designed to determine motivating factors is necessary to determine the impact of changing the behavior. All behavior—normal or abnormal, good or bad—serves a purpose with regard to the person committing the behaviors. Although we the observers of the behavior may deplore or see no positive benefits from the behavior, the possessor of the behavior is receiving some benefits, albeit in some cases the benefits may be negative and somewhat destructive. Regardless of the direction of the benefits to the helpee, there are ramifications for changing the behavior. An example of this point can be seen in a spouse who enables her alcoholic husband by relieving him of most family responsibilities because she takes on the responsibility of taking care of family matters, such as seeing that the bills are paid, maintaining the home, seeing that auto and personal insurance is paid, making sure the children are clothed, fed, nurtured, and so on. The professional helper enters the picture and convinces the spouse that she should require more from her husband. She complies with the helper's suggestions and gets her husband more involved in the daily family activities. One may think that life in this fictional home would be much happier and peaceful; however, the opposite occurs. To the amazement of the helper, more family discord began to appear. The reason for the spouse's unhappy state of mind is that, despite her previous complaints of the irresponsibility of her husband, she had become comfortable with being in charge of family matters. With her husband becoming more involved in family affairs, in her mind her role in family matters has diminished. The moral of this example is the helper must understand what the helpee's behavior means, emotionally and psychologically, to him or her and have some understanding of what may occur when the unwanted behavior is changed.

BECOMING CULTURALLY SENSITIVE

Whenever the topic of cultural sensitivity is mentioned, a common question is whether the helping professional should be of a similar background as the helpee. Some interpret this to mean whether the helper should be of the same race and social status and/or have had similar problems as the helpee. There can be little debate that a helper who has similar experiences and background as the helpee may have an advantage in relating to the helpee's situations than someone who has dissimilar experiences. This is evident in some substance abuse helping relationships. Some of the most effective help comes from former substance abusers. However, similar experiences and background do not guarantee a successful helping relationship. The helper being of the same ethnic/racial background of the helpee does not guarantee a successful helping relationship. The helper having a similar social or cultural background also does not guarantee a successful helping relationship. The helper having experienced similar situations and/or problems also does not guarantee a successful helping relationship.

As previously stated, former substance abusers often are effective in working with persons who are substance abusers. Likewise, helpers of the same ethnic/racial background and helpers from similar socioeconomic backgrounds can initially apply a level of understanding that someone who is not personally familiar with the background of the helpee can apply. What is being proposed is that a **cultural match** provides an initial advantage to the helper because the culturally matched helper has insight into the helpee's situation that the culturally mismatched helper does not have. However, in this author's opinion, this is where the advantage ends. Although some helpees may initially feel more comfortable and prefer a helper with a similar background, the vast majority of helpees want relief from the problems that are affecting their lives. If the helper can demonstrate cultural sensitivity as well as effective helping skills, most helpees will disregard the color of the helper's skin and/or his cultural background. A helper who does not or cannot demonstrate warmth and caring for the client and a professional understanding of the helpee's situation will not be successful regardless of whether there is a cultural match or mismatch. Therefore, it is imperative that professional helpers become culturally sensitive.

Cross, Bazron, Dennis, and Isaacs (1989) listed five things a helper must do to becoming culturally competent:

1. Acknowledge and value diversity: Recognize that cultural differences exist and that they play a role in development with regard to family, individual, and community development and functioning.
2. Conduct a cultural assessment: One must become aware of his or her own cultures and how these cultures have shaped his or her beliefs and attitudes.
3. Recognize and understand the dynamics of differences: Become aware of how differences in race and culture between clients and practitioners influence interaction and awareness of the ways in which racism and the current status and long history of race relations affect the interaction and establishment of rapport between racially and ethnically different clients and practitioners.
4. Acquire cultural knowledge: Develop an in-depth understanding of the cultural background of helpees.
5. Adapt to diversity: Adapt skills and techniques to fit within the helpee's culture and worldviews.

Sue and Sue (1990) also have suggested that "a culturally skilled counselor is one who is able to relate to minority-group experiences and has knowledge of cultural and class factors" (p. 165). They follow this suggestion with three intrapersonal skill developments that they believe a helping professional must develop to become culturally sensitive.

First, a culturally skilled counselor is one who is actively in the process of becoming aware of his/her own assumptions about human behavior, values, biases, preconceived notions, personal limitations, and so forth,

Second, a culturally skilled counselor is one who actively attempts to understand the world view of his/her culturally different client. In other words, what are the client's values and assumptions about human behavior, biases, and so on? Third, a culturally skilled counselor is one who is in the process of actively developing and practicing appropriate, relevant and sensitive intervention strategies/skills in working with his or her culturally different client. (p. 166)

The following are some additional suggestions about becoming culturally sensitive.

Understand clients' frames of reference: In almost any society of the world, one group will be dominant and that group's views and cultural standards will become the standard by which other groups are judged. Right or wrong, often subordinate groups' actions are deemed appropriate or inappropriate, normal or abnormal, and correct or incorrect by evaluating their actions against the cultural standards of the dominant group.

Helping professionals are not immune from falling into the trap of using one standard to judge behavior—failing to take into consideration the fact that environmental influences profoundly affects one's thought process and behavior. In the United States, the dominant culture cherishes independence and individuality, and those are good qualities; however, not all cultural groups in the United States view independence and individuality in the same manner as the dominant culture. Many Asian cultural groups view the well-being of the collective group as more important than individual accomplishments. Harmony among group members is valued more than individual accolades. Other examples are: the dominant culture values articulation of expressions more than silence; however, some ethnic/racial groups, such as some American Indians, value silence and short answers as the appropriate manner in which to communicate. Many African Americans, Asian American, Hispanic/Latino/Latina Americans, and American Indians depend on an extended family structure as the backbone of their family existence, whereas members of the dominant culture are often nuclear family-oriented.

To overcome the disadvantage of not being a cultural match with the helpee, the professional helper must educate him or herself with the helpee's frame of reference. This rule applies not only to a dominant culture helper working with a culturally different helpee, but also requires a minority helper assisting a helpee from the dominant culture.

Avoid stereotyping. For many good reasons and some not so noble reasons, we categorize people. We pool people together (based on some perceived and some real characteristics) and give the people labels. We identify characteristics such as dishonest, honest, lazy, industrial, violent, peaceful, stingy, generous, beautiful, ugly, happy, or sad, to mention only a few adjectives, and we attach them to people and groups of people. For those who are labeled as such, this becomes some of the ways they are viewed by the society of which they are part.

Stereotyping—whether depicting good or bad traits—often is incorrect, especially when it is applied to an entire group of people. A reason that stereotyping is often inaccurate relates to the obvious fact that everyone is an individual, and to pool people together because of perceived attributes and provide all with the same label represents prejudgment in its worse form. Labeling people based on known facts such as low income, middle income, wealth, or high risk for certain diseases are acceptable and often helpful. The key words are known facts. Thus, this does not constitute, in this author's opinion, harmful stereotyping.

Helping professionals must be careful with regard to accepting stereotypes and using those or allowing them to influence their helping process. The helping professional must be cognizant of the subconscious influence of stereotypes; therefore, the helper should, when working with someone of a different culture, conduct a personal internal analysis of his or her beliefs with regard to the cultural difference that exist between him or her and the helpee. Additionally, the key words that all helping professionals should remember when dealing with stereotypes is **known facts**.

Understand how clients express themselves. Most professional helpers who are sighted are visually oriented, meaning they observe and are aware of what they consider the individual's body language. As professional helpers, we are taught that the client's body language conveys as much information as the spoken word, if not more. In fact, some studies indicate that body language or nonverbal communication represents as much as 75% of one's communication. Certainly being aware of the client's body language is important; however, the helper should not make the mistake of misreading the nonverbal communication, especially when working with some ethnic/minority persons. Offered as an example, some minority individuals are very expressive with their hands and arms, and some are very vocal, especially by elevating the volume of their voices. To a helper who is not familiar with this behavior, the helper may misinterpret these nonverbal actions and, in some cases, verbal behaviors as signs of aggression and/or annoyance. An effective way of handling this is to ask the helpee if he is upset and inform him how you are interpreting this behavior. The helper may discover that the helpee is not aware that he is acting in this manner. The helper probably has reacted in this manner for such a long time that it has become a natural part of his repertoire of behaviors of which he is not aware of either the action or the influence it has on some people.

Most forms of helping are greatly enhanced if the helpee is verbal. A hallmark of talk therapy is an open exchange of information between the helper and helpee. Often when the helpee is somewhat quiet, answering questions, but not elaborating on the answers, the helper becomes confused—confused from the standpoint that most professional helpers are trained to expect an open flow of conversation between the helper and the helpee, and when this does not happen some helpers view the helpee as being resistant to the helping process. Culturally sensitive helpers will be aware that the limited flow of conversation may be part of a cultural trait; some cultures value silence, and some cultures view the professional helper as an authority figure and consider listening as appropriate and talking on their parts as disrespecting the professional helper's authority. Other culturally different helpees will not seek help unless their situation is beyond their control. Thus, when they seek help, they are expecting direct constructive advice aimed at resolving their problems. They are seeing a professional helper not to vent or use the helping process as a catharsis venue. Therefore, they expect answers and direction from the helper, not an exchange of conversation.

When the helper experiences what he considers to be inadequate communication from a culturally different helpee, he should explore at least three possibilities. One, is the silence based on one's cultural background? The answer to this question can be ascertained by researching the helpee's cultural heritage. Additionally, the helper may need to inquire of the helpee why he or she is reserved with regard to verbal communication. Two, has adequate rapport been established?

With regard to rapport, the helper may need to continue the efforts to increase the bonds of rapport. Three, is this an issue of lack of trust? If lack of trust is part of the problem, increasing the bonds of rapport will help, as will a frank discussion about whether the helpee has trust in the helper and the helping process.

UNDERSTANDING ACCULTURATION

As previously stated, within a given society, of all the cultural groups that exist, one will become the dominant culture, determining many of that society's activities, belief systems, values, and standards. In an attempt to be accepted by and be considered part of the society, subordinate cultures may attempt to emulate the dominant culture. This is a form of acculturation. Acculturation within the context of the U.S. society refers to the degree to which an individual identifies with the attitudes, lifestyles, and values of the dominant culture. In American society, there are numerous dominant cultural characteristics, and the extent to which individuals and groups of individuals deviate from those characteristics and standards determine how much they are devalued. Likewise, the closer they mimic and/or incorporate them in their lifestyles, the more they are valued. Many Euro-American cultural standards are so well woven into the fabric of American society that members of the dominant culture accept them as the correct standards by which to live, but in many instances the subordinate culture also makes the same judgment. There are many aspects of the Euro-American culture that are very good; therefore, generally speaking, there is nothing wrong with conforming to those standards. The lack of consideration given to other points of view and ways of doing things as well as lifestyles is what had been questioned, not the right or wrong of Euro-American cultural standards. Problems occur when the dominant culture refuses to recognize or devalues other legal cultural standards. From a helping relationship standpoint, the major problem is when the helping profession and/or the helping professional is either ignorant of other cultural standards or refuses to accept those cultural attributes as useful and productive ways of approaching life situations.

UNDERSTANDING SITUATIONAL CONTROL

Situational control means the forces or factors that have significant influence on the person's life. Although one can debate how much personal control we as humans have over our actions and behaviors, there can be no question with regard to the fact that our environment has a significant impact on our beliefs and how we carry forward those beliefs in the form of behaviors. Therefore, the professional helper should become aware of the factors that influence the helpee's behaviors. There are undoubtedly many factors that influence behavior, and those factors can be as individual as the person being impacted by their existence. I discuss three broad categories of faith, family, and friends. There are many more, too many to discuss here; in fact, an entire book could be devoted to this topic.

Faith, family, and **friends,** in this author's opinion, comprise the foundation of many ethnic/racial minorities/situational controls. This is not meant to imply that these three components are not important to Euro-Americans because for many they are. Faith, family, and friends are central to many ethnic/racial minorities because of the struggles that they have had adjusting to and advancing in American society. With regard to struggles, such as slavery, segregation, removal from one's homeland, poverty, language barriers, and many other obstacles, faith, family, and friends have sustained ethnic/racial minority individuals and groups through turbulent times. Let us take a look at the relevance of the three situational controls.

1. Faith. Regardless of whether a person attends church or religious services regularly, most ethnic/racial minority persons have been influenced by religion. Most have, either as a child, adult, or both, received instructions, inspiration, education, guidance, comfort, and love from religious teaching, leaders, family, and significant others. In times of extreme stress, many ethnic/racial minority persons return to their foundations of religious faith to support them.

For many ethnic/racial minority groups, the structure—whether it is referred to as church, synagogue, temple, mosque, or some other name—serves as more than a religious building. In many cases, some of these structures serve as meeting places to deal with issues the groups are facing. A classic example of this point is the fact that much of the discussion and planning for many of the civil rights movement's actions in America were developed in African-American churches. No doubt similar scenes have occurred in other ethnic/racial religious structures when those groups were encountering serious social issues.

It is true that for many ethnic/racial minority individuals, the religious structure and community serve the needs of many of its groups from birth to death, from baptism to burial, and many events between these two major life events. Therefore, professional helpers assisting ethnic/racial minorities would be wise to investigate the helpee's spiritual connections or lack thereof. In many cases, the spiritual connection could be a valuable resource that the helper could call on to assist in the helping process.

2. Family. Perhaps the oldest and most influential institution in the world is the family. Similar to religious institutions, for ethnic/minority individuals, the family is the strength on which many depend and lean. One of the things that the helping professional must understand with regard to some ethnic/racial minorities is that the concept of family may extend far beyond mother, father, and siblings, as is discussed in the section on family dynamics. The helping professional must become acquainted with who is considered family and the influence these individuals have in the life of the helpee. Again, these individuals may be valuable assets in the helping process.

3. Friends. As one probably can determine from the previous discussion with regard to many ethnic/racial minorities, faith, family, and friends are connected. Friends may be considered as part of the family. In the African-American community, such persons are fondly referred to as fictive kin. Likewise, church or other religious acquaintances may also be considered as family. There is a reason that many religious institutions refer to their members as "brothers and sisters."

With regard to youth and young adults, friends often play a significant role in the development of self-esteem. At some points in their lives, youth feel that friends and their peers understand them better than anyone including their parents. Consequently, the helping professional should explore friendships and how they are influencing beliefs and behaviors.

SUMMARY

In summary, it is noble to think that all humans are created equal. However, when we view humans from a group perspective, there can be numerous cultural factors that may cause some group of individuals to view events and other human interactions differently than another group of individuals. These events, which help shape our being, help determine our worldviews of situations and events. It is imperative that professional helpers become attuned to cultural differences because many of these cultural differences impact daily behaviors. Therefore, to be an effective and sensitive professional helper, becoming aware of cultural differences and taking some, if not all, into consideration when attempting to assist helpees are essential.

Chapter Review Questions

1. Why is it important to understand ethnical/racial groups' histories?
2. Why is it important in a helping relationship to understand a helpee's worldviews?
3. What are some of the things a professional helper can do to become more culturally sensitive?
4. Why is it important for a helping professional to understanding acculturation?
5. What do situational controls mean and how does it apply to a helping relationship?

Mental Exercise

1. What is your definition of culture?
2. List various cultures to which you identify as part of your life and identify the contributions these cultures have made to your life.
3. List some of the contributions your culture(s) have made to society.
4. List at least three stereotypes of your ethnic/racial and/or gender culture you do not like.
5. Do you believe that the melting pot theory of the United States is relevant in the twenty-first century? Defend your answer.
6. In your opinion, is a cultural match between the helper and helpee essential for a successful helping relationship? Defend your answer.
7. What are some of your prejudices? How did you acquire them? What, if anything, are you going to do to eliminate or at least modify them?

REFERENCES

Atkinson, D. R., Morten, G., & Sue, D. W. (Eds.). (1993). *Counseling American minorities: A cross-cultural perspective* (4th ed.). Madison, WI: Brown & Benchmark.

Bryan, W. V. (2007). *Multicultural aspects of disabilities* (2nd ed.). Springfield, IL: Charles C Thomas, Publisher.

Cross, T. L., Bazron, B. J., Dennis, K. W., & Isaacs, M. R. (1989). Toward a culturally competent system of care. Washington, DC: Child and Adolescent Service System Program Technical Assistance Center.

Pedersen, P. B., Draguns, J. G., Lonner, W. J., & Trimble, J. E. (Eds.). (1996). *Counseling across cultures* (4th ed.). Thousand Oaks, CA: Sage.

Sue, D. W., & Sue, D. (1990). *Counseling the culturally different: Theory and practice* (2nd ed.). New York: Wiley.

Suggested Readings

Cronk, L. (1999). *That complex whole: Culture and the evolution of human behavior.* Boulder, CO: Westview Press.

Morgan, D. (Ed.). (2008). *Key words in religion, media and culture.* New York: Routledge.

Richerson, P., & Boyd, R. (2005). *Not by genes alone: How culture transformed human evolution.* Chicago: University of Chicago Press.

Smith, P., & Riley, A. (2009). *Cultural theory: An introduction* (2nd ed.). Malden, MA: Blackwell.

Sorrentino, R. M., & Yamaguchi, S. (Eds.). (2008). *Handbook of motivation and cognition across cultures.* San Diego: Academic/Elsevier.

Williams, M. D. (2001). *The Black experience in middle class America: Social hierarchy and behavioral biology.* Lewiston, NY: Edwin Mellen Press.

Vacc, N. A., DeVaney, S. B., & Brendel J. M. (Eds.). (2003). *Counseling multicultural and diverse populations: Strategies for practitioners.* New York: Brunner-Routledge.

Chapter 6

UNDERSTANDING DISABILITIES

Chapter Outline
- Introduction
- Definition of a Disability
- Prevalence of Disabilities in the United States
- Historical Perspective
  - Treatments and Beliefs
- Perceptions of Disabilities
  - Current Perceptions of Disabilities
- Why Do We Feel the Way We Do About Disabilities?
- Things Not to Do When Assisting Persons With Disabilities
  - Additional Tips for Effectively Assisting Persons with Disabilities
- Summary
  - References

Chapter Objectives
- Provide information to increase the professional helper's understanding of persons with disabilities.
- Provide information with regard to effectively helping persons with disabilities.

INTRODUCTION

In the process of initially encountering information with regard to disabilities, one thought may be, why do I need to understand disabilities? This line of thinking may be followed by other thoughts of disabilities with regard to sheltered workshops, hospitals, and rehabilitation centers, which specialize in working with persons with disabilities as being the primary source of assistance for persons with disabilities. This kind of thinking about persons with disabilities is not uncommon for professional helpers and, in reality, for a major portion of the American population. With regard to professional helpers, when they give thought to persons with disabilities, they, generally speaking, think of persons with severe disabilities who need specialized care and assistance–care and assistance provided by medical and rehabilitation specialists. There is no doubt that medical and rehabilitation specialists play a major role in the caring and recovery of persons who have a disability. However, what is often missed by nonmedical and rehabilitation professional helpers is the fact that many of the persons they will see have some type of disability. The disability may not be a visible one, may not be a severe physical and/or emotional disability, and may not be considered by the helpee as a disability. All of the previously mentioned factors point to some of the reasons that, in the psychological and other helping arenas, disabilities and persons with disabilities are misunderstood.

The reality is many of the clients that psychological and other professional helpers will assist have some type of disability–perhaps not physically, perhaps not with severe mental and/or emotional problems; however, they will have some type of disability. The problem facing some clients may be alcoholism or alcohol-related problems, substance abuse, attention deficit disorder, inability to obtain a job because of some form of physical or mental problems, or inability to maintain a healthy family relationship because of emotional problems. The point to be made is that many of the issues with which clients come to a professional helper probably will have some aspect of a disability associated. Therefore, the helping professional should be aware of what constitutes a disability, as well as some of the problems encountered by a person with a disability that impacts the helping relationship.

A conservative estimate of the population of persons with disabilities in the United States is that approximately one-fifth of the population has some type of disability. Worldwide the numbers of persons with disabilities are much higher. In reality, no one knows the exact number–in either the United States or the world–of persons who have a disability. However, the application of common sense leads us to realize that, given health conditions, as well as living conditions in some parts of the world and to some extent in the United States, there is a large number of persons with disabilities. Given the numbers and the range of disabilities, the additional reality is that professional helpers will, at various points in their careers, interact with persons with disabilities.

In this chapter, I provide information that will assist the helping professional better understand what a disability is and some of the needs of those who have a disability. Additionally, suggestions with regard to effective ways of working with persons with disabilities and their significant others are discussed. Also in Chapter 8 (this volume), I present information about resources that can aid in the helping relationship with persons with disabilities.

DEFINITION OF A DISABILITY

There are a number of definitions for disabilities, and the appropriate definition depends, to a large extent, on the agencies and/or organizations and their functions as to how they define a disability. The U.S. Social Security Administration's definition may vary somewhat from the definition that the Veteran's Administration uses to conduct its business. Therefore, the definition will depend on the function and type of service rendered by the agency or organization. Despite the variety of definitions of disabilities, the one definition that is most commonly used and has the force of law is the definition put forth by the 1990 Americans With Disabilities Act. The Americans With Disabilities Act is a civil rights law that prohibits discrimination of persons with disabilities because of their disability.

The Americans With Disabilities Act provides what is considered a "three-prong" definition: First Prong–A person with a physical or mental impairment that substantially limits one or more major life activities such as walking, seeing, hearing, speaking, breathing, learning, working, or caring for oneself; Second Prong–A person is considered to have a disability if he or she has a record of such a physical or mental impairment; Third Prong–A person is considered as having a disability if he or she is regarded as having such an impairment. The first and second prongs are somewhat straightforward, identifying the life activities that must be impacted for the person to be considered to have a disability and whether a record exists identifying the fact that the person has a disability. However, the third prong introduced an interesting concept into the definition of a disability–that being the perception of having a disability. This part of the definition recognizes the fact that perception can have a similar impact as reality. Stated in other terms, if a person is perceived to have a disability, that person may be treated as if he has a disability; thus, any stereotypes, negative reactions, as well as possible sympathy associated with having a disability probably will be applied to the person. If a person is perceived to have a disability, this perception can be the basis for discrimination.

Helping professionals should know and care with regard to the definition of a disability because once the client has been classified as a person with a disability, he or she has certain protections, by law, from being discriminated against because he or she has a disability. Additionally, the person also has access to a number of advocacy groups to assist her, as well as other local, state, and federal government and private resources to assist in meeting appropriate needs. These resources can be of tremendous assistance to a professional helper.

PREVALENCE OF DISABILITIES IN THE UNITED STATES

As previously stated, at least one-fifth of the American population has some type of disability. Numerically, White Americans have the largest population of persons with disabilities. This is understandable given that White Americans numerically outnumber any other ethnic/racial group in America. However, the results of most surveys of the percentage of disabilities in America reveal a picture of a higher rate per capita of disabilities among ethnic/racial minorities and women than White males.

When viewed from the standpoint of ranking the prevalence of disabilities per capita among ethnic/racial minority groups, American Indians have the highest rate, followed by African Americans, with Whites being third. Persons of Hispanic origin ranked fourth, and Asian or Pacific Islanders ranked fifth. This same rank order occurs as one compares women and their ethnic/racial background. When women are viewed as an aggregate without respect for ethnic/racial background, survey results confirm that women have a higher rate of disabilities than men.

HISTORICAL PERSPECTIVE

In passing the 1990 Americans With Disabilities Act, the U.S. Congress acknowledged that persons with disabilities are a class of people who have been discriminated against, which has placed them in an inferior position within the United States. Among others, Congress acknowledged the following realities:

1. Society has isolated and segregated individuals with disabilities;
2. Discrimination against persons with disabilities continues to be a pervasive social problem;
3. Some of the acts of discrimination encountered by persons with disabilities are blatant and intentionally exclusionary; and
4. Persons with disabilities occupy an inferior status in American society.

Some of the discrimination to which the U.S. Congress was referring is long-standing; predating the establishment of American government. If we look backward through the long telescope of world history, we discover that persons with disabilities have experienced a mixture of treatment ranging from torture, abuse, and death to being treated as persons with special powers. The following provides a brief review of treatments that persons with disabilities have received and are currently receiving. This information is important to a professional helper because a historical review of treatments of persons with disabilities and beliefs about persons with disabilities provides the professional helper with a foundation for understanding some of the obstacles they had to overcome and, to some extent, still have to overcome.

Treatments and Beliefs

Obviously, it is difficult to trace the number of persons with disabilities in antiquity. However, given the living conditions, it is safe to postulate there have been disabilities from the earliest time of human existence. Therefore, the question isn't whether humans in antiquity experienced disabilities, but rather what was done with regard to those who had a disability? The answer to this question will help us better understand today's attitudes toward disabilities and those who have a disability. Haj (1970) reminds us that crude negative attitudes toward persons with disabilities, once deeply rooted in the superstitions and mythologies of the ancestors of modern human, have evolved into present-day sophisticated bigotry.

Although we are relatively certain that in some ancient social orders the belief with regard to persons who appeared to be different from the accepted norm was to avoid, isolate, and/or eliminate persons with significant disabilities, in all probability, there existed some societies that had more favorable views of persons with disabilities.

The point being made is that, in antiquity, there probably was no single belief with regard to disabilities and persons who had disabilities, which is the case for today's societies (Bryan, 2006). Later in this chapter, the reasons that we have such divergent beliefs are discussed.

Treatment: Similar to the fact that there have been and continue to be a variety of beliefs with regard to disabilities and those who possess them, there also exists a number of different ways persons with disabilities have been treated. In reviewing historical records with regard to treatment of persons with disabilities, one observes that the treatment falls within one of two categories—one, treated as evil, sinful, and or demonic; or two, treated as special people empowered, because of the disability, with powers to bring good fortune and/or possessing supernatural insight into life. The one way that few persons with observable disabilities have been treated is as normal people. Stated another way, rarely are disabilities treated as natural events that happen to some people, nor are persons with disabilities treated as "normal persons" (Bryan, 2006).

Elizabethan Poor Laws: Perhaps the beginning of a more consistent positive approach to treating persons with disabilities began during the late fourteenth and early fifteenth centuries; at least for those times, the treatment was considered a humanistic approach. Perhaps one of the best-known examples is the Elizabethan Poor Laws, which were enacted between 1597 and 1601. Although the Elizabethan Poor Laws were not specifically designed to aid and comfort persons with disabilities, some portions of the laws provided some protection for persons with disabilities, albeit by today's standards the protection would be considered degrading.

The Elizabethan Poor Laws were established to consolidate the previous English laws that had attempted to regulate relief for the poor. In earlier times in England, poor relief was the responsibility of the churches and the justice of the peace. Therefore, funding of poor relief came from tithe and some compulsory taxes that were under the jurisdiction of the justice of the peace. To a large degree, in addition to providing some relief to the poor, the church attempted to identify and keep track of those considered to be indigent, whereas the Justices of the Peace being a public entity also provided poor relief and also managed many of the relief efforts by categorizing the poor into the following groups: Those who would work but could not work, those who could work but would not work, and those who because of illness, age, and/or disability could not work.

Among other relief efforts, England attempted, with the Poor Laws, to regulate who would be allowed to beg in the streets. Among those were the acutely ill, the physically and mentally disabled, the very young, and the very old. Hence, one of the groups that was allowed to beg included persons considered handicapped. It is interesting to note that, as a result of being allowed to beg, some contend that the term *handicap*, or *cap-in-hand*, to a large extent became synonymous with beggars.

Early American Colonial Period: As we turn our attention to early American beliefs and treatments of persons with disabilities, we discover that after the colonies gained independence from England, the newly declared United States continued in many ways to implement the English methods of providing poor relief. It was clear that the United States, to a large degree, wanted to assist those persons, including persons with disabilities, who were needy. However, similar to the English Poor Laws, they wanted to limit the relief to those of their own (local persons). Offered as an example, in 1798, the U.S. Congress enacted the Seaman's Sickness and Disability Act:

> This law levied a twenty cents a month tax on each seaman (merchant marine) for the purpose of providing temporary relief of sickness to those who needed it. The money was supposed to be spent in the city that collected it and the surplus used for purchasing separate hospitals for use by the sick seamen. A year later the program was extended to the Navy. In 1837, congress acted to include the river-boatmen of the western waterways. Later these marine hospitals were to form the bulwark of the personal medical care system of the U.S. Public Health Service. (Campbell, 1974, p. 424)

During the following several decades, the young nation, through private organizations, developed several benevolent organizations that provided valuable services to persons with disabilities. Some of these organizations were: the American branch of the Salvation Army, hospitals for indigent and dependent children, and the forerunner of modern-day sheltered workshops, to mention only three.

Social Cleansing: Juxtaposition with some of the humanitarian efforts was some destructive efforts designed by their developers and promoter to create an "ideal world." Two of the most devastating efforts at social cleansing were social Darwinism and eugenics.

Social Darwinism: Toward the end of the nineteenth century, the English philosopher Herbert Spencer developed and promoted a theory called Social Darwinism. His theory stated that if commerce had fewer restrictions and interferences from governmental agencies, competition could be unrestricted, and thus those who survived would represent the strongest and fittest individuals and organizations. Spencer believed this would help develop what he considered to be an "ideal society." How Spencer's concept related to persons with disabilities was made clear as he discouraged governmental assistance to the poor. Spencer further believed that the poor and weak were drains on the resources of society. In his opinion, their lack of productivity caused public and private agencies to provide assistance, thus maintaining a group of people who could neither support themselves nor make significant contributions to society. Spencer thought it was better for society to allow the poor and weak to perish rather than sustain their existence and encourage their multiplication through government-supported public relief and health programs.

Although this philosophy did, for a period of time, gain favorable attention in the United States, clergy and disability advocates were able to curb its influence by denounced this philosophy as creating a "cruel society" rather than an ideal society. Despite Social Darwinism's short-lived success, it keeps alive in some people's belief systems the idea that the poor and weak (including persons with disabilities) were inferior people and society would be better served if they were removed and eliminated. This philosophy, to a major extent, was the foundation for the eugenics movement.

Eugenics: In more recent times, the government of Nazi Germany put to death persons whom the government believed to have a mental disability. In the United States, attempts to control reproduction occurred during the eugenics period.

The term *eugenics* was coined by Sir Francis Galton in 1883. The term literally means "well born." The term *well born* was the basis of Galton's idea, which he called a science. Galton believed that individuals inherited their good and bad qualities, thus he gave virtually no consideration to environmental influences on one's physical, emotional, and intellectual development. Therefore, Galton believed that only certain people should be allowed to reproduce. He believed that the human race could be improved through the process of selective breeding. This is similar to what farmers and ranchers do when they select animals with certain desirable qualities to breed in the hopes that a superior quality of animal will be produced. In essence, Galton was promoting the idea that persons with high intelligence and without major physical limitations should be encouraged to reproduce, whereas those considered to be of lesser intelligence and those with physical disabilities should be discouraged from reproducing. Another form of discouraging reproduction was sterilization, and many of the eugenics supporters vigorously supported this effort.

Sterilization: To accomplish their goals of limiting and/or decreasing the unfit population in the United States, as previously stated, the eugenics faithful promoted the ideal of sterilization and limiting immigration. Although restricting immigration of certain groups helped, in the minds of eugenic supporters, to decrease the number of persons entering the United States who had a mental disability and those who would become a burden on American society, there remained the issue of what to do with "unfit" Americans—namely, in their terminology, the feebleminded, criminals, and other degenerates. Eugenicists believed that persons with mental disabilities were a major contributor of illegal activities, such as prostitution and other criminal activities. In addition, they believed that allowing persons with mental disabilities, particularly those considered to be mentally retarded, to reproduce was not only producing more degenerates, but also was costing the government considerable amounts of money to support the offspring of those individuals. *Feebleminded* was the name given to persons considered to be mentally retarded by the eugenic group as well as others. Sterilization of the feebleminded was a solution that eugenicists proposed. In 1907, the state of Indiana became the first state to pass an involuntary sterilization law based on eugenic principles. According to Saunders (1998), by 1931, compulsory sterilization laws had been passed by 27 states.

It is estimated that in the United States, between the years 1907 and 1960, 30,000 to 60,000 persons were involuntarily sterilized. Many of these were persons with disabilities.

Gallagher (1990) also pointed out that the eugenicists sought not only to have persons with disabilities sterilized, they also, in their words, wanted them institutionalized for their own safety as well as the safety of others. The eugenicists promoted the idea that if these individuals were allowed to move about unrestricted, they would engage in criminal activities.

In an attempt to resolve constitutional issues evolving from these laws, an official of the Colony for Epileptic and Feebleminded in Lynchburg, Virginia, developed what the eugenic movement considered a model law of compulsory sterilization.

After the passage of the 1924 Virginia state compulsory sterilization law, the eugenic supporters knew there would be legal challenges to its constitutionality. The case selected to test the constitutionality of the law, as well as the legality of involuntarily sterilization, was *Buck v Bell.*

At the time of the passage of the Virginia law, Carrie Buck was a patient of the Virginia Colony for Epileptics and Feebleminded, having been placed there by her foster parents after she became pregnant as a result of an alleged rape by a relative of her foster family. Carrie gave birth to a girl whom the court declared feebleminded based on a psychological examination of the child prior to her first birthday. Perhaps because Carrie's birth mother had given birth to several children out of wedlock, including Carrie, she (Carrie's mother) also had been institutionalized and declared feebleminded.

Carrie Buck's legal case was chosen, in part, because there were considered to be three generations of feebleminded blood relatives, and the eugenic group believed this was an excellent example to prove their point of the passage of defective genes from one generation to the next. The case proceeded through the various courts and was finally heard by the U.S. Supreme Court. Writing for the majority (8 to 1), Justice Oliver Wendell Holmes issued the following opinion justifying the constitutionality of the Virginia law:

> We have seen that more than once that the public welfare may call upon the best citizens for their lives. It would be strange if it could not call upon those who already sap the strength of the state for these lesser sacrifices. It is better for all the world, if instead of waiting to execute

degenerate offspring for crime, or to let them starve for their imbecili-ty, society can prevent those who are manifestly unfit from continuing their kind. The principle that sustains compulsory vaccination is broad enough to cover cutting the Fallopian tubes. Three generations of im-beciles are enough. (as cited in Webb, Marshall, & Lombardo, 1998, p. 390)

The words used, the tone of the ruling, and the overall thoughts ex-pressed in Justice Holmes' opinion represents a high degree of insen-sitivity to persons with disabilities that one would not expect from a learned group of people, especially ones that represent the highest legal authorities of the United States. Later it was determined that nei-ther Carrie, her mother, nor her daughter were mentally retarded. It appears that Carrie's birth mother was declared feebleminded because she had several children out of wedlock. Additionally, interviews with Carrie indicated that she was not mentally retarded. Finally, an exam-ination of Carrie's daughter's school records indicated that at one point she had been placed on the school's academic honor roll.

Based on the U.S. Supreme Court ruling, involuntary sterilization was upheld in the United States, and as Albrecht, Seelman, and Bury (2001) remind us, it has been within recent years that the statutes have been removed. As previously mentioned, it is estimated that between the years 1907 and 1970, approximately 60,000 persons considered to be mentally ill and/or mentally retarded were involuntarily sterilized in the United States (Webb et al., 1998). The previously mentioned ex-amples as well as others not mentioned give us an idea of how some of our current perceptions and attitudes of persons with disabilities have been formed. Just as Chapter 5 (this volume) indicated that it is important for helping professionals to understand cultural differences, it is equally important for helping professionals to understand attitudes and perceptions of persons with disabilities.

PERCEPTIONS OF DISABILITIES

Sign of weakness: In today's society, it is not socially acceptable to label disabilities as evidence of a human weakness; however, our true beliefs with regard to illness and/or disability are demonstrated in how we treat persons with disabilities. As an example, the treatment modality of health care professionals with regard to their interactions with persons who are ill and/or have a disability is to amplify their limitations. To be more specific, the medical model requires the patient to become dependent on the health care professional. The patient, in effect, becomes an object. The patient is expected to totally submit to the health care provider's judgment. Test results become the evidence that determines the immediate direction of the person's life. In addition to the judgment of the health care professionals, others such as family members are counted on to make decisions about the person's well-being. Too often the patient is treated as if she does not have the capability of determining how she feels and what she would like to have done.

Patients' bill of rights and ethical standards, notwithstanding, health care professionals, through their behavior and in all probability unintentionally, often create in the mind of the person with a disability a feeling of helplessness and weakness. Additionally, this type of behavior, which also is fostered by family and friends, perpetuates the societal perception of disability as a weakness.

Disability associated with sin: Perhaps in ancient times, not having the knowledge of why people became ill, some died as a result of the illness, while others developed observable limitations. This lack of knowledge caused people of antiquity to associate disability with sin and/or evilness. The creation of evil spirits is often the result of our attempts to provide an explanation to unexplainable events. The human brain appears to be wired to think of cause and effect, and when we cannot determine the cause, we often invent one. In antiquity, with regard to disabilities, in the absence of an observable cause, too often the belief was that the person with a disability was being punished for some sin or evil acts he and/or his ancestors had committed.

In today's American society, most people do not associate disabilities with evil spirits. However, there remain some beliefs that disabilities are a result of our sins. This line of thinking is often supported by believers making references to disabilities created as a result of unlawful acts, such as car accidents resulting from the driver being under the influence of some illegal substance or someone becoming mentally ill after using some powerful illegal drug. Once one accepts this type of association, it is not beyond the realm of thinking to associate sins of the parents and foreparents to current disabilities, especially childhood disabilities, which seem to have no logical reason that the disability is part of the child's existence.

Current Perceptions of Disabilities

There is no unified worldview of disabilities and those who have them. The world's societal views appear to be somewhat schizophrenic with regard to persons with disabilities. On the one hand, some societies in an attempt to assist persons with disabilities attain some measure of freedom have taken a somewhat **paternalistic** approach. Although well meaning, this approach often subjects the person with a disability to unwanted sympathy and pity. Too frequently, the paternalistic approach smothers the person with good intentions and stunts the person's emotional and psychological growth. In contrast, some societies have tended to view persons with disabilities as expendable humans; persons of little societal value, to be segregated and separated from the mainstream of society and, yes, in some cases, persons to be exterminated. It is tempting to think that the treatment of persons with disabilities as expendable occurred exclusively in some of the so-called Third World—less economically and culturally developed counties. However, the fact is that this treatment has occurred in developed countries. In Nazi Germany, which was considered one of the most technological and economically developed counties in the world, the first group of people targeted for extermination were persons with mental disabilities. In the United States, some persons with disabilities have been segregated in the public schools. Additionally, some persons with mental disabilities have not only been segregated in mental institutions, but, as previously mentioned, some have been subjected to involuntary sterilization.

Neufeldt (2001) adds to the list of societal perceptions by identifying what are considered several of the main images societies around the world have of persons with disabilities: Persons with disabilities are not (a) able to contribute to the well-being of their society (worthless); (b) capable of heroic acts (hero); (c) the product of some evil (evil); (d) the product of some divine intervention (saintly); (e) limited in their capacity to make decisions on their own (fool); and (f) described as being sick (sick person). Similarly, Fine and Asch (1988) have pointed out that persons with disabilities are often regarded as impaired people, and that women with disabilities are regarded as damaged and asexual.

Obviously, the correctness of these classifications is debatable; however, what is not debatable is the fact that persons with disabilities throughout the world and throughout time have had many labels attached to their impact and worth to the societies in which they have lived. It is imperative that professional helpers understand what their personal perceptions of persons with disabilities are, as well as the perceptions of the society in which they the helper and the helpee live are. This understanding is vital to developing an effective and humane helping relationship.

WHY DO WE FEEL THE WAY WE DO ABOUT DISABILITIES?

Although we may not like to acknowledge the fact that as a society we perceive disabilities and those who have disabilities in the ways previously described, the reality is we do. Perhaps one of the major problems with regard to the human relationship with persons with disabilities is the fact that, for the most part, we as a society are in denial regarding disabilities. We do not like to think about disabilities, and unless we are forced to face the reality, such as having a disability or some significant person in our lives has a disability, we avoid the subject. It is this avoidance (denial) that has help to create and maintain a separation between persons with disabilities and persons without a disability. As long as we do not have to think about the subject, we do not have to deal with its reality. A relevant question is: Why do we have an avoidance complex regarding disabilities?

It is as if we have created, at least in our subconscious minds, two levels of humans: the normal and the abnormal. Those with disabilities are associated with the abnormal side of humanity. Fear is a major reason that we associate disabilities as abnormal, and because of this fear we separate ourselves from those who have disabilities. As humans, we tend to fear the unknown, and this is quite normal. This lack of knowledge brings on unreasonable fears, such as **fear of contamination**. The fear of contamination brings forth subconscious and sometimes conscious fears that if we associate with persons with disabilities, we will somehow contract the disability or some illness or disease associated with the disability. This is a reasonable fear if the disability is caused by a contagious disease that is not under control. In reality, this line of thinking began when some diseases were out of control and causing widespread plagues. However, today the vast majorities of illnesses that create disabilities are controlled and are of little, if any, threat to the public. Nevertheless, the fear of contamination continues. The more visible the disability, the greater the likelihood of this fear placing barriers between those with a disability and those without a disability.

The **fear of what could happen in one's own life,** which is more psychological than physiological in its origin, also creates barriers and impedes healthy human relations between those who have disabilities and those who do not. This fear has its foundation in the reality of the fragileness of life. It is a reality that all humans are one accident or one illness away from having a disability. From a psychological point of view, it is too psychologically painful to get to know the person with a disability because it creates sorryful feelings, which are subconsciously associated with one's own fragile state of life.

As previously stated, we often have fears of the unknown. Some disabilities occur as a result of disease or illness, the cause of which is unknown at its beginning; likewise, a cure or method to control also may be unknown. Because of the many unknowns associated with the illness, too often fear gives birth to panic, and once fear reaches the panic state, many times irrational behavior is the result. Frustration over not being able to adequately control the disease or illness frequently is projected onto the person with the disease. It is understandable that protective action such as quarantine may occur. However, once the cause and cure for the disease are known, the disease often remains stigmatized, as well as anyone who later contracts the disease. Diseases such as polio, tuberculosis, and leprosy prompt this behavior. Fortunately, in developed countries, many of these diseases rarely occur today, therefore a great deal of the stigma is not present. However, it is this author's belief that the stigma is resting below the surface of our emotions, ready to be released if a significantly large reoccurrence of the once dreaded diseases happen. Unfortunately, in less developed countries, these and other diseases exist, and the reaction is often devastating to those who have the disease and become disabled as a result.

Some disabilities such as AIDS as well as disabilities caused by alcohol abuse and strokes induced by the use of illegal drugs are often condemned because of the disability occurring as a result of socially unacceptable behavior. Thus, what one considers to have been the cause or contributing factor of the disability has an impact on how some people feel about the disability and the person who has the disability. From a psychological prospective, the often unspoken feeling about disabilities, under these and other morally considered circumstances, is that the person is receiving reasonable results for conducting him or herself in an immoral and/or unlawful, socially unacceptable manner. Stated another way, the person is receiving punishment for his or her sins. Therefore, disabilities are subconsciously and consciously associated with the undesirables and degenerate elements of society. In past years, in some societies, disabilities were considered to be punishment for sins—sins of one's ancestors or punishment for current sins. Today, in most societies of developed countries, this belief is not a conscious one but remains as a subconscious thought. As previously stated, some disabilities are caused by conditions that society considers to be immoral or undesirable. Unfortunately, as a society, we tend to be unable or unwilling to separate the action from the results of the action. Stated in other terms, we too often refuse to forgive the person for what may have been irresponsible behavior, thus the disability becomes the symbol of retribution. Therefore, disability becomes synonymous with punishment. This train of thought impedes rehabilitation.

Thus far, we have identified a definition of disabilities, and we have discussed how as a society we have developed some of the beliefs and attitudes toward persons with disabilities. Now let us turn our attention to inappropriate behavior that helping professionals should avoid when assisting persons with disabilities. Following that discussion, I discuss tips with regard to helping persons with disabilities.

THINGS NOT TO DO WHEN ASSISTING PERSONS WITH DISABILITIES

Do not use a paternalistic attitude in assisting persons with disabilities. One of the things that has hindered the progress of persons with disabilities effectively integrating in the mainstream of society is the well-meaning but overprotective attitudes and actions of persons without disabilities. Most persons without disabilities, because of their lack of knowledge of the potentials, desires, and abilities of persons with disabilities, tend to either avoid contact with persons with disabilities or overcompensate by inhibiting their emotional growth by trying to protect them from failing. It is my firm opinion that persons with disabilities have the same right to fail as any person. This may sound like a strange and insensitive statement. However, when one examines the underlying principle of the statement, one can see the statement is meant to be helpful rather than hurtful. The underlying principle is that by not allowing a person to attempt something that he or she would like to accomplish, you are not protecting her from failing, but rather blocking her chances of succeeding. Certainly there are limits to not interceding, just as one would prohibit a person from jumping off the roof of a three-story building because the person thinks he can fly; likewise, one would block ridiculous attempts by a person with a disability. Although the example is dramatic, the point hopefully has been made.

Most helping professionals will walk a fine line when working with persons with disabilities. The fine line is being of assistance, but not providing excessive help. Similar to the desire of the helping professional not to do things for the helpee without a disability that he can do for himself, the helper should not do things for the person with a disability that she can do for herself. Sometimes it is difficult to determine what reasonable expectations for the person with a disability are. However, it is imperative that the helper learn to gauge these situations. The operative word for professional helpers is *empowerment*, just as this is the key word for assisting a person without a disability.

Do not be afraid to ask about the person's disability and how it has impacted his or her life. One of the reasons that many persons with disabilities have had problems being accepted into mainstream society relates to the fact that many persons without disabilities fail to become acquainted with them. In too many cases, unless a person without a disability has someone close to them (a family member and/or friend) who has a disability, they tend to avoid meaningful contact. By meaningful contact, I am referring to getting to know persons with a disability on a first-name basis, socialize with them, and consider them as close personal friends.

Part of the lack of personal contact between persons with disabilities and those whom are considered as not having a disability is the fact that many persons without a disability are reluctant to get to know persons with disabilities on more than a superficial level. Part of getting to know persons with disabilities is becoming aware of their disability and some things about their life situations as a result of having a disability. After all, the disability is part of the person.

Some persons without a disability seem to feel that if they inquire about the person's disability, the inquiry will create a state of depression or feelings of shame within the person with a disability. As a professional helper, one can be assured that inquiring or commenting about the person's disability, unless the inquiry or comment is patronizing, rude, and/or insensitive, generally speaking, will not cause the person to become depressed or hate himself. There probably are few questions that the person has not been asked previous to your questions and/or comments. In fact, most persons with disabilities prefer that they be asked about their disability rather than someone staring and avoiding contact. This author has had polio and walks with a limp, and I prefer that interested people ask me about my disability so that we can discuss my situation, get this part of my life in the open so that we can move onto other conversation and human interactions.

There is one exception to the rule of not avoiding asking a person with a disability about his disability and that relates to employers interviewing and hiring persons with disabilities. To avoid the possibility of discrimination against persons with disabilities in employment, the Americans with Disabilities Act prohibits employers from asking persons seeking employment whether they have a disability. Therefore, human resources helping professionals as well as any helping professional functioning in the role of hiring should become familiar with the Americans with Disabilities Act, particularly Title 1 Employment.

Do not express sympathy to the person for having a disability. Although it is acceptable to express sympathy to persons on the death of a family member or close friend, generally speaking, it is unacceptable to show expressions of sympathy because a person has a disability. Persons with disabilities do not need sympathy; they need understanding and assistance to overcome some of the stumbling blocks of negative attitudes and paternalistic attitudes toward their life situations.

Expressions of sympathy may make some persons with disabilities temporarily feel good; however, sympathy does nothing with regard to improving the person's self-esteem. In fact, sympathy, in the long-term, lowers one's self-esteem because it negatively impacts one's self-concept.

Do not treat the person with a disability as being a special person for having the disability. The opposite of expressing sympathy is to praise the person for moving forward with his life despite the fact that he has a disability. Everyone, with or without disabilities, face obstacles and difficult times in their lives. Most people, some with professional help and some without professional help, overcome their obstacles. Treating persons with disabilities as special tends to set them apart from other people who have overcome or learned to live with obstacles. The most important thing a professional helper can do with regard to persons with disabilities is to treat them as human beings, no better or no worse than any other human. A major objective of most persons with disabilities is to be treated as their nondisabled brothers and sisters, no more courageous and stronger than they are.

Do not assume that because the person has a disability she needs assistance—ask. In this discussion, I am referring to physical assistance, such as with a wheelchair, and opening doors as well as other types of physical assistance. Rather than assume the need for assistance, simply ask. For example, rather than clutch the arm of a person who has visual limitations and guide him across a street, ask if he would like to have you assist him across the street. The reality is that many persons with disabilities do need some assistance and will be grateful for any kindness shown to them. However, let the decision about whether there is a need for assistance be theirs rather than assistance being forced on them. Most persons with disabilities prefer to be as independent as possible, but they also know their limitations and are willing to ask for and accept assistance.

Do not stare; if you want to know something about the person and his or her disability—ask. Curiosity is a normal human trait. Therefore, it is not inappropriate to want to know the why and how of the situation. However, what is inappropriate is staring at the person as if he is a freak of nature. Equally as insulting is to move away from the person as if he has a contagious disease. As previously stated, most persons with disabilities are willing to discuss their disability.

When communicating, talk directly to the person with the disability, not to the person or persons accompanying her or him. A major mistake that some helping professionals make when verbally assisting persons with disabilities, particularly persons who have a hearing impairment or has mental limitation (thus have an interpreter or someone to speak for them accompanying them) is to talk directly to the accompanying person. Even if the person with the disability cannot hear you or may not completely understand what you are saying, it is appropriate and best to address your comments to him rather than the interpreter. By doing this, you are acknowledging the person with the disability as a human being. It is inappropriate to talk directly to the accompanying person or persons, thus treating the helpee as if she is not in the room. I have seen this behavior, too many times, in medical settings, where the medical helping professional will talk to family members while the patient/helpee is sitting or lying and experiencing every word.

Do not be afraid to say the word *disability* or *handicap* to a person with a disability. Some professional helpers avoid saying the word *disability* or *handicap* as if these words represent death or nonexistence. These are words that describe a condition of life. If the person with a disability is not in denial of his life condition, the uttering of these words should not place him/her in a state of shock.

It is a truism that there is some debate with regard to whether to say disability or handicap to describe the person's condition. Some prefer the term *person with a disability*, others prefer the term *person who has a handicap*, and others have no preference. The thing on which most people agree is to emphasize the person rather than the disability, thus the term **person first**. To be more specific, say person with a disability, rather than a disabled person, or say person with a handicap rather than a handicapped person.

Additionally, the helping professional must be aware of the terminology she uses to refer to the helpee with a disability. Terms such as *cripple, lame, idiot, imbecile,* and *dumb,* to mention a few, should not be used when referring to persons with physical and/or mental disabilities; also, the term *retarded* should be used sparingly, if at all.

Additional Tips for Effectively Assisting Persons with Disabilities

Vash (1981) offers some helpful tips to the helping professional with regard to determining the most appropriate ways to assist persons with disabilities.

Emotional and behavioral reactions to disablement depend importantly on characteristics of the person who becomes disabled. What remaining resources do they have for developing effective and gratifying lifestyles? For those whose disabilities adventitiously, what activities and behavior patterns are interrupted by disablement and how central are these to their happiness? What kinds of temperaments do they have? What is the spiritual or philosophical base in their lives? What personality traits do they have that will influence the type and intensity of their reactions to disablement? (p. 14)

Quinn (1998), while referring to the specific helping profession of social work assisting families of children with disabilities, offers some important information that could be useful for other helping professionals with regard to assessing the needs of families who have children with a disability.

Social work with families of children with disabilities has been an important intervention for more than 40 years. The social worker needs to examine the family's strengths and its needs. Information should be gathered about the organization of the family and its income level, the health of the parents and the role each family member plays. In addition, the social worker should investigate just how much overload the parents can manage and what are the unresolved conflicts regarding having a child with a disability in the family. Cultural forces that are operating within the family should be identified as should the constructive attitudes and strengths of the member. The answers to these questions will help in determining what services and assistance would be helpful. (pp. 7–8)

From a behavioral standpoint, Greif and Matarazzo (1982) have identified some basic goals of helping professionals with regard to working with persons with disabilities: (a) as much as possible, reestablish the helpee's predisability skills; (b) assist the helpee learn new skills for achieving previous goals; (c) assist the helpee with regard to setting new goals and facilitating their achievement; (d) assist the helpee with regard to adjustment to the new condition; and (e) assist the adjustment of the person with disabilities' significant others.

SUMMARY

In summary, helping professionals must expand their concept of disabilities from the commonly considered views of someone with severe physical and/or mental conditions. Certainly, persons with severe physical and/or mental disabilities need assistance and will be part of some helper's caseload. Additionally, there will be others seeking or being referred who have issues where disability is not readily seen, but as the helper proceeds with evaluation aspects of disabilities will appear. Therefore, it is vitally important that the helper have some basic understanding of disabilities and how to work with helpees who have disabilities.

Although in the United States it is not likely that many, if any, persons would openly admit that they are biased against persons with disabilities. In America openly expressing negative feelings with regard to persons with disabilities is closely akin to being against motherhood and educating children; however, if one looks closely at some of the problems persons with disabilities encounter, most on a daily basis, one can easily make a strong case supporting benign neglect of thousands of persons with disabilities in the United States and millions more around the world. As proof of this statement, using only the United States as an example, on any given month of a year the unemployment rate for persons with disabilities is in double digits and this often is not counting persons with severe disabilities. When one considers persons with severe disabilities the unemployment rate reach astronomical percentages such as in the 30% range. In part the indefensible high rate of unemployment is a result of many people's lack of understanding of the capabilities of persons with disabilities and a result of this lack of understanding is the lowering of the self-esteem of many persons with disabilities. Part of the solution for increasing the self-esteem of many persons with disabilities is for both the nondisabled and persons with disabilities to change many of society's attitudes with regard to what persons with disabilities can do, or stated in other terms, remove some of the negative attitudes which the society either consciously or unconsciously holds.

With regard to removing negative attitudes and replacing these attitudes with positive and more realistic attitudes about capabilities of persons with disabilities, as a society we should began with educating nondisabled and persons with disabilities about disabilities. A realistic question to this proclamation is how do we accomplish this task? The answer is to begin with the youth. To answer the next logical question is how do we accomplish this goal and what proof exists that the effort will be successful? To answer these questions I use the example of racial integration in the United States. In the not too distant past, the United States was faced with the enormous problem of segregation of human races–to be more specific, the unequal opportunities and treatment of African Americans and to a lesser degree other ethnic groups such as American Indians and Asian Americans. Because of the unequal treatment and opportunities of African Americans, they were relegated to second-class citizenship in the United States. During the period of segregation African Americans had very high unemployment and the employment that many African Americans received was dangerous and very difficult work. Additionally, the pay they received was considerably less than Caucasian Americans. These factors as well as many others portrayed African Americans as second-class citizens. Although it has taken considerable time to partially remove this stigma; however, racial relationships with regard to African Americans have improved and a major reason is integration of youth in public schools. Youth of various ethnic and racial groups being educated side-by-side as well as enjoying each other's company in and out of class has, to a significant extent, eliminated the old attitudes that African Americas are less intelligent than non-African Americans. The point being made is this success can be duplicated with regard to changing and improving attitudes about persons with disabilities.

Currently, many youths with disabilities attend public schools in the same classroom with nondisabled youths and as a result of this interaction friendships are developed based upon personality compatibility rather than differences. These types of friendship developments allows young minds to accept persons on who they are and not based upon faulty perceptions upon years of adult bias and prejudices. Additionally, this close interaction has caused nondisabled youth to view youth with disabilities as equals. Stated in other terms nondisabled youth have learned to look beyond the disability and see the person as a human being with similar strengths and weaknesses as themselves. They view them as friends not someone to segregate and shun. The youth tend to see young persons with disabilities as potential friends with strengths and weaknesses similar to their own. This is not to say that nondisabled students do not see and/or not aware of some physical limitations that some students with disabilities have; however, their friendship with them is based upon personality compatibility rather than physical differences.

One cannot discuss school-age youth with disabilities without pointing out the reality of disabilities such as intellectual disabilities and other disabilities that require "special education." In many of these situations, students are placed in separate classrooms for part of a day or in some instances perhaps the entire day. However, this does not mean that this separation negates the development of understanding and friendships between nondisabled and persons with disabilities. Most teachers, both special education and other classroom teachers, diligently work to educate and sensitize students with regard to the strengths as well as weaknesses of all students. This approach tends to help students, both nondisabled and students with disabilities to develop genuine respect for each other.

This author is not unaware that some nondisabled school children are not very sensitive with regard to disabled children as well as disabled adults with disabilities. This is not a perfect world and some things of this nature are going to occur; however, it is also this author's opinion that the majority of school-attending children are less prejudiced with regard to their counterparts in school and persons with disabilities than many adults. The major point being made is that as adults, if we would follow the lead of most nondisabled school children, many of the negative attitudes as well as neglect of persons with disabilities would not be of significant concerns in the United States.

It has been proven time and again that when children are allowed to study and play together, differences of color, race, ethnicity, social status and disabilities often become of lesser concern than one's personality and compatibility. It is we adults who tend to place qualifiers on friendships. It is we adults who are the major offenders of discrimination. It is we adults who create the society in such a way that life becomes, in part, a game of competition, and the competition becomes hardcore where we select our friends based upon what they can materially do for us. Stated in other terms, as adults, the world in which we live becomes so competitive that too often we neglect to assist those that may have less than we have. In fact, we tend to take pride in seeing our fellow human beings having less than we have, unless we have our goals set to utilize what those having more than we have as an opportunity to improve our life status. One may say that there is nothing wrong with improving ones' status in life's arena; however, it is this author's contention that there is a problem with this approach when we neglect other's need and fail to assist them. How does this relate to persons with disabilities; the simple answer is that too often we magnify their weakness and fail to see their strengths. No one is perfect and everyone has strengths and potentials; therefore we should search for the strengths in a person and help that person utilize those strengths. When we have done that, we become better human beings and are on the correct path to helping create a better society.

It is this author's belief that if the United States continues to develop ways in which school children (kindergartner to graduation) continue to learn, study, and play together, many of the negative attitudes about persons with disabilities will fade away, and those that remain will be less effective in perpetuating negative attitudes and beliefs with regards to persons with disabilities. If we observe and listen to the youth, they will teach us that no one is perfect and we all have limitations. They will also teach us that as human beings we are all more alike than different, and this certainly is true for persons with disabilities.

The previous discussion has dealt with youth and the fact that school children, tend to be more accepting of perceived differences than adults. School children tend to accept others based upon friendship. Stated in other terms, if you are a nice person, have a good personality and is friendly, children view acceptance in these terms more than viewing and basing friendship upon one's limitations. Having made that distinction, this part with regard to education discusses how we educate persons with disabilities and how this is done impacts not only their education also impacts self-confidence.

Educators in the United States must be given credit for working hard to give children with disabilities opportunities to maximize their potentials. Federal and state governments have implemented Individual Education Plans (IED) which require public schools that have children with disabilities to develop education plans that will help maximize their potential of being successful in their academic work. The development of these plans require input from parents of the child with disabilities as well as input from the educators. This approach is very good in that it requires involvement of the parents, thus hopefully the plan or plans are realistic with regard to the child's abilities to successfully navigate and complete the plans. This type of involvement is very good and certainly should be continued. Other educational plans that complement this approach could begin at an early age and introduce children to future goals such as understanding of what college education is as well as trade schools. Certainly at a very early age children will not completely comprehend the many aspects of either a college curriculum and/or vocational education; however by introducing them to these things they will likely develop images in their minds of what they would like to be as well as develop an image of self-determination. This will be the beginning of developing self-awareness and self-confidence. The noted psychologist Alfred Alder in developing his Adlerian psychological theory posits that children at an early age of about six years began to think in terms of what they would like to be. This does not mean they fully understand the many aspects of careers, but they are beginning to develop an image of themselves as future adults. Parents and educators should take these early learning opportunities to encourage mental and physical exploration careers and what is required to achieve those dreams.

Children begin at an early age to think of, visualize, and dream of being adults. In this process many thoughts flood through their minds with regard to what they want to be when they become adults. This is a critical time in all children's lives and certainly persons with disabilities are no exception. This is a period when a child's self-confidence can be built and sustained, or depleted and destroyed. This early age, around six to ten years of age is very critical, especially to youth with some type of disability. This is the time when they began to believe in their abilities to complete difficult tasks or become victims of self-doubt. This is also a critical time when children should be encouraged to explore the limits of their physical, mental and emotional boundaries. For many, if not most, nondisabled youth are given these opportunities; however, unfortunately some—and one is too many—youth with disabilities are discouraged from exploring. They are often told they cannot accomplish these tasks, and encouraged not to attempt to accomplish same. If the child with a disability does attempt and fail, this is pointed out to him/her that the task is beyond his/her abilities. The major difference is when a nondisabled child ties and fails he/she is often encouraged to try again and again until accomplishment has been achieved. This success does wonders for the nondisabled child's self-confidence. On the other side of the coin, the first failure the nondisabled child experiences and if he is not encouraged to try again, loss of self-confidence begins to grow within the child. Certainly, there are limits to any child's abilities, and some actions are attempted before the child is physically, mentally and/or emotionally prepared to take on such tasks. The difference between the non-disabled and the child with a disability is how the initial defeat is handled. The child with a disability not being given another chance at the task, and/or the task not being modified in ways that the child can in some manner succeed, are the beginning of loss of self-confidence.

The need for building self-confidence is not exclusive to youth with disabilities; the need is equally important to adults with disabilities. A strong case can be made that increasing self-confidence of youth with disabilities could be negated when they become adults and life-enhancing resources are not available namely adequate employment and/or employment training that leads to meaningful employment.

An example of lack of employment for adults with disabilities can be seen at almost any point in time when one compares the employment rate of nondisabled persons to the employment rate for persons with disabilities. It is not a fabrication of reality to state that the unemployment rate for persons with disabilities is very near or exceeds three times that of nondisabled persons. That statistic does not include persons with disabilities who have been unemployed for long periods of time. Without providing reasonable employment opportunities for persons with disabilities, some of the efforts to increase the self-esteem of youth with disabilities will be negated. The question thus becomes how do we as a nation and society increase employment opportunities for adult persons with disabilities? To answer that question the following are some things that can be done: 1. Continue and improve sheltered workshops. 2. Increase and promote supported employment. 3. Provide assessable and reasonable cost public transportation. 4. Assist persons with disabilities who qualify with good housing.

Collectively, persons with disabilities from prehistoric times to the present have been handicapped not as much by their physical, mental or emotional disabilities, but by society's perceptions of them as human beings. The proof of this statement is magnified in some of the terminologies used to identify them. Terminology such as cripple, handicapped, crazy, dumb, deranged, lunatics, and gimps (to mention only a few uncomplimentary words) were used in the past and unfortunately to some extent today. Although we proudly speak of individual differences and the uniqueness of each person, we live in an ambivalent world where, despite these differences, we continue to categorize certain traits and assign each a name, frequently condemning those different from what is considered "normal." Names may not only display how we feel about a situation or someone at a given time, but also send messages to a group or an individual about how they are perceived. It may be argued (and truthfully so) that the use of certain names are not deliberately used to debase anyone; however, the fact remains that certain words are steeped in traditionally unglorified meanings to the point that a person or group of people affected may be very sensitive to their use. Perhaps words not meant as negative messages may, in fact, be received as such.

Sheltered workshops such as Goodwill Industries were for many years the primary source of training and employment for some persons with disabilities, particularly those persons with severe disabilities. One of the disadvantages of these types of workshops was because they were exempt from paying minimum wages based on the belief that employees with disabilities were not as productive as nondisabled persons. In some and probably in many cases this was true; however, today as a result of automation, computerization, and other labor-savings methods, many persons with disabilities with appropriate education and training can, if given the opportunities, be as productive as nondisabled persons.

Numerous studies have shown that persons with disabilities are some of the safest, reliable and productive employees when they are given a chance to be gainfully employed. Because of these proven facts, some persons with disabilities are being hired whereas in past years they would not have been hired. On the positive side more persons with disabilities are able to secure employment, many of these are persons with less severe disabilities. However, some persons with disabilities such as those with mobility problems, intellectual and mental disabilities, continue to have difficulties securing meaningful and gainful employment. Therefore, more sheltered workshops such as Goodwill Industries need to be developed and equipped with up-to-date technology so that employees can be trained and prepared for employment in the nonsheltered employment environment. One way of accomplishing this is to have private industries partner with sheltered workshops in training persons with disabilities for jobs in their work environment. These industries can help provide modern equipment that represents what is used in their business, for training in sheltered workshops. Additionally, these businesses could work with prospective employees with regard to things such as how to interview, and so forth. Some other things private employers can do in cooperation with sheltered workshops are: 1. Increase and improve employment skills. 2. Help persons with disabilities build resumes. 3. Help persons with disabilities learn good interviewing skills.

Perhaps the most discriminated groups with disabilities are the persons with mental and emotional disabilities. Many of the old stereotypes which plagued persons with disabilities for centuries have been removed; but those beliefs continue to plague many persons with mental and emotional disabilities. Perhaps the most disabling thought about persons with mental and/or emotional disabilities is that they are "crazy" and dangerous. This concept was derived, to a large extent from movies and televisions' display of persons with mental and emotional disabilities. Too often they are displayed as mass murderers, rapists, and evil people. There is no question that some persons with mental and emotional disabilities do commit horrendous crimes. However, the fact is these are the exceptions. One must acknowledge the fact that some persons who are not mentally ill also commit horrendous crimes.

The negative perceptions of persons with mental and emotional disabilities often are roadblocks for them to receive appropriate and adequate mental health care. Therefore, what is needed is appropriate mental health attention. Instead of closing institutions that care for persons with mental and emotional problems, there should be increased emphasis on operating more facilities for the help and treatment of these issues. More study and research is needed, which will lead to better understanding and treatment of physical, emotional and psychological issues.

Chapter Review Questions

1. What is the Americans With Disabilities Act's definition of a disability?
2. Approximately what percentage of the United States' population has a disability?
3. What is the relationship of the Elizabethan Poor Laws to persons with disabilities?
4. What was the intent of Social Darwinism?

5. What is eugenics?
6. Was involuntary sterilization ever lawful in the United States?
7. What was the relationship of the legal case *Buck v. Bell* with regard to disabilities?
8. What does the concept of fear of contamination mean?
9. What does the term *paternalistic attitude* mean with regard to persons with disabilities?

Mental Exercise

1. Under certain circumstances, students with learning disabilities may be given extra time for tests. Do you believe this is fair to students without learning disabilities? Is this giving an unfair advantage to persons with learning disabilities? Defend your answers.
2. List some of the stereotypes, of which you are aware, with regard to persons with disabilities.
3. Do you think that eugenics could return within the United States?
4. In your opinion, should persons who have cognitive mental disabilities (often labeled mental retardation) have children? Defend your answer.
5. You are the human resources director (personnel director) for a clothing manufacturing company. Your company's primary products are women's dresses and men's casual jeans. Your company employs 50 persons, 10 in management and 40 involved in the sewing and assembly of the previously mentioned products. Financially, your company has had no problems in making payroll in the 15 years you have been the human resources director. For the last five (5) years, the company for which you work has used all of its earnings in giving raises and upgrading equipment. This year is no exception. Your boss has informed you that one of the goals of the company is to continue with pay increases and equipment upgrade.

   You are currently interviewing to fill a position of a sewing machine operator. You have narrowed the search to two persons, both males, and both have essentially equal qualifications. However, one of the candidates is a person who is paralyzed waist down, thus he uses a wheelchair as his mobility device. Your company has never employed a person with a physical disability, and the work area is on the second floor of the two-story building;

however, there is room on the first floor for a limited number of machines and operators. There will be expenses to modify the area to accommodate the machines and operators. Additionally, the current machines are not wheelchair accessible. The restroom and break area are on the second floor, the building doesn't have any elevator, and the restrooms are not wheelchair accessible. **Whom will you hire?**
Justify your decision.

References

Albrecht, G. L., Seelman, K. D., & Bury, M. (Eds.). (2001). *Handbook of disability studies.* Thousand Oaks, CA: Sage.

Bryan, W. V. (2006). *In search of freedom* (2nd ed.). Springfield, IL: Charles C Thomas.

Buck v. Bell (1927). United States Supreme Court case.

Campbell, H. J. (1974). The Congressional debate over the Seaman's Sickness and Disabilities Act of 1798: The origins of the continuing debate on the socialization of American medicine. *Bulletin of History of Medicine, 48* (3), 423–426.

Campbell, R. N. (1987). The new science: Self-esteem psychology. In J. T. Super & J. R. Black (1991). Self-concepts and need for achievement of men with physical disabilities. *Journal of General Psychology, 119* (1), 73–80.

Fine, M., & Asch, A. (Eds.). (1988). *Women with disabilities: Essays in psychology, culture and politics.* Philadelphia: Temple University Press.

Gallagher, H. G. (1990). *By trust betrayed.* New York: Henry Holt.

Greif, E., & Matarazzo, R. G. (1982). *Behavioral approaches to rehabilitation; coping with change.* New York: Springer.

Haj, F. A. (1970). *Disability in antiquity.* New York: Philosophical Library.

Neufeldt, A. H. (2001). Quoted in Leavitt, R. L. (Ed.) *Cross-cultural rehabilitation: An international perspective.* London: W. B. Saunders.

Quinn, P. (1998). *Understanding disability: A lifespan approach.* Thousand Oaks, CA: Sage.

Saunders, Jr., D. E. (1998). Lessons from eugenics for the neoeugenics era. *Journal of the South Carolina Medical Association, 9,* 383–388.

Vash, C. L. (1981). *The psychology of disability.* New York: Springer.

Webb, S. A., Marshall, M. R., & Lombardo, P. A. (1998). Eugenics in the South: The Carrie Buck case. *The Journal of the South Carolina Medical Association, 9,* 389–391.

Suggested Readings

Clements, L., & Road, J. (Eds.). (2008). *Disabled people and the right to life: The protection and violation of disabled people's most basic human rights.* New York: Routledge.

Erickson, P. E., & Erickson, S. K. (2008). *Crime punishment and mental illness: Law and the behavioral sciences in conflict.* New Brunswick, NJ: Rutgers University Press.

French, S. (2008). *Disability on equal terms.* Los Angeles/London: Sage.

Gabel, S. L., & Danforth, S. (Eds.). (2008). *Disability and the politics of education: An international reader.* New York. Peter Lang.

Guernsey, T. F., & Klare, K. (2008). *Special education law* (3rd ed.). Durham, NC: Carolina Academic Press.

Haugen, D. M., et al. (2008). *Rights of the disabled.* New York: Facts on File.

Leavitt, R. L. (Eds.). (2001). *Cross-cultural rehabilitation: An international perspective.* London: W. B. Saunders.

Serene, F. H. (2008). *Making archives accessible for people with disabilities.* Washington, DC: National Archives and Records Administration.

Siebers, T. (2008). *Disability theory.* Ann Arbor, MI: University of Michigan Press.

Chapter 7

UNDERSTANDING RELIGIONS

Chapter Outline
• Introduction
• What is Religion?
• Religion and Culture
• Christianity
• Judaism
• Islam
• Buddhism
• Hinduism
• Commonalities
• Other than Religion
• Implications for Helping Professionals and Others
• Conclusion

Chapter Objectives
Make helping professionals aware how various religious beliefs may and can influence the helping relationship.

INTRODUCTION

Religion in most parts of the world is a very important and powerful force in many people's lives. Even though some countries, including the United States, attempt to separate the function of its governments from religion, the fact remains that in indirect ways religion has some impact upon the political, social, and to some extent, fiscal activities of these countries.

In countries which attempt to separate religion and government, often the role of religion is left to the religious organizations, i.e., church, temple, mosques, and so forth. While these religious organizations have varying degrees of impact they, in fact, have an impact on some governmental actions. Regardless of how a government attempts to keep religion separate from political actions, the undeniable truth is governments are conducted by people. Regardless of how a government attempts to separate government and religion, if those persons making and/or influencing governmental policies, laws and actions, some of the religious beliefs of those making or influencing the decisions will have impact on some if not many of the decisions. Therefore, anyone who believes that their government is immune to some religious beliefs is taking a naive view of how governments work.

Many, if not most religious leaders take pride in sharing their religious beliefs knowing that the sharing will in many instances have a significant impact on governmental actions. In the United States, politicians seeking political office and/or local and state leadership positions often seek the support of religious leaders. One of the reasons for these attempts to gain the support of the religious leaders is the influence these persons have via their congregations and the American society's belief that religious doctrines provide divine directions with regard to moral and correct ways to live. Some countries have the foundation of their governments based upon certain religious doctrines.

In the United States and other countries which attempt to separate religion and government, the role of religion and its influences are delegated to religious institutions. With regard to helping professionals, too often we view their roles and contributions to the well-being of society as helpers in religious organizations or organizations founded and based upon religious precepts, such as the Salvation Army, church operated food and clothing distribution facilities, and hospitals. These organizations may continue to offer services based upon religious precepts.

Quite often helping professionals, if they are not employed by or providing free services to religious-based hospitals, clinics, etc., may tend to overlook the importance of being aware of the many ways religion impacts persons they are attempting to help. Despite the fact that the United States and other nations attempt to separate church and state does not mean that persons who are in need of help is not impacted by religion. Their religious beliefs can have significant impact upon how they respond to the type of help you are attempting to provide. Offered as an example, if you as the helping professional is working in a health facility counseling patients that use that facility, it is important that you know something about their religious beliefs, if they have any. Their religious beliefs may influence how they respond to certain types of treatments as well as whether they will follow medication instructions. The patient may believe in divine healing and/or is not willing to take certain medication because of the composition of the medication. Some patients may feel strongly about having their religious leaders involved in the treatment regimen and are not willing to proceed without their consent.

As discussed in this text, the United States of America as well as some other countries has had significant immigration where persons come to the nation for various reasons and have various beliefs that may be somewhat different than some persons born and reared in the United States. Therefore, it is imperative that helping professionals become aware that the way things are done in the United States are not always the way immigrants have been taught and believe. In fact, there are some citizens born and reared in the United States that have different views than the majority of American-born and reared citizens. Therefore, it is imperative that helping professionals maintain an open mind with regard to various religious beliefs. For some persons, their religious beliefs are the most important guiding forces in their lives, therefore it is important to have a broad understanding of various religions. Having made that statement, this author realizes that no one is, or can be an expert on the many religions and their beliefs. It is this author's opinion that it will be wise for helping professionals to learn about the five major religions in the world: Christianity, Islam, Judaism, Buddhism and Hinduism. Therefore, in this chapter, some basic information of the previously mentioned religions will be discussed.

WHAT IS RELIGION?

Some people define religion according to their spiritual belief preferences such as Christianity, Islam, and Judaism to mention three. An obvious fault is that the definition basically declares the other religions as inaccurate representations of religion without providing an accurate operative definition of religion. Others may define religion by identifying, traditions, practices, and beliefs which constitute a specific religion or several religions. Again those that do not follow the specified traditions, practices and beliefs are in effect declared as nonreligions. Others simply describe religion as "a belief system." This has an obvious flaw of not describing a belief–if one says a belief in religion, then one is not describing what religion is. Tylor (1871) defined religion as "the belief in spiritual beings. Geetrz (1973) identifies religion as a cultural system and Asal (1982) defined religion as "an organized collection of belief systems, cultural systems and world views that relate humanity to spirituality and sometimes to moral values." Makinde (2013) points out that religion is envisioned to give meaning to life, clarify the source of life, and the origin of the world. He further points out that in all societies around the world, the belief in supernatural power exists, therefore, what influences human beings influences society. Asal (1982) in earlier comments serve as a foundation for Makinde's position when he stated "in most cases, humans develop morality, ethics, laws, and way of life from religion." Although more of a fact than a definition, religion has for many people the impact of motivating and inspiring people to do good things and achieve things that goes beyond benefiting oneself but inspires and motivate others to do honorable things. According to Geertz:

> Whether anyone likes it or not, religious beliefs are unavoidable aspects of life with respect to cultural values, politics, even finances. These relationships between religion and society are visible in Islamic religion and Muslims social cultures. The relationship between religion and society is also obvious in Christian social cultures, morality, ethics and governance. It is reflected in Buddhism social cultures and governance in society. (1973)

There are no definitions of religion known to this author that does not have some flaws; therefore I shall not attempt to provide a definition. However, I will point out that defining religion is somewhat like trying to define the wind. One cannot see the wind, however, one can feel and see the impact of the wind. Similarly, religion is not something one can visually see; however for persons who consider themselves religious they can feel and see the impact of religion. Continuing with the analogy of wind and religion, similar to each person's personal preference with regard to experiencing wind, some people like a very calm and quiet day, others may like the wind blowing vigorously against their bodies. Likewise, with regard to experiencing religion some like a very smooth and sedate flow of religious services, while others like loud, animated religious services. While religion tends to escape an accurate or definitive definition, the effects of religion are a powerful force in many people's lives.

For many people who consider themselves religious or have some religious faith, it is very difficult to imagine human life without some connection to a supernatural faith. Perhaps they have difficulties comprehending the development of the universe and its continual existence without superhuman involvement. Likewise, they may have difficulty believing that their lives, to some extent, are not guided by a power or powers greater than their own. Also, for some, having a faith in powers beyond their own adds additional meaning and comfort to their lives as they encounter difficult times. The belief in an afterlife for some gives additional meaning to their relatively short existence.

RELIGION AND CULTURE

Religion or the expression of faith in something or someone greater than one's self goes beyond attending religious services. The expression of faith includes adhering to some, if not all, of the basic principles and beliefs that serve as the foundation of the faith. The expression of faith also includes recognition and at least occasional celebration of important historical events. Similar to ethnic/racial groups who celebrate or recognize significant events related to that part of their culture, individuals of a religious persuasion also place great importance in significant events related to their faith. Therefore, for some people, their religious faith transcends all the other variables of their cultural composition.

It has been stated that religion unites humans, which is partially true, and this would be a completely great act if everyone agreed upon what is the best interest of human kind. Unfortunately, there is no oneness and never will be, with regard to this issue. A religion's views will set standards of decorum, however, true to the mental makeup of humans some of those views will be questioned which will lead to a break away from some of the precepts of those views. Thus a new group of religious concepts will be formed. Many times this type of action is berated by those that do not agree with the newly formed religious concepts; however, this is how cultures are established, likewise this is how various religious views and concepts are formed.

Another fact that explains a reason there are numerous different religions is testament to the mental versatility of humans. Stated in other terms, humans are endowed with the ability to process information.

One may ask the question: "how relevant is religion in today's society?" An answer is found in the fact that there are a large number of beliefs and philosophies which are tagged as religions. Thus, if religion is not relevant in today's society, then religion would disappear; instead more and more religions appear almost yearly if not more often.

Brief overview of the following faiths/religions: Christianity, Judaism, Islam, Hinduism, and **Buddhism.** This author is aware that scores of books have been written about each of the faith/religions mentioned in this chapter, which indicates that there is a tremendous amount of information on each subject. Therefore, no attempt is being made to give detailed coverage of the previously mentioned faith/religions. It is hoped that the reader will be inspired to do additional research to increase his/her knowledge.

CHRISTIANITY

Brief History of Christianity

Jesus of Nazareth was born and reared a Jew and when he began his ministry he differed with the Jewish religion when he proclaimed himself as the Son of God. His preaching of salvation upset the Jewish religious structure of that time. Jesus of Nazareth had disciples who assisted him with his ministry as they began to convert followers from the traditional Jewish religion. Some of the differences in the teaching of Jesus Christ brought him into conflict with many in the Jewish establishment as well as the Roman Empire. According to Blainey, (2012). "Palestine at that time was on the outpost of the Roman Empire which was ruled by leaders that preached that man should obey the gods of the Roman Empire." Blainey continues by stating that the start of Christianity was very turbulent for the first Christians when they began to shun the gods of the Roman Empire. He further contends that the division between the first Christians and the Roman Empire is what led to the death of Jesus of Nazareth. After the death of Jesus it was his disciples who continued to spread the word of God. In 313 AD, the Edict of Milan was signed between Constantine (the Roman emperor in the West) and Licinius (the emperor in the East), which allowed Christians to openly practice Christianity without the fear of persecution. Later, Constantine embraced Christianity and the Christian religion became the preferred religion of the West. Blainey, in his time frame of the development of Christianity moves forward by pointing out that during the Reformation of the 1600s, the Christian church with regard to some of its doctrines were challenged by Martin Luther and John Calvin, and as a result the Protestant church of the Christian religion was formed by Martin Luther. According to Bryan (2007), Martin Luther viewed salvation as a gift from God through the forgiveness of sin and should not be dictated by the Pope and the Bishops of the Roman Catholic Church. Nail (2013) makes us aware that these basic beliefs gave everyone, no matter their social class or gender, the right to practice religion. This split which is referred to as the Protestant Reformation was the first major split of the Roman Catholic Church. Rome and the Roman Empire's army during the time of Jesus Christ's physical appearance on earth were the military and political rulers of the region in which Christianity developed. Christianity and its influence spread throughout the Roman Empire and later throughout the rest of Europe; as we know today, Christianity has also spread throughout the rest of the world. Christianity, which is one of the most influential of the major world religions, is also one of the youngest religions.

There are three main divisions of Christianity: (1.) Roman Catholic, (2.) Eastern Orthodox, and (3.) Protestant. The first of the three divisions that existed was Roman Catholicism. Many of the first churches were established by the Apostle Paul, but were persecuted and even considered by some to be illegal. However, in the fourth century, Constantine won his place as Roman emperor and gave praise to the Christian God for his victory in battle by proclaiming his conversion to Christianity, thus its status as the official religion of the Roman Empire. This gave Christianity a strong footing and ensured its survival. The Roman Empire fell in 476 A.D. and the Eastern and Western Christians were no longer unified by the centrally located Rome. The differences in their beliefs and practices began to create even more divisions between them. After many years of debate between the two regional groups, in 1054 A.D, a split between the Roman Catholic and the newly formed Eastern Orthodox religions, which did not recognize the authority of the Roman Catholic Church occurred. The differences in doctrine led to the creation of the second major division.

The third division came about in Europe. As previously mentioned a German Monk named Martin Luther posted what later came to be called 95 Theses, which called out any who wished to debate on certain doctrines and practices of the Roman Catholic Church. The movement that occurred as a result of Martin Luther's actions is referred to as the Protestant Reformation, which has led to the development of what is termed Protestant churches.

As previously mentioned, currently there are three major divisions within the Christian faith: Roman Catholic, Eastern Orthodox, and Protestant. Within the Protestant group are numerous denominations such as Baptist, Methodist, and Church of Christ, to mention only three. Within the various branches of these denominations are further divisions such as the Southern Baptist and Free Will Baptist to mention only two. Further division can also be seen along ethnic/racial lines. While most Protestant denominations have become open to persons of all ethnic/racial groups, most, however, remain segregated, perhaps not by edict, but by tradition. This is especially true in the case of African Americans. During the period of slavery and reconstruction, primarily in southern American states (although not exclusively in those areas), African Americans were not welcome in churches where the congregations were predominately Caucasians. Denied access to their home countries' religions, many African Americans adopted and developed branches of the Caucasian-dominated churches to help serve their religious inclinations. Thus, the separation of religious congregations along racial lines in America continues today. Regardless of the division or denomination of the church, the Holy Bible is the sacred text of all groups.

As previously stated there are three major divisions of the Christian religion. The Eastern Orthodox formed the second division when it broke away from what some consider the original Christian church, the Roman Catholic Church in 1054 A.D.; the division occurred as a result of disagreement over doctrine and ecclesiastical authority. Even though most Eastern Orthodox churches have common beliefs, principles, and doctrines, each tends to be oriented toward the nation in which it resides–Russian Orthodoxy, Romanian Orthodox, and Bulgarian Orthodox to name three as examples.

Some Basic Beliefs of Christians

Although there are three divisions and numerous denominations within the Christian religion, there are some beliefs that are held in common by all. Some of them are:

- All Christians believe in one God, who is the Father and Creator of all humankind.
- All Christians belied in the Trinity: the Father, the Son and the Holy Spirit.
- All Christians believe that Jesus of Nazareth is the Christ and is the Son of God, born of a Virgin and was sent to Earth to live a sinless life, thus setting an example for earthly faithful to follow.
- All Christians believe in the Virgin birth.
- All Christians believe that Jesus was crucified for humankind's sins and was buried and resurrected in three days and later ascended to Heaven.
- All Christians believe the Bible is the Holy Scripture provided as encouragement and guidance by which they are to live.

Significant Events of Christianity

There are numerous events and significant dates that are important to Christians; however, not all Christians observe each of them. Despite this, the two most important events in Christianity and, generally speaking, observed by all Christians are Christmas Day, which represents Jesus Christ's birthday, and Easter, which represents the resurrection of Jesus Christ.

Summary

One of the major precepts in which most, if not all, Christians and Jews believe is the Ten Commandments.

1. You shall not have other gods before me.
2. You shall not carve idols for yourselves in the shape of anything in the sky above or on the earth below or in the water beneath the earth; you shall not bow down before them or worship them.
3. You shall not take the Lord's name in vain.
4. You shall keep holy the Sabbath day.
5. You shall honor your father and mother.
6. You shall not murder.
7. You shall not commit adultery.
8. You shall not steal.
9. You shall not bear false witness against your neighbor.
10. You shall not covet your neighbor's house. You shall not covet your neighbor's wife.

Commandments one through four are guides with regard to love and worship of God. The last six are guidelines for loving and caring for others. All of the commandments can be considered culturally based.

JUDAISM

Brief History of Judaism

It is impossible to understand the history of Judaism without discussing the history of the Jewish people. Much of the early history of Judaism is told in the first five chapters of the Old Testament of the Bible (Torah). Abraham is considered the founder of the faith, which is called Judaism. When one traces the lineage of Abraham, it is recognized that some of the best known persons of the Torah are of the seed of Abraham. Isaac, and Jacob, also known as Israel, whose decedents were called Israelites, all are of the lineage of Abraham. According to Scripture, descendants of Jacob migrated to Egypt where they were enslaved, and Moses received the Law from God and led them from bondage.

The word Jew can refer to any person of Jewish parentage; this means any one born of those descendants of the group described in biblical and post-biblical sources. Jew is also used to refer to an ethnic, cultural, and religious group who adhere to a body of beliefs known as Judaism.

The history of the Jews is replete with conflicts, victories, and defeats as they struggled to attain and retain the "promise land." Today, the nation of Israel, which was established in 1948, is recognized by Jews as their homeland. The word homeland is somewhat misleading in that not all Jews originate from the current state of Israel. To better understand what a Jew is, one needs to understand that from a cultural standpoint, the term Jewish is not a designation of a race of people. Anyone through the process of conversion can become a Jew; therefore, a Jew can be of any race or ethnicity. Additionally, one does not have to be born in Israel to be a Jew. Also one does not have to be born a Jew, as previously stated, he/she can become a Jew by going through the process of converting to Judaism. Given this information, to a large extent, being a Jew is a way of life and perhaps a state of mind. Furthermore, one does not have to be religious to be a Jew.

To further understand Judaism, one must understand that currently there are three major sects or versions of Judaism: Orthodox, Reform, and Conservative. Orthodox Judaism believes in the teachings of the concepts in the Torah and further believes that they are unchanging and should be followed unaltered as outlined in the Scripture. Reform Judaism does not strictly adhere to all Jewish traditions as do the Orthodox Jews. Conservative Judaism believes in the scholarly study and interpretation of the Torah. Stated another way, followers of the Conservative philosophy believe that the beliefs of Judaism should be open to evaluation and interpretation and be changeable based upon contemporary scholarly findings, study, and interpretation.

One can see that defining Judaism is both complex and a multifaceted endeavor, and is almost impossible to define without defining what a Jew is. For Orthodox and Conservative Jews, a Jew is defined as any person whose mother was or is a Jew, or any person who has completed the process of conversion to Judaism; whereas, for the Reform Jews, children whose mother or father was or is a Jew is Jewish as long as they were reared as a Jew.

Some Basic Beliefs of Judaism

In listing some of the beliefs of Judaism, only some of the beliefs held by the three major sects of Judaism have been listed. There are other beliefs held by Orthodox Jews that Conservative and/or Reform Jews may view in different ways.

The basic theological premise of the Jewish faith is namely that God exists, that He created the world by His will, and that He revealed His will to Israel and mankind at Sinai (Donin, 1972). Jews believe in one God. As previously stated, the Torah, or the first five books of the Hebrew Bible (Old Testament), is the foundation of doctrine, customs, and observances. The Oral Torah served to provide clarification for many of the commandments; this served as the cornerstone for what was to become the Talmud.

The bond between the Jewish people and the land of Israel began during the time of Abraham. When the children of Israel fled oppression and slavery in Egypt, they sought the land that had been promised them in Deuteronomy 34:4 (Trepp, 1980).

In summary some of the basic beliefs of Judaism are:

• God exists.
• God is the Creator of all that exist.
• God is incorporeal (without a body)
• God has communicated through prophets.
• The Torah was revealed by God to Moses.

Significant Events and Traditions

Halackhah: The system of Jewish law is Halackhah; its major emphasis is on deeds as it asks for a commitment in behavior. The law also deals with ethical obligations and religious duties.

Sabbath: A day of rest, starting at sundown on Friday evening and lasting through sundown Saturday.

Kosher: Kashrut, more commonly known as keeping kosher, sets forth what Jews may eat, the acceptable method of slaughter of animals, the cooking utensils, and cleaning methods that may be used. With regard to acceptable foods to eat, the rule is that Jews may eat any land mammal that has cloven hooves and chews its cud; this includes sheep, cattle, goats, and deer. From the water, they may eat anything that has fins and scales. Shellfish such as lobsters, oysters, shrimp, clams, and crabs are excluded. With regard to fowl, birds of prey may not be eaten; however, fowl such as chicken, geese, ducks, and turkeys are permitted. Rodents, reptiles, amphibians, and insects are forbidden (Rich, 2005).

There are restrictions with regard to combining foods. One may not eat meat and dairy together; however, eating fish and dairy, or dairy and eggs is acceptable. These are a few of the rules and/or restriction; for more information, one should consult a Jewish dietician or Rabbi. Also one must be aware that not all Jews adhere to all of these practices.

Jewish Festivals: Some of the festivals observed by Jewish **people** are **Rosh Hashanah, Yom Kippur, Sukkoth, Hanukkah, Passover** and **Shavuot.**

Rosh Hashanah is the Jewish New Year, which occurs in the fall.

Yom Kippur, the Day of Atonement is the climax of the High Holy Day season. It is considered a day of spiritual reckoning where Jews spend the entire day in the synagogue in prayer, meditation, and fasting.

Sukkoths is a thanksgiving festival. This is a time of rejoicing, engaging in hearty meals which symbolize a bountiful harvest.

Hanukkah is perhaps the second most observed Jewish holiday. This holiday is based on a historical story of a miracle. The story relates that the Greeks had entered the temple and desecrated all of the holy oil except for one flask. Based upon volume, this oil should have lasted only one day, instead it lasted eight days. Thus the tradition of lighting candles for eight days.

Passover is the most observed holiday for the Jewish people (Rich 2005). Passover celebrates the Jewish peoples' exodus from Egypt and their bondage in that area. On the eve of the exodus, the Jews marked their doorpost with lambs' blood, and the angel of death which killed all Egyptian firstborn children passed over the houses marked with the blood. As a result of this event, it is written that Pharaoh released the slaves and allowed them to leave Egypt.

Shavuot celebrates the giving of the Torah to the Jewish people (Rich, 2005).

Summary

As previously stated, the Ten Commandments which are in the Torah is a guide for all Jews.

ISLAM

Brief History of Islam

Islam is the youngest of the major religions of **Christianity, Judaism, Hinduism, and Buddhism.** The faith that we know as **Islam** began in Mecca during the Seventh Century A. D. The city of Mecca is situated close to the Red Sea, which in earlier times this location made travel to Mecca easier for persons of the Islamic faith. This is where many of the early Muslims lived and where Islamic culture began.

The Islamic **Prophet Muhammad** was born around 570 A. D. in Mecca, Arabia and is said to have had a revelation from the Archangel Gabriel which led to the establishment of the religion **Islam**. According to Berry (2007), in 610 C. E., **Muhammad** visited the caves outside Mecca to meditate. The angel Gabriel appeared and spoke the word "Iqraa: which means recite or read. Also according to Berry this was the first revelation within the series of revelations given by **Allah (God). Allen and Toorawa** (2011) also inform us that these revelations lasted for the next twenty-three years. The revelation among other things revealed to **Muhammad** that there was only one God, Allah, and He is the Creator of the world. It should be noted that during that period of time in the Arabic region of the world, as well as other parts of the world, belief in and worship of more than one god was common.

After the initial revelations, the **Prophet Muhammad** was able to convert some of his relatives, including some in-laws and his wife Khadija, to Islam. The Arabic word Islam means the submission or surrender of one's will to the only true God worthy of worshiping, Allah, and anyone who worships Allah is called a Muslim. Additionally, the word Islam means peace, which is a natural consequence of total submission to the will of Allah.

According to the Islamic religion, Adam was the first prophet sent by Allah. It is noted that Muhammad is a prophet, not a god nor considered the Son of God. Additionally, the Islamic religion considers Jesus and Abraham as prophets; however, Muhammad is considered to be the greatest and major prophet.

After the death of Muhammad in 632 A. D., Abu-Bakr became the leader; some Muslims did not accept him as the successor thus there was an ideological split in the Muslim world. The division produced two major groups: the Sunni and the Shi'a. The division appears to have been primarily over earthly leadership of the Muslim faith. Today, there are a number of Muslim sects around the world. In the United States, within the past century there has been a development among African Americans groups, commonly referred to as Black Muslims or Nation of Islam. Regardless of the sect, all follow many of the teachings of the Prophet Muhammad and acknowledge Allah as the one and only God.

Basic Beliefs and Traditions

The **Qur'an** is the holy scripture of Islam which was revealed to the Prophet Muhammad by Allah. The Qur'an contains valuable information, practices and scriptures for practicing Muslims. To Muslims, the Qur'an is the word of God and these words express to them His will. The relevance of the Qur'an to Muslims can be compared to the relevance of the **Torah** to Jews and the **Holy Bible** to Christians. The Qur'an is divided into 114 chapters and the chapters are divided into verses.

According to John Sabini (1990), there are **Five Pillars of Islam** and the foundation of the Islamic religion is based upon these five pillars. These actions are ones that all Muslims must perform, if possible, to remain on the correct path. These pillars are giving testimony to faith, prayer, almsgiving, fasting, and pilgrimage. The following explanation of the five pillars is based upon the writings of John Sabini.

Testimony: (Shahada) This is the profession of faith. "There is no god but God; and Muhammad is the messenger of God."

Prayer: (Salah) Every adult Muslim, male or female, of sound mind and body, is required to pray five times a day: at sunset (beginning of the Muslim day), in the evening, at dawn, at noon, and in mid-afternoon. The Qur'an promises that those who pray and perform good deeds will enter Paradise, and tradition also states that each prayer absolves one of minor sins. An important fact that helping professions should know is that a Muslim at prayer should not be interrupted, stared at, or photographed, and a person should not walk in front of the praying person (Sabini, 1994).

Almsgiving: (Zakat) Benevolence and giving to the less fortunate is highly valued. Not only is it valued, it is mandated by the Qur'an.

Fasting: (Sawm) According to Sabini, fasting is meant to test the self-denial and submission of the faithful Muslims and permit those that have abundant resources to experience the deprivations of the poor. Both men and women and all but the youngest children are required to fast. Once a year for a period of one month, Muslims are required to abstain from food, drink, smoking, and sexual relations during the hours of daylight. This occurs during Ramadan, the ninth month of the Islamic calendar. It is noted that the Islamic calendar is based on the Lunar months which have twelve months in a year; however, the Lunar year is shorter than the solar year by about ten days.

Pilgrimage: The major pilgrimage is called the **Hajj**. The Qur'an requires that every adult Muslim of either gender and in sound body and mind make a pilgrimage to Mecca at least once in a lifetime, if possible. The destination is the Holy Mosque in Mecca.

Significant Events

There are a number of celebrations and events associated with Islam, and as is the situation with the other major religions, not all Muslims fully participate. Also, some events are celebrated more fully within one Muslim country and not so in another. Most of the major events have been outlined in the belief section.

Summary

In recent years, for a variety of reasons, persons of Muslim faith have received considerable negative press; however, it is important to separate the religious faith of this religion from actions by persons and/or governments which interpret and use violent acts as part of the requirement to be a Muslim. We should recognize that this religion is based upon peace and recognize other religious leaders such as Jesus

Christ and Abraham to mention only two as holy persons. While some may debate the action of some persons considered a Muslim as defining the religion, again the fact is the religion is based upon peace.

BUDDHISM

Brief History of Buddhism

The founder of **Buddhism**, or as he referred to himself, the way-shower, was Siddhartha Gautama. He was born in approximately 560 B. C. in the area that is present-day Nepal, India. Gautama's father was a local ruler who practiced Hinduism; therefore Siddhartha Gautama was reared in the ancient Hinduism religion. Much of the narrative of Gautama's life is weaved with legends in that most of his history was written long after his death. By way of legend, it is said that a white elephant touched the side of Gautama's mother and by this action she knew she was with child. The white elephant was considered a divine animal, and its action of touching the side of his mother became evidence of the divine destiny of the coming child. Legend also records that his mother gave birth to him in a standing position while holding on to a branch that had miraculously lowered itself to assist her. With regard to his birth, it is also reported that he did not emerge through the womb, but emerged painlessly from the side of his mother, thus saving him the trauma of a vaginal birth. This method of birth is important in that it is believed that a vaginal birth wipes out the memory of past lives and is further believed by Buddhists that Siddhartha Gautama retained memory of all of his previous lives. It should be further explained that Buddhists believe that one is born, dies, and reborn until he/she attains Nirvana. Nirvana is considered to be a state of existence where suffering no longer exists.

As previously stated, Siddhartha Gautama was born into royalty, privilege, and affluence, but at approximately age twenty-nine, he had a life-changing experience that provided direction to the rest of his life. While out riding, he encountered four sights that would change his life and began his quest for enlightenment, or Buddha (the term Buddha means enlightenment). The sights he saw were an old man, a sick man, a dead man, and a holy man (Ganeri, p. 10). Because he had led a sheltered life, he had not experienced many of the realities of life: infirmity, death, and illness. These sights gave him cause to contemplate the many aspects of life. Because of this contemplation, Gautama decided to leave the comfortable life he had known in search of answers to the question of how to find the positive counterparts of the suffering states of birth, aging, illness, death, sorrow, and corruption (Armstrong, 2001 p. 5). He then began to devote his life to extreme asceticism, which he later abandoned because he was not finding the answers to the perplexing questions. Thus, he began to devoted his life to meditation.

While meditating under a tree, Siddhartha Gautama found the answer. This discovery became known as the middle way. The middle way is the principle that between extreme asceticism or depravity and indulgence is a rationed life in which the body is given what it needs to function optimally, but no more (Novak & Smith). A result of his meditation, and what contemporaries call revelations, there have developed within the Buddhist tradition Four Nobel Truths and an Eight-Fold Path, which will be explained in the next section on basic beliefs.

Some Basic Beliefs

As previously mentioned, Siddhartha Gautama was reared in the Hindu religion, but he did not think that some of the precepts of the religion answered some basic questions of life, such as why do humans suffer? Although he did not find the answer to this and other questions of life through Hinduism, he retained one of the basic Hindu beliefs, that being reincarnation after death. Gautama believed, and this became a major part of Buddhist belief, that one is born, dies, and is reborn again and again until one attains the state of Nirvana. As previously mentioned, Nirvana is considered to be a state of existence where suffering no longer exists and the causes of suffering have been removed.

Buddhists believe there are **Four Nobel Truths** and these truths explain suffering. They are (1) life is suffering. This basic truth is saying that suffering is part of living and being human, (2) cravings cause suffering, (3) to end suffering, one must end cravings, (4) the means to end cravings can be found by following the Eight-Fold Path. If one follows the Eight-Fold Path, it will lead him/her to Enlightenment (Buddha). The steps along this path are (a) Right Views, (b) Right Intentions, (c) Right Speech, (d) Right Action, (e) Right Livelihood (occupation), (f) Right Effort, (g) Right Contemplation, and (h) Right Meditation. As one can extract from these steps to Enlightenment, they deal with morality. If one has the correct morality and intentions, he/she is on the correct path to Enlightenment.

There are a number of versions or sects of Buddhism and some appear to have elevated Gautama to the status of deity; however, he did not proclaim himself a deity. He said he was a way-shower.

Significant Events

As is the case with the other major religions, there are a number of celebrations and the two most important festivals for most Buddhists are **Wesak and Dharma Day**. Wesak is the celebration of the Buddha's enlightenment, and is considered the most important celebration in the Buddhist year. Buddhists plan most things around a lunar calendar; therefore, this festival is held on the full moon of May/June. Dharma Day celebrates the day in which the Buddha arose from his session of enlightenment.

Summary

The person who many refer to as Buddha, (he considered himself as the way shower), saw several forms of life which distressed him and he dedicated his life to finding ways of living which counteracted suffering. In this process he developed Four Nobel Truths and the Eight-Fold Path. Some may consider this similar to the Ten Commandments of Christianity and Judaism and the Five Pillars of the Muslim faith.

HINDUISM

Brief History of Hinduism

Identifying the history of Hinduism is more difficult than identifying the history for the other major religions because there is no one central individual or figure to which one can associate its development. Some Hindu individuals say the religion has existed forever. Hinduism is henotheistic with regard to its identification of deities. Stated another way, Hindus believe in a central deity, called **Brahman**, which is a pervading spirit or oneness of the universe, present in all things considered sacred and honored. In addition to Brahman, some may also worship what is considered minor deities.

The few historical things that are known about Hinduism indicate that the basis of the religion is a mixture of an ancient civilization of people, and their religious beliefs, who lived over 5000 years ago in the Indus Valley region of the Indian continent and the religious beliefs of Aryan people who invaded the Indus Valley region approximately 3000 years ago. Although the history of Hinduism is difficult to identify, what is known is Hinduism is the oldest religion of the major religions, Christianity, Judaism, Islam, and Buddhism, and perhaps the oldest religion in the world. Hinduism is the dominant religion of India.

Hinduism differs somewhat from the other major religions discussed in this text in that there is no one defined founder, no single scripture, and no universal set of teachings. Many of the teachings of the religion throughout its history have differing philosophies, and there have been many different holy books written. Some Hindus do not consider Hinduism to be a religion, but a way of life. However, the followers of Hinduism follow a basic set of principles and concepts and believe in Brahman, whom they consider to be the Supreme Being.

While Hinduism recognizes only one Supreme Being, there is a triad, to be more accurate, one God with three persons: Brahma, who is considered the creator of the world and all creatures; Vishnu is considered the preserver of the universe; and Shiva is considered the destroyer to assure that re-creation can be achieved. It has been said that Hindus worship multiple forms of the one God, but there are several other secondary gods or deities that Hindus may or may not worship because of the differing teachings. One thing that separates Hinduism from other religions is that there are many different practices and beliefs within the religion itself. Some of the deities that may be worshiped are:

Surya–God of the Sun
Kali–Goddess of time and death
Bhuvaneshwri–Queen of the phenomenal world
Indra–god of thunder, rain as well as other events. Hardon, J. (2013).

There are four sacred Hindu Vedas texts and they are: **Rig Veda, Sama Veda, Yajur Veda** and **Atharva Veda**. Veda means wisdom, knowledge or vision. The laws of the Vedas regulate social, legal, domestic and religious customs. The Vedas are the most sacred books of India and are the original scriptures of Hindus teachings. Each Veda contains four separate parts, which include hymns, rituals, theologies, and philosophies. These Scriptures are the doctrines that encompass all facets of Hindu life. Dharma is considered the divine power that makes things possible and is regarded as the morality that steers humans to act ethnically and in service to humanity and to God.

According to Hardon (2013), the Rig Veda is the oldest Hindu literature and contains hymns. The earlier writings in the Rig Veda spoke of gods of the earth, gods of the air, and gods of the bright heaven. By the end of the Rig Veda writing, it began to speak of and worship unknown gods. The Sama Veda was written to compliment the Rig Veda and provided four chants and tunes for some of the hymnal prayers. The Yajur Veda addressed not only the gods, but also the cultic objects that acquired sacred character by reason of invocation. The final book in the Veda is the Atharva Veda which is considered to be very similar to the Rig Veda, but incorporates magical spells or witchcraft.

Using Hardon's information base with regard to Hindu religion, Karma is generally thought to govern the cycles of reincarnation. Karma is a Sanskrit word whose literal meaning is "action" and refers to the law that every action has an equal reaction, either immediately or at some point in the future. Hindus believe that human beings can create good or bad repercussions for their actions and Karma determines how they live their next life—good karma results in rebirth to a higher level while bad karma can cause a person to be reborn at a lower level or even as an animal.

Some Basic Beliefs

Perhaps the best understanding of the Hindu religion does not come from its history, but from its basic beliefs and goals. A major goal of people who are Hindu is to attain **moksa**, or enlightened liberation of the Atman or self from the wheel of rebirth or the cycles of birth and death. **Reincarnation**, or **samsara**, is the belief that one is reborn after death. The physical form of rebirth is determined by the level of spiritual purity that the person has achieved by the time of his or her death.

The belief in **Karma** is a major aspect of the Hindu religion. Karma is the law of action and reaction. For every action taken, we face a reaction in the future. Therefore, chance and luck, from the Hindu perspective, does not exist. Consequently, everything happens according to the positive or negative energy stored from our actions in the Karma. In coordination with Karma, the Dharma is used to assure spiritual growth toward moksa. Dharma is a set of moral codes and correct behaviors that are taught in ancient texts and rituals. Hinduism promotes the belief in meditation and rejection of the material world as the final step to Nirvana where the Atman (self) and Brahman (absolute spirit) are reunited, resulting in the individual attaining moksa (enlighten liberation).

As previously stated, the Hindu religion is a henotheistic religion which believes in the oneness of spirit (Brahman) but may worship that spirit by way of a multitude of gods who are seen as coming from a divine source. The sacred texts of the Hindu religion are the Vedas (wisdom). The Vedas are four collections of religious writings, believed by Hindu followers to be inspired, composed approximately 3000 years ago. Vedas are considered the oldest and most profound source of Hindu wisdom available to study. Vedic chants are used in modern worship ceremonies. The Brahmans and Upanishads are texts that seek to explain the Veda and are often used as reference material and are the basis of specialized branches of Hinduism. The religion does not have explicit doctrine or institutional forms of worship; therefore, the practices have become regional in expression. Stated in other terms, in different areas and regions of the world where the Hindu religion is practiced, each has developed its own expression of the faith.

Considering the fact that expression of the Hindu faith is regionalized, one source of identity is which creator god they choose to follow. The three major figures of the modern creation gods are Brahma (the creator), Vishnu (the preserver), and Shiva (the destroyer). These three represent a Trimurti (trinity) of perspectives about the universe. Vishnu is the generative and positive force. Shiva is a destructive force which is necessary in the creative process. Brahma balances these two opposing forces. The three are not separate beings, but different aspects of the one universal spirit.

Significant Events

Because Hindu religion is regionalized, it is virtually impossible to list all of the significant events and festivals.

Summary

The Hindu religion is the oldest of the five major religions and in some way the most difficult to explain to persons not of the Hindu faith. As is the case with the other four major religions the Hindu faith promotes peace and harmony in life.

COMMONALITIES

All of the five major religions have codes of conduct.

1. **Restrictions on consumptions of certain foods:** Muslims abstain from eating pork; this is also true of some persons of the Jewish religion. Other religions avoid eating the flesh of animals for various reasons. Hindus avoid eating beef because they view cattle as sacred. Buddhists avoid eating the flesh of some animals because they believe the killing of animals is a cruel practice.
2. **Belief in an afterlife:** Christians believe in heaven and hell; they believe the direction of one's afterlife depends on how one lives his/her life on earth. Islam and Judaism have similar beliefs although they may have a different name for heaven and hell. Hindus and Buddhists believe in reincarnation. The Buddhist believe that one is reincarnated until he/she has lived a life of Nirvana where reincarnation ceases.
3. **End of time:** Islam, Judaism, and Christianity believe that a savior will come when the world ends. It should be noted that Christians believe that a savior, Jesus, has come and will return at the end of time.
4. **Holidays:** All of the five major religions have holidays/special days and or occasions set aside to honor or emphasize specific past events that are considered central to the religion. Provided as examples: Christians celebrate the birth of Jesus, Muslims cele-

brate the birth of their major prophet Mohammad, and Buddhists celebrate the birthday of Buddha, Siddhartha. Jews celebrate Hanukkah, and Hindu celebrate Bikrami Samuat (Hindu New Year).

5. **Differences:** Each of the five major religions has different holy guidelines to which they adhere. Jewish faith has the Tanakh and the Talmud. Christianity has the Holy Bible. Islam has the Qur'an. Hindu has several books including Vedas and Upanishads. Buddhism also has many books including the Tripitaka and the Mahayana.

Similar Teachings Found in Christianity and Hinduism

The following information was extracted from Parallel Teachings in Hinduism and Christianity, Wolfe, G. (1995) Austin, TX: *Jomar Press:* Pages 1-4.

(**Christian**) **Acts 17:27, 28:** Yet [God] is not far from each of us, for in Him we live and move and have our being. (Hinduism) Upanishad: The whole universe came forth from Brahman and moves in Brahman. . . . In Brahman it lives and has its being.

(**Christian**) **John 8: 12:** I am the light of the world; he who follows me will not walk in darkness but have the light of life. (Hinduism) Bhagavad Gita, Chapter 10 verse 11: I destroy the darkness born of ignorance with the shining light of wisdom.

(**Christian**) **Revelation 22: 13:** I am the Alpha and the Omega, the first and the last, the beginning and the end. (Hinduism) Bhagavad Gita, Chapter 7 verse 6, and Chapter 10 verse 20: I am the origin of the whole world and also its dissolution . . . I am the beginning, the middle, and the end of all things.

OTHER THAN RELIGION

Although it may be difficult for many to believe what we see and experience in life is all that exists of our being occupants of this planet, there are those that either do not subscribe to religion and an afterlife, or have serious questions with regard to the existence of religion and a supernatural force or forces. Some of these nonbelievers and doubters are called either Atheists or Agnostics.

Atheism is not a religion, because persons who consider themselves as atheist do not believe in a god or gods or supernatural beings; however, they have a belief system which makes them unique from a cultural standpoint. As previously stated, they do not believe in a supreme being. For those who believe in a supreme being or beings it perhaps is difficult to comprehend the thinking of atheists, particularly from the standpoint of how life events beyond human control occur. How did the universe form? Why did the universe form? Do life events occur randomly? What controls do humans have over their destiny? Those and many other questions are the essences of the thinking of those that do not understand atheism.

What is Atheism?

A simplified definition of an atheist is one that does not believe in the existence of a god or gods and a lack of belief in an afterlife. A major reason for this lack of belief in a god or gods from the atheist's viewpoint is because there is no evidence that such Supreme Being or beings exist. One common factor in many religions is the belief in some type of life after physical death; however with regard to the belief of atheists, there is no life after death. Stated in other terms, the atheist's point of view is once a person dies that is the end of his/her existence. This viewpoint appears to be based upon their belief that there is no proof that life exists or will exist after death. Persons of various religious faiths may argue this from the standpoint of their religious documents which specifically discuss life after death. An atheist's response may be this is a belief without concrete documentation of such existence. The end result of this argument relies on one's belief system.

As one reviews his/her beliefs of right or wrong, acceptable or nonacceptable behavior in a given society, one will find that what is deemed acceptable or nonacceptable is based upon a given societies rules of appropriate behavior. One may argue that many of these rules have been extracted and perhaps modified from religious precepts. An atheist's viewpoint with regard to how right and wrong is developed is that each society develops it's views of what is acceptable regardless of where they are based, and this is what helps govern the behavior of all people.

Some atheist's viewpoint with regard to how the world began is very straightforward—"they do not know." Although some, if not many, religious persons believe in the "big bang" theory, others believe in the "creation theory." The bottom-line with regard to this controversy is no one at this point in history really knows the answer. The question of how the world began presents an interesting balancing act for some religious people, on the one hand they are professing their beliefs with regard to creation of the world brought forth by a Supreme Being and on the other hand they are accepting scientific information that moves one to believe that there is scientific evidence that supports an enormous event that set the world on track to develop life as we currently experience life. Given this possible contradiction, the atheist's answer "they do not know how the world began" appears to be a reasonable answer.

What is Agnosticism? While some people may think of agnosticism and atheism as being the same philosophy, there is a significant difference between the two concepts. Atheists do not believe in God/Supreme Being whereas agnostics simply say they do not know whether there is a Supreme Being. Agnostics without totally rejecting the existence of a Supreme Being and concepts such as afterlife, basically state they do not know whether such exists. From this statement there is an appearance that Agnosticism holds out hope that some religious precepts are true and mention only one—life after death which would allow the possibility of experiencing past loved ones.

Both agnostics and atheists sometime suffer similar discrimination by being labeled as "God Haters," which appear to be an incorrect evaluation of their beliefs. Both appears to be saying that there is not sufficient evidence for them to accept concepts and beliefs of traditional religious beliefs.

Some atheist's viewpoint with regard to how the world began is very straightforward—"they do not know." Although some, if not many, religious persons believe in the "big bang" theory, others believe in the "creation theory." The bottom-line with regard to this controversy is no one at this point in history really knows the answer. The question of how the world began presents an interesting balancing act for some religious people, on the one hand they are professing their beliefs with regard to creation of the world brought forth by a supreme being and on the other hand they are accepting scientific information that moves one to believe that there is scientific evidence that supports an enormous event that set the world on track to develop life as we currently experience life. Given this possible contradiction, the atheist's answer "they do not know how the world began" appears to be a reasonable.

IMPLICATIONS FOR HELPING PROFESSIONALS AND OTHERS

What does religion have to do with the helping process? What does religion have to do with cultural diversity? As helping professionals, when we delve into religious background or lack of same, aren't we getting into a sensitive area? As helping professionals, don't we have enough to consider when analyzing clients without involving ourselves in perhaps a controversial area such as religion? These are perhaps similar questions that were either asked or crossed the minds of professional helpers when the issue of considering race and ethnicity as variables in the helping process emerged.

As a helping professional, involving one's self into a client's religious beliefs can be risky. However, what is being proposed is not trying to change a client's religious beliefs, but understanding those beliefs and their impact upon the client's behavior. This understanding is necessary when attempting to develop a reasonable helping plan. This understanding is similar to considering one's race and/or ethnicity and the experiences associated with these variables as well as some of the beliefs and values to which the person's cultures expose him/her. Likewise, beliefs and values learned from religious association provide powerful influences on a person's belief systems.

This author contends that if a client/patient believes in a power or powers greater than oneself, this devotion and the beliefs and rules associated with this devotion are a stronger force upon one's behaviors than racial and ethnic influences. For persons who have some devotion to religious beliefs, these beliefs have an impact upon their health belief system. Some clients/patients, if they are influenced by religious beliefs, may feel that their illness and/or disability are the will of God; therefore, their recovery and/or rehabilitation is determined by His will. Similarly, where the person's religious doctrine promotes cause and effect, the person may believe that past behavior is the reason for his current situation. Do these predestination beliefs mean there can be no helpful intervention? The answer to this question is intervention is possible. One goal should be to help them (the helpees) understand that intervention is not meant to change their beliefs, but there are numerous dimensions to human life that should be pointed out to them and that spirituality is a very important dimension that can be used to aid in the healing, recovery, and helping process. The approach a helper should take will be determined by the type of help that is being offered. If the helper does not feel comfortable involving himself in the client/patient's religious life, he should seek the assistance, with the permission of the client/patient, of a helper who is trained in this area.

An important fact the helper should remember is that he does not have to become an expert on religion and religious beliefs. However, as it is important to understand some things with regard to a client's racial and ethnic cultural background, it is equally beneficial to have basic information about religious background and/or orientation. If one does not know, ask.

CONCLUSION

Unless one is involved in some type of religious counseling, religion as a cultural variable is often overlooked. The truth of this statement is greater perhaps in the United States than it is in some other countries, which do not promote separation of church and government. Despite the separation of religion and governmental affairs, for many people in the United States, religious doctrines provide considerable guidance and comfort. The influence of one's religious faith often is demonstrated at times of crisis and conflict. Despite the impact that religious faith can and does have on some persons' decisions and actions, especially in times of discomfort, helping professionals often overlook this important variable. Through the process of failing to recognize the influence and impact of this variable, the helping professional may be overlooking a component which can have significant influence on the outcome of the helping plan.

The purpose of this chapter was not to recommend a process by which the helping professional could incorporate religion in the helping plan, nor was it intended to recommend ways to minimize the impact religion may have in the helping process. The purpose of this chapter has been to make the helper aware of the possible importance of religious faith with regard to working with some clients. Additionally, the purpose was to increase the awareness of helping professionals with regard to the major religions in the world, their meanings, and importance to those persons who live by their precepts.

There is no question in this author's mind that if we followed the major precepts of the five major religions we would have a peaceful and productive world where love and obedience would prevail. However, it is the wrongful interpretations and selfish intents that have caused religions to be used in ways not intended by the Holy ones and have caused many dreadful acts to be perpetrated in the name of religion.

Chapter Review Questions

1. What are the three (3) major religious divisions within the Christian faith?
2. What are the three (3) major beliefs of the Christian faith?
3. What are the three (3) major sects or versions of Judaism?
4. What is the name of the five (5) books of the Hebrew Bible?
5. Within Judaism, what does Kosher mean?
6. What is the meaning of Yom Kippur?
7. Within the Islam faith, who is the Prophet Muhammad?
8. What are the Five Pillars of Islam?
9. What does the term "the middle way" mean in the faith of Buddhism?
10. What are the Four Nobel Truths in the faith of Buddhism?
11. Within the Hindu faith what does the term "Dharma" mean?
12. Within the Hindu faith what does the term "Karma" mean?

Mental Exercise

1. Discuss with someone of the Christian religion some of the basic beliefs of his/her religious faith.
2. Discuss with someone of the Jewish faith some of the basic beliefs of his/her religion.
3. Discuss with someone of the Islamic religion some of the basic beliefs of his/her faith.

4. Discuss with someone of the Buddhist faith some of the basic beliefs of his/her religion.

5. Discuss with someone of the Hindu religion some of the basic beliefs of his/her faith.

References

Allen, R., & Toorawa, S. M. (2001). *Islam: A short guide to the faith.* Grand Rapids, MI: William B. Eerdmans Publishing Company.

Armstrong, K. (2001). Buddha. New York: Penguin Groups.

Asal, T. (1982). The construction of religion as an anthropological category: In *Genealogies of religion: Discipline and reasons of power in Christianity and Islam* (2nd ed.). Baltimore, MD: John Hopkins University Press.

Berry, D. L. (2007). *Pictures of Islam: A student's guide to Islam.* Macon, GA: Mercer University Press.

Bryan, W. V. (2007). *Multicultural aspects of disabilities.* Springfield, IL: Charles C Thomas.

Donin, H. (1972). *To be a Jew: A guide to Jewish observance in contemporary life.* New York: Basic Books.

Ganeri, A. (2001). *Buddhism Srl.* Florence, Italy: McRae Books.

Geertz, C. (1973). *Religion as a cultural system: In the interpretation of cultures.* (12th ed.). London: Fontana Press.

Hardon, J. (2013). Retrieved from http://catholiceducation.org/karticles/religion/re0707.html

Makinde, J. A. (2013). Religion. Unpublished paper, University of Oklahoma.

Nail, E. (2013). A brief history of Christianity. Unpublished paper. University of Oklahoma.

Novak, P., & Smith, H. (2003). *Buddhism: A concise introduction.* New York: Harper-Collins.

Rich, T. (2005). Judaism 101. Kashrut: Jewish diatary laws. Retrieved June 20, 2005. http://www.Jewfag.org/kkashrut.htm.

Sabini, J. (1990). *Islam. A primer.* Washington, DC: Middle East Editorial Associates.

Trepp, L. (1980). *The complete book of Jewish observances: A practical manual for the modern Jew.* New York: Simon & Schuster.

Taylor, E. B. (1871). *Primitive culture: Research into the development of mythology, philosophy, religion, act, and custom* (1st ed.). London: John Murray.

Wolfe, G. (1995). *Parallel Teachings in Hinduism and Christianity.* Austin, TX: Jomar Press.

Chapter 8

UNDERSTANDING RESOURCES

Chapter Outline
- Introduction
- Knowledge of Helpee's Rights
- Cutting Through Red Tape
- Support Groups
- Advocacy
- Community Leaders
- Resources for Inadequately Served Populations
  - The Elderly
  - Persons With Disabilities and Their Families
  - Women
  - Ethnic/Racial Minorities
- Summary
- References

Chapter Objectives
- Emphasize the importance of the professional helper understanding resources available to helpees

INTRODUCTION

Attempting to understand the concepts of Freud, Maslow, Adler, and other psychological theorists often is exciting to a new professional helper. The new helper may have visions of applying these various concepts toward the resolution of the client's problems. No doubt many helpers will have these opportunities; however, many will discover that one of the most important and frequently needed tools of the helper is to understand community and other resources. The frequently stated saying "can't see the forest for the trees" is often a truism with regard to persons engaged in significant life events. To be more specific, frequently, when clients are experiencing problems, they become so engrossed in the unfolding events that they overlook some solutions to the problems. These possible solutions may be seen and understood by someone who is not intimately affected by the troublesome life events. Therefore, a helping professional's knowledge of resources that the helpee is overlooking can be part of the solution to the helpee's problems.

For many clients, when they seek assistance from a professional helper, they are not looking for, or in some cases not expecting to hear, psychological jargon, nor are they seeking what they may consider a long period of time to elapse before a resolution is reached with regard to their needs. What they often are expecting is a rapid conclusion to their issues. Although a rapid conclusion may not be in order, however, what the helper will discover is that part of a resolution to the client's issues is referring the client to appropriate resources. Effective professional helping is not about the helper being the know-all and complete provider of services; rather, an effective helper is at his best when he or she is aware of appropriate resources and is able to connect the client with those services. Similar to a primary care physician, she is able to provide a number of services to her patients. However, there are times when she must refer the patient to a specialist. Likewise, the professional helper should be aware of resources so that she can refer her client to the appropriate community specialist.

There is not a way to identify all of the helping resources in one chapter, if one knew about those resources. Therefore, a few resources will be identified by name, and the resources will be discussed in generic terms with the intent of making the readers aware of the need to become familiar with resources in particular areas. The hope is to heighten the awareness of readers for the need to become familiar with various resources, and have them firmly in their minds as well as the psychological, sociological, and educational theories. As a professional helper, I have spent decades assisting helpees and have found that one of the most important tools in the helping process is the knowledge of resources.

Queralt (1996) sums up my views with regard to the importance of resources with the following comments:

> You will likely be more effective in assisting your clients to overcome deficits and to deal with their problems if you help them construct a better life for themselves by discovering and using their strengths and by reaching out for resources available to them in their environments. This is the essence of empowerment. (p. 11)

KNOWLEDGE OF HELPEE'S RIGHTS

Awareness of resources available to the helpee will depend on several factors: the type of life situations the helpee is encountering; the location in which the helpee lives; the resources available in the helpee's town, city, and state; and the type of helping relationship in which the helper is involved. Given the previously mentioned qualifiers, one of the first things the professional helper should do is become acquainted with the local, state, and federal laws that pertain to the helpee's situation. Provided as an example, if the helpee's concerns relate to disability issues concerning himself and/or a significant other, the helper should become knowledgeable with regard to local, state, and federal laws pertaining to this subject. Every state has some type of committee or council that advises and/or enforces disability rights of persons with disabilities. At the federal level, the helper should become acquainted with the American's With Disabilities Act (ADA), as well as other federal legislation related to disabilities, such as the Individuals Disabilities Education Act (IDEA) if the issues relates to a school-age person with a disability. Additionally, the helper should become familiar with other agencies such as the Equal Employment Opportunities Commission to assist with helping protect the helpee's civil rights. As previously stated, these agencies and organizations are identified as examples of the way a helping professional could and should think when identifying resources for the helpee.

The helping professional should not only identify resources, he should make a directory of these and other resources. One might respond to this suggestion by stating that there often are printed directories; in those cases, that is good and will save some time for the helper. However, the helper must be vigilant with regard to keeping the directories updated and supplement the directories with resources not covered within the printed directories.

CUTTING THROUGH RED TAPE

For helpees who are thinking clearly enough to identify resources as well as those who are having difficulties determining the availability of resources, being able to navigate through policies, procedures, institutional and agency jargon, as well as other legal and nonlegal requirements often becomes a daunting task. This task becomes more daunting given the sometimes distressed emotional state that the helpee is experiencing. One only has to think about the frustration and difficulties experienced when attempting to complete federal and state income tax forms or completing health insurance forms; now add to this frustration some physical and/or emotional stress resulting from some personal problem and one may obtain a glimpse of what a distressed helpee feels when attempting to obtain resource help.

The professional helper can provide considerable support to helpees in distress by not only directing them to appropriate resources, but also by helping them to understand the dimension of the help. Stated in another term, assist the helpee "cut through the red tape." This does not mean that the helper has to become an expert in reading and understanding difficult-to-understand forms, policies, and procedures, but the helper should be aware and/or able to locate resources that can interpret these documents.

SUPPORT GROUPS

Families as well as individuals experiencing long-term problems or issues often state the most important resource is support groups. The process of talking with someone who is either experiencing or has experienced similar issues is both therapeutic and rewarding. Psychologists, social workers, counselors, and educators, (to mention only four), are helping professionals with many therapeutic and helping techniques, and often cannot be as effective as the helpee experiencing others who have navigated their way through similar situations.

Helpees connecting with support groups have numerous advantages, such as the feeling of equality, comforting feelings, empathy, and understanding. **Feeling of equality** relates to the fact that, once the helpee overcomes the reluctance of sharing information, he begins to feel on an equal footing with others in the support group. This feeling of equality is based on the fact that all within the group are sharing similar experiences. At this point, the reader may be questioning whether the helpee can have a similar feeling of equality when in a formal helping relationship with a professional helper. The answer is no! Regardless of how well rapport is established and the professional manner in which the professional helper conducts herself, there will always be a difference in the power structure of the helping relationship. An effective professional helper will always be viewed by the helpee as being an authority figure, thus the balance of power resides with the professional helper. This does not mean that this relationship is bad, nor does it mean that the professional helper cannot be effective. This simply means that support groups can be a valuable supplement to the formal helping process and, in some cases, can be the primary helping tool.

Comforting feelings may occur because helpees become aware that others have experienced similar issues and have been successful in either overcoming those issues or have found resolutions to the issues with which they could accept and adapt to their situation. The development of feelings of comfort often is associated with the beginning of acceptance of the situation. It is not uncommon, when problems or issues arise, for persons involved to attempt to avoid acknowledgment of the issues. In some cases, they are hoping that the issues will go away or they are either in denial of the issues or their seriousness. Again, by experiencing others who have metaphorically traveled similar roads, the helpee begins to see the value in being a realist and accept the existence of the issues, realizing that this is the best way to find acceptable resolutions to those issues.

Unfortunately, too often when a person or family encounters significant life issues they receive sympathy from family and friends. Although the expression of sympathy is often meant as a positive show of support, sympathy, regardless of how well intended, does little to help the person or family find acceptable solutions to issues. Also, another unfortunate fact is that some support groups do offer a generous dose of sympathy; thus, the professional helper should carefully investigate support groups before she recommends them to helpers. As all professional helpers are taught, **empathy**, not sympathy, is what the helpee needs. Well-constructed and well-informed support groups provide an **understanding** of the issues that only someone who has experienced the issues can offer. Additionally, effective support groups discuss issues in ways that refuse to support self-pity.

As previously stated, it is imperative that the helper, in advising helpees with regard to support groups, conducts a careful investigation of the groups. Investigate how they have been established and why they have been established. Also, as previously eluded to, all support groups are not established for therapeutic support. Some support groups are established to vent frustrations, and this may be appropriate, but often does not provide therapeutic support. Some support groups are established for therapeutic support; however, sometimes they may venture into sympathetic pity support. Therefore, as previously stated, it is imperative that the professional helper thoroughly investigate and evaluate support groups before recommending to a helpee.

ADVOCACY

Similar to support groups, advocacy groups can provide valuable assistance to helpees who are experiencing life issues. Whereas support groups, generally speaking, consist of persons who are either experiencing or have experienced similar problems as the helpee, advocacy groups often will consist of those who have and/or are currently experiencing similar problems, as well as persons who have an interest in, and strong feelings for the issues being debated and are working toward solutions to problems.

Advocacy groups range from small community-based organizations to large in numbers, and the scope of their involvement may be statewide or national. Many large advocacy groups have branches in various (if not all) states, and they deal with issues that draw national attention. Regardless of the size of the advocacy group, most serve useful purposes and can be assets to professional helpers and their clients.

COMMUNITY LEADERS

Understanding the community in which the helpee lives and the leaders of those communities is essential resource knowledge for a helper to have. Certainly, knowledge of a community helps with regard to becoming aware of resources within that community. Similarly, awareness of community organizers and other community leaders is also valuable information. However, it often is much easier to identify community resources than community leaders, specifically leaders who are effective and can make differences with regard to your client's issues. In large metropolitan areas, there will be several people who consider themselves community leaders. In fact, each may claim leadership to certain factions of specific issues. The point being made is that, in some instances, it is not always easy to decide from whom to ask for support. A mistake often made is to seek the assistance of persons who appear to have the support of the town, city, or state leaders. The reason this can be a mistake is that often these city and state officials will support and promote people with whom they feel comfortable. This means the leadership is supporting people not because they are the most effective, but because they are people who create the least number of problems for them. Likewise, as a helper, one should not assume that the person or persons who get the most headlines in the various media are the community leaders. It has been this author's experience that local church leaders have a good understanding with regard to whom the effective community leaders are.

RESOURCES FOR INADEQUATELY SERVED POPULATIONS

In this section about resources, I discuss specific populations, such as ethnic/racial minorities, women, persons with disabilities, elderly, and the homeless to emphasize the need for understanding resources for these and other special groups. The reason for this discussion is the fact these populations as well as others are often overlooked with regard to the need for specific and sometimes special resources.

One thing the special populations previously mentioned as well as others not mentioned have in common is discrimination. In this discussion, discrimination does not necessarily mean vicious, hatred, punitive actions that are often associated with discriminative action. There is no doubt that in some cases, hopefully rare, the previously mentioned type of discrimination does take place with regard to special populations. However, in most instances, the kinds of discrimination these populations encounter are neglect, needs not being met, and inadequate consideration given to their circumstances.

In cases such as the homeless people, as well as persons with life situations brought on by abusing one's body and mind with destructive substances and perhaps destructive actions, the helping professional will be required to set aside some of his cultural orientations and view the helpee as a person who has the potential for growth and change. As stated elsewhere in this book, helping professionals are humans before they are helping professionals; therefore, they are subject to many of the beliefs and attitudes that exist in the overall society. It is not an uncommon thought, in the minds of some people, that homeless people and substance abusers are "reaping what they have sown." The point being made is that helping professionals are not immune to having these thoughts. If we have those types of thoughts with regard to persons in need of help, the way we react to them may represent those thoughts and feelings. This is why the humanist therapies emphasize the points that as helpers we do not have to agree or condone clients' behaviors. However, we should be compassionate and accept them as persons who can change and are worthy of our efforts to assist them in their growth process, leading to change. Part of the process of change with which the professional helper can assist clients often relates to directing them to appropriate resources.

The Elderly

The population that is 65 years and older is one of the fastest growing groups within the United States, and this fact is true for most of the other industrial developed countries in the world. Improvements in medical technology, advanced education of medical personnel, improved physical fitness, and advancements in mental health services are only a few reasons for the increase in lifespan of the group identified as the elderly.

The lifespan for many elderly persons is increasing, and with this increased longevity comes unique opportunities and challenges for professional helpers as they attempt to meet some of the needs of this growing population of inadequately served people. I discuss only a few of the resource needs of many elderly persons: mental stimulations, recreation, assistance with changing technology, resources for elderly living in rural areas, and financial resources.

Mental stimulation: When one is young, rearing a family and building a career often dominate one's attention; therefore, one becomes engrossed in events of the moment to the point that little thought is given to what life will be like when one becomes an elderly person. When a person does think of the future, often he thinks of retirement from the prospective of a young person. At that point, retirement thoughts relate to things the person dreams of doing when he attains elderly status. Often the problem with these thoughts is that the dreams of what will be done during retirement years does not take into consideration the aging process, such as loss of strength, stamina, and possible health problems that may limit physical and mental activities. Stated in other terms, the person often thinks of retirement activities in relationship to being able to do the same things and at the same level of accomplishment when he was much younger.

As the person grows older, she often discovers that things she used to do become more difficult to accomplish, and takes longer. The decrease in physical prowess is often accompanied by a decrease in mental acumen. Not always the case, but in many instances, as a person's age limits her physical activities, opportunities for mental stimulation also decrease. The helping professional must be aware that aging does not equate to mental deficiency, and one of the most important things he can do when helping elderly clients is to assist them with engaging themselves in activities that not only mentally stimulate them, but also provide a mental challenge.

The type of helper one is determines the extent of the help given in this regard. In some cases, such as art therapists, recreational therapists, and occupational therapists, the helper is directly responsible for creating many of these mentally stimulating opportunities. However, in other cases, such as social workers, counselors, psychologists, psychotherapists, community organizers, and other community advocates, they should be prepared to identify the resources that can best provide the mental stimulation needed by some elderly persons.

As we grow older, one concept becomes of paramount importance to the aging population: **independence**. In fact, most resources that the elderly population requires relates to some form of independence.

It is a truism that some people are fortunate to be active well into their 80s and 90s. However, for a large number of the elderly population, decreased vision, decreased hearing, broken bones, aching muscles, and decrease in strength and stamina are a few of the factors that serve to limit their independence. The previously mentioned factors, as well as others, too often serve as a roadblock to driving automobiles, taking walks, and visiting friends and family as often as one would like. These limitations, as well as others not mentioned, lead the elderly person to become more dependent on family, friends, and others than they ever imagined.

The loss of independence—having to rely on others for helping meet some of the needs that they were previously able to handle with their own initiative—frequently becomes a source of embarrassment and can lead to depression. The helping professional can help eliminate embarrassment and hopefully prevent periods of severe depression from becoming a major part of the elderly person's life by a thorough assessment of the person's needs and locating resources to meet those needs. The helper must handle the introduction of those needs to the elderly person in a manner that will not increase the person's feelings of dependency. To be more specific, I have previously pointed out that having to rely on others to help them do things that they once were able to handle in a solo manner often causes elderly persons embarrassment. Therefore, the helper must, as much as possible, not create situations where the elderly person becomes dependent on her. One method of avoiding creating a feeling of dependency is to engage the elderly person in searching for the resources on her own. The helper can serve as a guide, directing the elderly person to appropriate resources, letting the person make her decision regarding which services to utilize. The helper should also remind the helpee that she, the helpee, is the final decision maker with regard to which service to utilize and to what extent they will be utilized. Certainly, this author recognizes that there are some decisions over which the helpee may have little control, such as some emergency services. Even in those cases, the helpee can have considerable control, if she has had a chance, in advance, to identify what she wants done in emergency situations. This leads to an important resource with which the helper can assist the helpee, that being legal services to document one's desires. The key to assisting the elderly with maintaining independence is, as much as possible, to have them make their own decisions, not having those decisions made for them.

Even by keeping the elderly person on track with regard to making her own decisions, there will be times when the elderly person will feel that she is a burden on others. She will think back to the days when she felt she was in control of her life and made all of her major life decisions. This is not an uncommon feeling and belief of young active adults; however, the truth is, as John Donne (*For Whom the Bell Tolls,* 1623) so poetically stated, "No man is an island, entire of himself." All humans need help throughout their lifespan, and this is a point that the helper should make to the elderly person when she begins to feel like a burden on family, friends, and society.

One of the resources that can be useful to the elderly is **continuing education**. As previously mentioned, mental stimulation is useful to helping keep the elderly active. Many colleges, universities, and trade schools have begun to offer courses specifically targeted to the older population. In many instances, the educational institutions offer courses at either no or reduced cost to the elderly. The previously mentioned institutions of education recognize that many elderly are not searching for a second career but simply want to keep up with the changing world in which they live. One of the needs many elderly recognize is to keep up with the changing technological world. Computers, the Internet, cell phones, and text messaging are only a few of the changing technological innovations that some elderly feel is making them less knowledgeable than their younger counterparts. Some elderly view some of these technological devices as being too complicated to learn to use, whereas others view them as a challenge they can conquer. Regardless of the viewpoint from which the elderly handle the current technology, they are excellent resources to keep the elderly in touch with their environment, help eliminate boredom, and possibly avoid depression.

In some cases, such as trade schools, elderly learn new trades to be used as hobbies, and some may use them as a means for a second career to supplement a fixed income. Regardless of how education is used, it is a tremendous resource and the professional helper will be wise to be aware of these resources and assist the elderly in utilizing them.

Perhaps the most underserved elderly populations are **rural elderly** and those elderly who live in sparsely populated areas. Although the isolation of rural and sparsely populated areas often afford a peaceful contrast to the hurried life of a major metropolitan area, this peace and solitude sometimes has its disadvantages for persons as they grow older. Often rural areas are devoid, or at best significantly limited of many resources, which make metropolitan areas hurried and noisy and convenient, such as taxi and bus services, as well as large libraries, medical and dental facilities, movie theaters, shopping centers, and other social and entertainment outlets.

The lack of the previously mentioned facilities and services, as well as others, will present a significant challenge to the helping professional as he attempts to connect the rural elderly with the needed resources. The combination of lack of resources and possible limited access to means of obtaining distant resources will challenge the most creative of helpers. However, creativity is what is required. Locating resources, regardless of the distance in accessing them, becomes the first order of business for the helper. The second order of business is locating resources to make accessibility possible. With regard to the second order of business, one resource that most small towns and communities have are religious and civic organizations. In most cases, these organizations are interested in helping their citizens. Also, in most small towns, the citizens, generally speaking, know each other, and they take pride in helping each other in times of need. Perhaps the major problem a professional helper will face in small towns is the person in need of assistance that allows his or her pride to block seeking and asking for help from friends and neighbors.

Additionally, the professional helper should research state, federal government, and private programs and organizations designed to assist underserved elderly persons. Every state in the United States has a human services department that is charged with the responsibility of assisting persons throughout the state who have needs. Also, there are increasing numbers of other services and organizations targeting this population, and it becomes incumbent on the professional helper to become aware of these resources.

Another needed service that some elderly persons require is assistance with navigating the medical care system. Accessing appropriate **medical care** is one issue; perhaps a larger issue for the elderly is their understanding of the volumes of paperwork, understanding the terminology, and understanding the rules and regulations associated with receiving appropriate medical care and payment of services. With regard to payment of services, understanding who pays for what and how much each entity pays is at best a challenging effort. To be more specific, understanding how much insurance companies pay and how much Medicare or Medicaid pays can be difficult to interpret. Professional helpers are not required to have answers to these and other questions; however, they should be able to connect the helpee with the appropriate resources to answer these questions.

The final resource need with regard to the elderly that is discussed is **social** and **recreation**. Most humanistic psychological therapies and theories discuss the need for humans to have appropriate social connections in order to develop a balanced life and develop and maintain normal human relationships. This concept applies not only to young persons, but also to the elderly. Unfortunately, because of the previously mentioned variables, as some people grow older their social and recreational connections become limited. With the possible exception of attending religious services and functions and seeing family members, many elderly persons have few social contacts.

In the past, our society has revered the concept of youthfulness, perhaps not fully realizing the impact this has had on older persons. This worship of youthfulness has overlooked the need for recreation and social contact for the elderly. Because the population of persons over the age of 65 is one of the fastest growing populations in the United States, perhaps this concept will change. Also, because of the increase in life longevity of the elderly, professional helpers will need to increase their awareness of recreational and social resources designed for the elderly.

Persons with Disabilities and Their Families

Equal to the elderly, persons with disabilities are one of the most underserved populations, not only in America, but also in the world. As discussed in Chapter 6 (this volume), persons with disabilities make up approximately one-fifth of the U.S. population and an unknown percentage worldwide. Regardless of the percentages, persons with disabilities and their families have significant needs that a professional helper can meet by understanding those needs and providing resources to meet them. The families of persons with disabilities are included because of their involvement in the daily life activities of persons with disabilities; consequently, the family is significantly impacted by the needs of the person with a disability. In some instances it is difficult to separate the needs of persons with a disability from the needs of their family members.

To avoid duplication of discussion provided in the chapter on disabilities, I have limited my discussion of resource needs to the following: **respite care, advocacy, inclusion, employment,** and **protection of rights**. I acknowledge that this is a limited list of resource needs, and most advocates for persons with disabilities can attest that an entire book could be written on this subject.

Families that have a member who has a disability that significantly restricts use of some or all extremities and/or have significant cognitive limitations (to mention only two types of severe disabilities), often experience restrictions of their time away from home. The family member's disability may serve as a handicap to family activities. Although most families, in the previously mentioned situation, do not believe that caring for a family member with a disability is a burden, over periods of time the family may begin to feel the stress of being on call 24 hours each day. It is during these stressful times that they need a break from the daily responsibilities of caring for their loved one.

Respite care is a means by which family members, on a short-term basis, are relieved of the responsibility of caring for their loved one. There are several types of respite care. Some are very short-term, in that the respite caregiver comes into the home during certain periods of the day to allow family members, who are the full-time care givers opportunities to relax and/or take care of other family needs. Another type of respite care involves removing the person with a disability from the home for short periods of time, such as a week or perhaps longer, again to relieve the family from the rigors of daily caregiving. Most family members find respite care to be rejuvenating, thus helping them to return to providing quality care to their family member.

Professional helpers who work with persons with disabilities and their families should be aware of the benefits of respite care and investigate the types of services available. Additionally, the helping professional must be aware that when introducing the idea of respite care to families, some may be resistant. They may feel guilt thinking they are abandoning the family member with a disability or that they are not being good caregivers by acknowledging they need help. Therefore, the helping professional must be prepared to deal with guilt feelings, assuring the family that this will help their mental health, and help them to continue to provide quality care.

Protection of rights: Resources pertaining to the protection of rights and the understanding of the same are of paramount importance to persons with disabilities and their families. Within most, if not all, industrialized developed countries, efforts are put forth to ensure reasonable rights are afforded to persons with disabilities. In the United States, laws such as the Americans with Disabilities Act (ADA) and the Individuals with Disability Education Act (IDEA), to mention only two, have been put forth to protect rights of persons with disabilities. Other laws, such as those related to the social security of the American people, and the transportation laws that cover more than persons with disabilities, also provides services and protects rights.

There are numerous laws designed to protect persons with disabilities that can be enforced to protect the rights and ensure services to this population. Helping professionals who work with this underserved population should become aware of these laws. Obviously, it is next to impossible for a helper to become knowledgeable with regard to these laws; however, the helper should know about the general areas of protection that these laws provide. Additionally, the helper should become aware of agencies and organizations that enforce and/or use these laws to promote the well-being of persons with disabilities.

With regard to protection of rights for persons with disabilities, there are two major areas that should be of paramount concern to helpers of this underserved population—**discrimination** and **employment**. In the United States, as discussed in the chapter on disabilities, most discrimination of persons with disabilities is not malicious or designed to be hurtful. In many instances, acts that are meant to help often have the result of being discriminatory. Provided as an example, placing school children who are considered to be slow learners into classrooms where all of the children are diagnosed with the same limitation is often done to enhance their chances of being academically successful. However, the result is segregation of these children from the stimulation they might receive from various levels of intellect. Although intended to be helpful, the end result often is retardation of the children's potentials. Certainly, there are cases where some of these children benefit from the previously mentioned grouping. It is this author's opinion that too often the grouping is done more for convenience than sound educational reasons. The point being made is that discrimination, for whatever reason, places the recipients of discrimination at a disadvantage. Helping professionals working with persons with disabilities must carefully view how these helpees are treated, and be able to connect them with the appropriate resources to protect their rights.

Employment: To be more accurate, the lack thereof is a major obstacle to persons with disabilities more fully participating in whatever society in which they live. In the United States, the unemployment rate for persons with disabilities is often 10 to 20 points higher than the national average and even greater when persons with severe limitations are included.

In all industrial countries, work is important not only to the economy but also to the well-being of the worker. Work serves as more than a means to receive currency that is used to purchase goods and services; work is often essential to one's self-concept and self-esteem. Work helps define who we are and our place within the society in which we live. Considering the significance of not only being employed, but also being both gainfully and meaningfully employed. It is essential that helpers are aware of laws that protect the rights of persons with disabilities in the area of employment. The helper should not only be aware of these laws but also the agency and/or organizations that enforce them. Given that some of these laws and the enforcement arms often have considerable paperwork involved, the helper should either be in a position to assist, or be able to refer the person to someone who can assist in navigating through the various steps involved in obtaining their rights.

As discussed several times within this book, some psychological theorists emphasize the importance of humans contributing to and being part of their society. Likewise, most humans want to be part of the society in which they live. At first glance, this may seem to be a reasonable and easily attainable desire. Unfortunately, for too many persons with disabilities, the desires for **inclusion** become an unfulfilled dream. Helpers attempting to connect with resources necessary to include persons with disabilities in societal activities can become a touchy and difficult situation.

There are laws that prohibit discrimination with regard to persons receiving goods and services that a helper can utilize to ensure inclusion in employment and access to most public, and some private facilities. However, laws cannot, do not, and should not force people to socialize with other people. The act of socializing should be a personal matter. Therefore, the helping professional will have to skillfully utilize community resources in including some persons with disabilities in community activities. For a variety of reasons, there probably will always be some people who avoid persons with disabilities; however, it has been this author's experiences that the vast majority of people welcome contact with people from a variety of backgrounds.

The other side of inclusion is getting some persons with disabilities to break away from their comfort zone and seek contact with their societal neighbors. For many years, persons who look different from the majority of the population and/or acted differently were, in various ways, discouraged from becoming part of the general population. Fortunately, today those reactions no longer are the dominant views of most societies. However, for some persons with disabilities, especially those with disabilities that cause noticeable deviations from societal norms, reluctance to engage in societal activities is not uncommon. Because of this fact, helping professionals may experience more reluctance with regard to some persons venturing into society than lack of acceptance of society.

Advocacy: As is the case with all the other underserved populations being discussed, this is a major resource need for persons with disabilities. One word of caution to helpers working with persons with disabilities is, in the process of advocating for or encouraging others to do so, there needs to be a measure of restraint involved. To be more specific, for centuries many persons with disabilities have had others determining what was, and is best for them. This action has resulted in many persons with disabilities becoming dependent on their advocates. Therefore, if the helper or other advocates do everything for the person, they are reinforcing dependency. Most persons with disabilities are capable of determining what their needs are. However, they, like many persons without disabilities, may not know how to satisfy those needs. When possible, the helper should have the persons with a disability express what he views as his needs, and if reasonable, the helper should engage in helping the person fulfill those needs. Therefore, the helper should advocate *with* the person, not *for* him.

Women

Historically, throughout the world, women have been discriminated by and subject to male domination. Today, in some parts of the world, women are severely restricted with regard to their abilities to participate in society, thus they remain subjected to male domination. Fortunately, in the United States and many industrialized countries, women's rights have increased. Despite improvements in women's rights and even in the most industrialized country in the world, women continue, in many areas such as employment, not to be treated on an equal status as males.

Although women are not numerically a minority in the United States, many women in America and around the world are inadequately served because of inequity and status when compared with males, particularly with regard to employment. It is a well-documented fact that, within the United States, on average women receive less pay than their male counterparts for the same or similar jobs. Additionally, it is also a truism that many women are not given equal opportunities with males for Fortune 500-type jobs as well as other higher paying jobs.

As distressing as the previously mentioned facts are, some women also encounter perhaps more disturbing human encounter actions—that being physical and mental abuse. Certainly, there is no attempt in this chapter to minimize any other discrimination against women by emphasizing abuse as an area on which helping professionals should concentrate their increase of knowledge of resources for women. However, when we view women's issues from an underserved prospective, various forms of abuse, including physical, emotional, and sexual abuse should be prominent on that list of issues.

Helping professionals who attempt to assist women should become familiar with resources developed to protect women from abuse. They should also become familiar with how to access those resources. Safe houses, legal services, medical services, and religious services are but a few of the resources that are available to abused women. One might think that the obvious is being stated and that most women are aware of these resources. It may be true that many women are aware of these and other resources; however, for a variety of reasons, some women fail to utilize them. Reasons such as being afraid of additional abuse from the abuser if she reports the abuser to appropriate authorities, attempts to protect children, and being ashamed to acknowledge that she is in such a situation are only a few of the reasons that some women fail to utilize appropriate resources.

Women with small children who do not work outside the home, and women with disabilities too often are targets of abuse. These women are some of the most likely persons to be abused by spouses, family members, and/or caregivers. Mention has been made that some women refuse to seek help because of their desires to protect their children. Additionally, they may be at a disadvantage because they do not work outside the home; therefore, they have considerable economic dependence on the employed spouse. Unfortunately, this feeling of dependence and the desire to protect the children sometimes cause women to live in an abusive situation.

Women who have some type of disability are too often overlooked victims of abuse. Certainly as vulnerable to abuse, and perhaps more so than any other group, women with disabilities are at risk of being abused. Because of their state of mind and/or their state of dependency, too frequently they become victims of various forms of abuse. Additionally, to elevate a bad situation to critical, these persons often do not have anyone to whom they can report the abuse or seek relief from the abuse.

The question may be asked, if these persons are isolated from the general population, how does a helper become aware of this abuse? The answer is that social workers and other human service workers, such as rehabilitation counselors and medical facilities' social service workers, should be aware of the existence of women with disabilities, thus they should keep contact with these persons. They should pay close attention to the physical condition of the women, noting any bruises and unusual marks, as well as changes in personality regardless of how slight these changes may be. These and other helpers should know of resources to keep tabs on these women and make reports of expected abuse to appropriate authorities.

Ethnic/Racial Minorities

This discussion of resources for underserved ethnic/racial minorities relates specifically to economically disadvantaged ethnic/racial minorities. In fact, some of the discussion also applies to economically disadvantaged persons of any ethnic/racial group. Reasons for concentrating on economically disadvantaged persons are: (a) many economically disadvantaged persons do not have necessary contacts and/or influence to attain needed services, (b) some economically disadvantaged persons may not have the educational background to access needed services, and (c) many economically disadvantaged persons are so overwhelmed with daily living that they have difficulties concentrating on needed services until the need becomes critical. As previously stated, these three conditions are not exclusive to economically disadvantaged ethnic/racial minorities; rather, they are too often conditions common to many economically poor persons regardless of race or ethnicity.

SUMMARY

In summary, several, but certainly not all, of the resource needs of economically disadvantaged and underserved are: (a) assistance with **protection of their rights**, (b) assistance with **identifying and securing adequate employment**, and in some cases, (c) assistance with regard to **being connected with and included in their larger society**. Lack of financial assets too frequently disenfranchises some people from receiving the many goods and services that could and should be available to them. One only has to view health statistics in the United States and observe where the majority of preventable illnesses are concentrated. Additionally, if one views the educational statistics and observes public school and college graduation rates to see which groups of people do not complete their educational courses of study, a clear picture emerges with regard to the need for assistance with resources for certain groups to become more competitive in society.

It is a well-documented fact that some people are incarcerated or otherwise punished for crimes and actions for which they are not responsible. Being economically disadvantaged too often contributes to them not receiving the justice they deserve. Undoubtedly, there are a variety of reasons that economically disadvantaged people are poor; some probably are the result of their own actions or lack thereof. However, most do not cherish the conditions in which they live and desire, and would benefit from the helping hands of knowledgeable helpers who know the appropriate resources available to help, and in some cases save their lives, and in most cases improve their lives.

Unemployment or **underemployment** too frequently is the future for some economically and educationally disadvantaged individuals.

In an economically driven society, one's employment status often determines the person's economic and social status within the society in which she lives. Assisting persons with access to resources such as education and training can become humanitarian gifts that empower the person and her family, as well as provide a motivational platform for future generations to be successful.

Chapter Review Questions

1. Why is having knowledge of a helpee's legal and civil rights important?
2. What are some of the benefits of support groups in a helping relationship?
3. How can advocacy groups be a resource in a helping relationship?
4. What are some of the resource needs of the elderly and how can these resources help?
5. What are some of the resource needs of persons with disabilities and their families?

Mental Exercise

1. Think of three different helping scenarios, such as a helpee who is an alcoholic, a helpee who is being physically abused, and an elderly person with Alzheimer's disease. List at least 10 resources for each that you could use in the helping process. The three listed are submitted as examples; you should select your three and identify the type of helper you would be, such as case manager, social worker, vocational rehabilitation counselor, and so on.

References

Donne, J. (1623). *For Whom the Bell Tolls.*
Queralt, M. (1996). *The social environment and human behavior: A diversity perspective.* Boston: Allyn & Bacon.

Part II

CULTURAL EVOLUTIONS AND THE HELPING PROFESSIONAL

Chapter 9

HELPING PROFESSIONAL'S ROLES IN CULTURAL EVOLUTION

Chapter Outline

INTRODUCTION

The word progress is closely associated with the word change. One of the things that has made America a strong nation and world leader with regard to civil and human rights is its citizen's abilities to recognize inequalities and correct same. Some may justifiably point out that sometimes the corrections occur slowly and also occur as a result of much anguish as well as not being the corrections some in American society prefer. Regardless of the qualifiers one may use to explain how changes occur in America, the fact remains that changes do occur and in most instances the changes have been the correct human relations actions. Bryan (2014) referred to these human relations changes as cultural evolution and made the following statement:

> No society has ever been perfect nor will there ever be a perfect society. This statement is true if for no other reason that perfection is in the eyes of the beholders and humans have free will and the ability to be independent thinkers. Because societies are composed of humans and these humans have opinions, ideas and beliefs there will always be some level of disagreement with regard to the rights of other individuals and disagreement as how a society is supposed to be conducted. Despite the truth of these statements most progressive societies should and do attempt to right wrongs and open its society to various view points as well as provide opportunities for expression of these rights, taking into consideration how the expression of these rights will impact society as a whole. p. 240

A role for the helping professional in the cultural evolution is to assist clients with regard to understanding and appropriately responding to the evolution which is occurring. Thus the assistance can take various forms, such as learning to accept and adapt to the changes, understanding the changes, opposing the changes, and/or help modify the changes.

Some of the changes that are discussed in this chapter relate to changes that have occurred; other have not occurred but, in this author's opinion, will occur within the future and some that should occur to help those involved obtain better access to goods and services. In developing a rationale for the need of the helping professional's involvement, I will provide a brief historical overview of the subject and discuss how and why helping professionals' expertise are needed.

The following are the subjects which will be discussed: same-sex marriages, lesbian, gay, bisexual, transgender, immigration, race relations, women's rights, disabilities, ageism, elderly, legalization of marijuana, and social equality. There are other areas where professional helpers' expertise are needed; however the ones listed are (in this author's opinion), greatly needed at this time in American history.

LESBIAN, GAY, BISEXUAL AND TRANSGENDER RIGHTS AND SAME-SEX MARRIAGES

Sexual relationships between persons of the same gender has been occurring for generations. Historical information informs us that same-sex relationships occurred in ancient Egypt, Rome and Greece. Likewise, persons of one gender (male or female) have permanently or at various times chosen to live as a person of the opposite gender. This and other actions have been cause for some to condemn as immoral same-sex relations and/or living occasionally or permanently as the gender of which they were not born. Much of the objections are based on religious/moral grounds. Some objections are based upon beliefs that having sexual relations with someone of the same gender is immoral and many of those that make this proclamation use religious scriptures as their main source as documentation of the inappropriateness of this behavior.

It should be recognized that there are some differences between same-sex marriage rights and the broad topic of Lesbian, Gay, Bisexual and Transgender Rights; however, for most discussions of same-sex marriages a common thread occurs that link same sex marriages with LGBT rights. Often the dominant discussion of same-sex marriages relates to the perceived morality or lack thereof with regard to sexual relationships between two persons of the same gender. There can be little to no question that sexual relations occur in same-sex relationships, however, with regard to same-sex marriages, without trying to deny sexual acts in the relationship, same-sex marriages goes much beyond this action. Too often (in this author's opinion), the objections relate too much to the sexual acts and disregards the legal aspects that are afforded persons who are legally married. This (again in this author's opinion), is and should be the central concern with regard to same-sex marriages. Some of the rights gained via legal marriage status are: (a) Marital communication privilege (b) Right to transfer property ownership from one spouse to another without paying taxes on the value of the property as is the case with regard to the sale of land involving a male and female marriage. (c) Right of next of kin. Dayna Lovett (2013) frames this rights issue as a civil rights struggle:

Throughout history in the United States there have been many struggles of individual's rights who are by someone's definition not as equal.
The struggles have been tragic in so many ways and in all ways they
were unnecessary because these struggles were for each individual living here in the United States to have the basic human rights that should
be given to all: the right of life, liberty and the pursuit of happiness. This
sentence does not have a 'but' or 'only' if you believe like the majority
or act like the majority. It is a right that should be given to all. It seems
that over the many years of struggles and horrible tragedies as a nation
we still have not learned anything. p. 241

Bryan (2014) points out that much of the objection to same-sex marriages and gay rights in general are based on religious/moral grounds.
Some objections are based upon beliefs that having sexual relations
with someone of the same gender is simply immoral and many of
those that make this proclamation use religious documents such as the
Holy Bible or other religious documents as their main source as documentation of the inappropriateness of this behavior. Whether one
subscribes to this type of objection is a personal belief and those that
disagree with using religious documents as justification for their beliefs
can point to the fact that in years past some persons justified enslaving
and separating persons based upon their racial classification on words
taken from the Holy Bible. Additionally, some may point out the fact
that the Holy Bible speaks against strong drink, commonly referred to
as intake of alcoholic beverages; however, the sell and consumption of
alcohol is legal in the United States. Others justify their objections to
some gay rights and same-sex marriages based upon what they believe
is nature never intended for persons of the same gender to marry
and/or have intimate sexual relations. Regardless the method of objection and ways of protesting gay rights and same sex marriage, there
appears to be a movement within the United States to be tolerant and
accepting of gay rights and since the United States Supreme Court on
June 26, 2015 rules same sex marriage legal it is reasonable to expect,
over a period of time, more acceptance and understanding of gay
rights. Currently, there are roles for helping professionals with regard
to this subject and one can reasonable expect the roles to increase. Regardless, the belief of the helping professional, he/she must conduct
oneself in a professional manner as he/she would with regard to any
issue.

THE PROFESSIONAL HELPER'S ROLE WITH REGARD TO
SAME SEX RELATIONSHIPS.

Same-sex marriages in the United States are becoming legally accepted as well as gradually becoming socially accepted. This is not to say that everyone in the United States, regardless of whether same-sex marriages is legal, is going to accept this as an acceptable part of society. This is human nature just as not everyone is accepting of interracial marriage. Certainly this is not meant to equate same-sex marriages with interracial marriage; the point being made is that regardless of what social concept and action occur there will be some that disagree and certainly in an open and free society they have that right. Some, if not many, professional helpers will encounter clients who are in same-sex relationships, some legally married and others in nonmarried arrangements, but none the less in same-sex relationships. Some of the issues these persons will have relate to their relationship and others will not, nonetheless their relationship will be a factor that the professional helper will have to take into consideration. Stated in other terms, the helping professional will have to be aware of his or her beliefs and attitudes with regard to same-sex relationships. As is the case with many helping relationships, the helper (if he truly wants to consider himself a professional) must not allow the possibility of negative thoughts regarding the relationship to affect his willingness and ability to help the persons. Some may take exception to this statement if they have strong religious beliefs against these types of human relationships. If the issues the persons are presenting have nothing to do with religion (in this author's opinion), there should not be any reluctance working with the person or persons. If the contact relates to religious issues and the helper believes he cannot provide nonbias help, he should refer the client to someone who does not have these social and religious limitations. Religious counselors may have the latitude to discuss the subject on what they consider moral basis; however, some persons who are not employed by religious organizations most likely will not have this latitude. Part of being a professional involves being objective, and as much as possible keeping personal bias out of the helping relationship. Truth and honesty in the helping relationship must prevail. If and when persons who are in same-sex marriages or relationships come to the helper with problems/issues that have nothing, or very little, to do with their marriage arrangement, the helper should not bring their marriage arrangement or relationship into the situation, just as they would not if the marriage or relationship was heterosexual.

DISABILITY

Chapter 6, provides a good overview of definition of the disability, as well as identifying some of the treatments persons with disabilities have had to endure in part because of how we perceive persons with disabilities. The following discussion presents an evolution with regard to treatment and interaction with persons with disabilities as well as some of the current and future needs of persons with disabilities, which bring us to some of the techniques professional helpers should use to assist persons with disabilities.

The general population of persons in the United States probably think that persons with disabilities in America are well protected with regard to their needs being met. This false sense of well-being to persons with disabilities is occurring because persons with disabilities continue to be the hidden minority. Too often many persons in America think of disabilities as those persons who have visible severe disabilities and/or mental disabilities which incapacitate the person. Persons with disabilities are often not considered as a minority population such as racial minorities. The real fact is that persons with disabilities are the largest minority group in the United States, they consist of persons from every demographics of the United States as well as in the world except nondisabled. Persons with disabilities are part of every demographic that we compile. Persons with disabilities are part of every ethnic group, both genders and sexual preference, all social groups, every economic group, and the listing could continue. A conservative estimate of the population of persons with disabilities in America is fifty-four to fifty-five million persons, representing one-fifth of the United States population.

One may think that the previously mentioned demographics would cause most Americans to become more aware of persons with disabilities; however, the truth is that unless we have a disability, or have a family member who has a disability, or know someone who has a disability, we do not think of disabilities. Additionally, if we think of disabilities, the following thoughts come to mind, just to mention a few. (a) Persons with disabilities are "taken care of" by state and federal government. (b) Persons with disabilities have access to a handicap sticker, thus their access to goods and services are made accessible for them. (c) Persons with disabilities are severely disabled, thus they are either institutionalized; hospitalized or being cared for at home. All of the previously mentioned views of persons with disabilities represent limited views, many of which are incorrect. Many persons with disabilities do not receive "public or state or federal financial assistance, but this does not mean that they could not benefit from a better understanding of their needs.

Because the Americans with Disabilities Act and its amendments as well as other legislation have been enacted, this has given a false sense of feeling that the well-being of persons with disabilities is acceptable to persons with disabilities, their families, and supporters. This belief can easily be proven incorrect if one views the unemployment rate of persons with disabilities. In 2013, the unemployment rate for persons with disabilities was approximately 13%. Additionally, for those persons with disabilities who had some type of employment, over 30% were working part-time. In comparison, during the same period the unemployment rate for persons without a disability was approximately 7%. It is this author's contention that the unemployment rate for persons with disabilities is much higher than the 13% rate when one takes into consideration those persons with disabilities that have discontinued the search for employment. To be fair with regard to the comparison of unemployment between persons with disabilities and those that are considered nondisabled, the same consideration exist. However, with any comparison of unemployment rate between persons with disabilities and nondisabled persons, the rate is approximately double with persons with disabilities having less employment than nondisabled.

In this text, **Chapter 6** provides considerable information regarding the progress that has been made for the betterment of persons with disabilities, especially through legislation. This fact is true; however, if one reviews things that have been accomplished for persons with disabilities, the facts will show that since the Americans with Disabilities Act in 1990 there has been (at least in this author's opinion) a decline in attention to the needs of persons with disabilities. This is not to say that nothing has been done because to the credit of the United States

legislators and the United States Executive branch, some progress
have been made. However, since the Americans with Disabilities Act
(to which I refer as the Civil Rights Act for persons with disabilities),
there appears to be less attention given to some of the significant needs
of persons with disabilities, such as employment, needs of school-age
children with various types of disabilities, needs of elderly persons
with disabilities, and persons with intellectual, mental and emotional
disabilities.

Considerable attention has to be placed upon organizations which
represent persons with disabilities. To elaborate on what needs to be
done to assist persons with disabilities, one must look at the efforts and
attention that brought forth and made successful the passage of the
Americans with Disabilities Act (ADA). Before the ADA most attention for persons with disabilities including actions that brought to the
public's attention with regard to the needs of persons with disabilities
were done by various organizations which represented specific disabilities, such as the Lung Association and the Cerebral Palsy Association. There was very little intermingling of the various organizations,
and organization was promoting their particular disability needs.
These various organizations began to realize that what would benefit
all persons with disabilities was strong organized efforts that represented and had the best interests for all types of disabilities Many organizations began to work together to encourage the United States
Congress to consider legislation that represented the needs of most, if
not all, types of disabilities. This success led to the Civil Rights Act for
persons with disabilities–the Americans with Disabilities Act. There
has been other legislation since the 1990 ADA that has passed such as
the 1999 Developmental Disabilities and Assistance Act and the 2008
ADA Amendments that took effect 2009. However, since the strong
and effective efforts by persons with disabilities and their supporters
that led to the development and passage of the Americans with Disabilities Act, there seem to be relaxing of the efforts to maintain the
momentum that led to the development and passage of the previously mention ADA. It appears that organizations which work with and
support persons with disabilities have gone back to pre-ADA efforts.
Stated in other terms, today the primary push with regard to disability advocacy is primarily related to promoting the needs of persons
with specific needs. Certainly, this is important work and should be
continued; however in addition to this work, these various organiza-

tions need to join together to promote the overall issue of needs of persons with disabilities, such as employment or lack of employment, nursing home abuse, homelessness, lack of adequate transportation and lack of adequate assistance for persons with disabilities that live in rural areas. What is needed is the revitalization of the spirit and drive that led to the development and passage of the ADA. These are only some of the areas of helping that professional helpers are needed. In some instances professional helpers may need to be the main spokesperson for the needs and rights of persons with disabilities, and in other instances there will be need to advocate with persons with disabilities so that their voices can be heard.

Additionally, to promote the cultural evolution of persons with disabilities, professional helpers are needed in the following areas.

1. Assisting with employment of persons with disabilities. To be more specific, helping professionals need to work in making the American public aware of the high unemployment rate of persons with disabilities. In this effort the helping professional can provide valuable service by expressing the reality that many unemployed persons with disabilities are capable of working if given a chance and additionally pointing out that in many cases very few, if any, modifications have to be made at a worksite to help make them productive employees.

2. Associated with employment, the professional helper can assist with regard to not only educating employers about their abilities, they can also assist in educating the American public of the capabilities of persons with disabilities.

3. Professional helpers are needed, and will continue to be needed with regard to assisting persons with disabilities with vocational training as well as securing higher level education.

4. Provide assistance for severely disabled persons. This is the group that has the highest unemployment rates. It is a reality because of the degree of disability that some persons have. They are and, in all probability, will not be able to secure gainful employment. However, in some cases assisting them with working from home, perhaps on a part-time basis will be a significant improvement from the boredom of being home alone with very little to occupy their minds.

5. Provide assistance with care and concerns of treatment of persons with disabilities living in nursing homes. Unfortunately, there has been sufficient documentation of some nursing home abuse of persons with disabilities. This is an area that greatly needs a helping professional's attention.

6. Helping professionals are currently and will continue to be needed with regard to assisting families that are adjusting to family members who have a disability. Statistics indicate that a large number of abuses of persons with disabilities occur at home. In many, if not, most cases of home abuse of persons with disabilities occur because of frustration more than dislike of the person. Assisting families of persons with disabilities with respite care often can make a significant difference in family relationships.

7. Advocating for improvement of education of students with intellectual disabilities.

8. Assisting persons with disabilities in rural areas.

Another very important topic that requires helping professionals services will be the emerging results of the study of human genes. To be more specific, as science progresses and we are able to diagnose early in the pregnancy birth defects, families will have to make decisions whether to continue the pregnancy. Without any doubt these are types of decisions which will be some of the most psychologically important decisions those concerned will ever have to make. Helping professionals who are educated and trained in this area can be of invaluable assistance to those concerned with decisions of this nature.

These are only a few of the roles helping professionals can and will need to provide for assisting persons with disabilities. The key to working with persons with disabilities is assisting and advocating, not taking over their lives by doing for them.

IMMIGRATION

Some form of immigration occurs throughout the world virtually every day and immigration occurs for various reasons. Some immigrated to escape from oppression and others immigrate to secure opportunities for a better life for one's self and/or family. The United

States has been the immigration destination for various groups of people for many years, and this process likely will continue well into the current twenty-first century.

Currently, the majority of immigration to the United States has come from the nation of Mexico and several South American countries. The vast majority come to help secure a better future for themselves and their loved ones. No doubt some come for much less than honorable reasons, thus the thought of immigration sometimes places negative thoughts in the minds of some, if not many, citizens of the United States. Regardless of the reason and the good or bad feelings that immigration may engender, in some person's minds the act will continue.

In ten or fifteen years, the United States will likely experience increased request for immigration from areas today not known for large numbers of immigration to the United States, such as some countries in Africa, Asia and Europe. Some of the reasons for the desire for immigration will be economical, and to seek opportunities for more freedom of life activities. One may question this projection on the basis of the distance these countries are from the United States. The response to that question is that distance has not, in past years, been a determent to Korean, Japanese, and Chinese people seeking improved life opportunities. As long as people aspire to improve their life situations many will find ways to attempt to make those aspirations and dreams become realities. In the process of immigrants attempting to make life better for themselves and their loved ones, unfortunately some problems and conflicts will occur. Conflicts will occur as different social values and different ways of conducting one's life will clash with established American values. Helping professionals are and will continue to be needed to assist both sides of the social divide. Americans will have the opinion that the new immigrants should conform to American standards, and the immigrants will be reluctant to give up centuries-old customs, beliefs and actions. Somewhere among the differences there must be a compromise that will benefit all sides. The role of many helping professionals, especially those who are engaged in social issues, will have to become educated about customs and beliefs of persons which have been unknown and of little interest to them in previous years. As is discussed in Chapter 7, many social beliefs and actions, regardless of country of origin, are often based in religious doctrine which has been taught as truths not to be broken or compromised. Therein is a role in which helping professional's sensitivity and expertise will be required. The helping professional must be sensitive to various viewpoints presented by both the immigrants and the established citizens.

AGEISM

When discussing ageism, often we think in terms of older age or more specifically elderly. In this brief discussion I will discuss ageism in relation to current issues and future issues helping professionals will encounter with regard to older persons, not elderly, remaining in the workforce and what that means to older workers. Additionally, I will discuss another side of ageism–the impact of older workers staying longer in the workforce and its impact upon younger workers as they attempt to obtain employment and their attempts to secure job promotions that could be impacted by older workers remaining in the workforce.

A variety of things such as new and improved health care, including new medication, new health procedures, more persons being involved in physical fitness programs via exercise, healthier eating habits, and improved health check-ups which identifies potential medical problems early, thus improving the chances of avoiding medical issues which in past years decreased individuals' length of life. Because of the increase in lifespan and many more persons (than in past years) staying employed longer than in previous years, this will present some problems for younger employees securing employment and moving up the employment ladder. Also for those that chose not to be employed longer, many are engaging themselves in hobbies, extended vacations, developing new learning experiences, such as developing new hobbies, returning to college for advanced education, or going to college for the first time.

From the standpoint of how does this information impact helping professionals, the simple answer is they will be needed to help older persons move into a new phase in their lives. In past years, one worked until he/she was sixty or sixty-five years old then you retired and begin to prepare for the end of life. In the past ten to fifteen years there has been increased emphasis on working longer for a variety of reasons, such as being healthier, therefore able to continue to work, and financially unable to live a comfortable and psychologically re-warding life. Helping professionals, especially those in financial indus-try will be needed to help persons be financially prepared for the longer lifespan. Other helping professionals such as persons in the fit-ness industry will be needed to assist with helping persons to remain physically and psychologically prepared for a longer and productive life.

Another issue that has developed and has become an issue that helping professionals can provide service for is the impact on younger persons as older persons maintain employment longer. As previously stated in past years one could count on persons retiring at ages sixty to sixty-five; however, today (also as previously stated) many persons are working past the previously mentioned ages of retirement. This has begun to cause some frustration on the part of younger workers be-cause their work advancement potential is being delayed. It is this au-thor's prediction that this issue will continue to be a concern and the prevalence of this concern will increase in the upcoming years. Psy-chological counselors as well as other helping professionals will be needed to deal with some of the frustration and psychological issues associated with these concerns.

Because of good health and economic reasons persons fifty-five years and older, will remain in the workforce longer. The Sloan Cen-ter on Aging and Work at Boston College predict by 2019, workers 55 years and older will be 25% of the workforce. Similarly the U. S. Cen-sus project between years 2015 and 2040 a 67% increase in persons 65 and older in the workforce. To protect the older person's employment rights in 1990 the United States Congress amended the Age Discrimi-nation in Employment Act of 1967 by enacting the Older Workers Benefit Protection Act of 1990. This amendment makes it illegal for an employer to: (a) Use an employee's age as the basis for discrimination in benefits, (b) Target older workers for their staff-cutting program, and (c) require older workers to waive their rights without observing cer-tain safeguards.

ELDERLY

As previously stated, a variety of factors have increased the lifespan of many Americans, and as research continues and lifestyles continues to improve, the life expectancy for many will continue to increase. The impact of persons continuing to remain on their jobs longer has been discussed; however, in addition to that fact, the reality is at some point persons will retire and they and others will have to make adjustments with regard to living out the remainder of their lives. Some will be financially and physically able to remain in their homes while others will need some types of assisted living arrangements. There currently is a need for helping professionals who are trained to provide assistance to older persons, and this need will continue to grow as the population of older persons continues to increase. This will require increased study and education with regard to understanding some of the needs of elderly persons. This is not to imply that helping professionals will encounter different type of clients; however, with longer lifespans comes a variety of issues that many helping professionals have not encountered. Stated in other terms, it will not be different types of clients the helping professional encounters, rather some, if not many, different types of issues with which to help the client handle. Issues such as resource management, vacations and other types of recreation that are appropriate for persons of their age, physical and possibly emotional conditions, physical fitness, intellectual fitness, and end of life issues to mention only a few areas of concern to persons who may be considered elderly. There currently is educational training for geriatric specialists and in the not too distant future this area of specialty will continue to expand.

WORKING TOWARD SOCIAL EQUALITY

In order to effectively discuss social equality it is helpful to explain and discuss social inequality. Social inequality exists when members of a society, for a reason or a variety of reasons, do not have equal opportunities as the dominant group to conduct their lawful daily life activities in ways that allow them to support their daily and future life needs. Additionally social inequality often occurs when persons are unable to rise above or remove the restrictions that are handicapping them with regard to improving their stations in life.

Within the United States much progress has been made with regard to various ethnic, racial minorities, and women to mention only three groups improving their lives. Some of the discrimination that once existed which prohibited the previously mentioned groups from moving up the socioeconomic ladder has been moved. Examples are women in previous years being treated as servants of their husbands and African Americans punished and controlled as one would an animal, certainly not a pet animal. Stated more succinctly these two groups as well as others that are not mentioned are examples of past treatment that in many respects, thankfully have been significantly changed.

William Kornblum and Joseph Julian (2007) offer their perspective on how social change occurs.

> It is worth noting that the idea that a society should intervene to remedy conditions that affect the lives of its citizens is a fairly recent innovation. Until the eighteenth century, for example, most people worked at exhausting tasks under poor conditions for long hours, they suffered from severe deprivation all their lives, and they often died young, sometime of terrible disease. But no one thought of these things as problems to be solved. They were accepted as natural, inevitable conditions of life. It was not until the so-called 'enlightenment' of the late eighteenth century that philosophers began to argue that poverty is not inevitable but a result of an unjust social system. Through legislation, education and attitude changes stumbling blocks which use to hinder the advancement of some of the members of the previously mentioned groups have been either eliminated or lessen by virtue of legislation, education and social awakening. This social awakening has not eliminated prejudice and basis; however what has happened is a majority of the population realizes that discrimination based upon ones ethnicity, racial background and gender does not enhance the image of the United States, in a world where we are promoting fairness and equality to other countries and at the same time treating certain segments of our population in ways that make us appear to be hypocrites. p. 5

An example to which Kornblum and Julian are referring relate to the fact that some ethnic, racial minorities and women for decades have not received equal status and treatment in American society as Caucasian males. From the beginning of American colonization these three groups have at many times been relegated to at best second-class citizenship. Women were in effect treated as second-class citizens, primarily wards of their spouses. They were not given the vote in the majority of states until 1920. African Americans for many years were legal servants to Caucasians and unofficial servants for many more years. Other minority groups such as persons of Asian descent also for many years did not have full rights as citizens of the United States. Persons with disabilities and some American Indian tribes often were treated as sympathetic wards of American society.

PHILOSOPHICAL EXPLANATION OF POVERTY

In an attempt to explain how poverty in America occurs Kornblum and Julian (2007) identify philosophical explanations of how some experts explain persistent poverty.

> Structural explanations: Those that ascribe to this philosophical approach attribute poverty to the functioning of the dominant institutions of society, such as markets and corporations. When these major social structures change, conflicts arise as large members of people attempt to adjust to new conditions and new forms of social organization. For example, in a society dominated by agrarian production and agricultural markets, the poor tend to be people who lack land or whose land is unsuitable for farming. Or they may be people who have been forced off their land and have come to towns and cities to look for work. In industrial societies, the poor tend to be those who have been unable to acquire the skills or knowledge that would enable them to find and keep jobs in factories or other businesses.
>
> During various periods of American history, some groups migrate to the cities in an attempt to escape from an impoverished rural life. Others migrated when they were forced off the land by the mechanization of farming, by the consolidation of farms into larger units, and by the pressure of competition with large agribusinesses. (p. 210)

The point being made with regard to a structural explanation for poverty is structural conditions, often beyond the control of certain populations which caused significant changes in their lives resulting in loss of income and often loss of the ability to maintain an acceptable standard of living. Stated in other terms, the structure of their lives change in ways that made being able to maintain a livable wage virtually impossible. Additional examples of this theory is the mechanization of jobs and technological advancements that require advanced education.

The second explanation identified by Kornblum and Julian (2007) is referred to as Cultural Explanations. The following remarks provide an explanation of that philosophy.

> Cultural explanations of poverty are based on the interactionist perspective in sociology. In this view, through the ways in which they are brought up and socialized and through their interactions in everyday life, people become adapted to certain ways of life, including poverty. These ways of life persist because they become part of a group's culture.
>
> Proponents of the cultural approach argue that a "culture of poverty" arise among people who experience extended periods of economic deprivation. Under these conditions, new norms, values and aspirations emerge and eventually become independent of the situations that produced them, so that eliminating the problem does not eliminate the behaviors that have been developed to deal with it.

This approach that proposes there is a "culture of poverty" as Kornblum and Julian acknowledge, is very controversial and many experts in the field of social sciences reject the concept. There are very few that would disagree that sustained poverty can impact individuals and families' hopes for a brighter future. However, sustained poverty does not often decrease their drives to improve their living conditions for themselves and future generations of their families. Helping professionals are and will continue to be needed to assist and advise persons with ways to move themselves from poverty. Additionally and associated with this issue, helping professionals encouraging the power structure of America to make available a helping approach to assisting persons in their attempts to remove themselves from poverty.

The Effects of Poverty

The saying "the rich get richer and the poor stay poor" has been around for many years and is as relevant today as the saying was when it was first spoken. As we look at social transition within the United States societies, we note that some portions of ethnic minorities have reached the middle-class economic structure with a smaller number reaching above middle-class status. While at first glance this is notable progress; however, when we take a more in-depth view we begin to realize while discrimination based upon ethnicity and race is not as prevalent as in past years, what we actually are witnessing is social class inequality. In past years social classes were, in broad and general terms, identified as low social class, middle social class, and upper social class. In some cases the middle-class groups were the largest group and they were divided into lower middle-class, and upper middle-class. Regardless of the classification one's status was based upon his/her personal and/or family's economic status. There is nothing wrong with class stratification if all citizens have equal opportunities and access to the economic ladder that allows one to progress. This is and will continue to be a major role for helping professionals. To be more specific persons at the lower rungs of the economic ladder will need some assistance from professional helpers to prepare themselves for the difficult climb that await them as they try to improve their lives and their families lives. It is this author's belief that the struggle to move up the social and economic ladders will no longer be a struggle of certain racial and ethnic groups against the economic majority class. (One should note that I have not said racial and certain ethnic groups struggling against Caucasians.) In the not too distant future the upper social and economic group will be an increased mixture of races and ethnic groups. One could argue, and be correct to say that the upper economic class currently consists of ethnic and racial groups. The current problem is while the current composition consists of a variety of ethnic and racial groups, the reality is that the upper levels of the economic class is not composed of many ethnic and racial persons. The point to be made is this will change and more ethnic and racial persons, in the not too distant future, will become part of the elite and powerful decision makers. This to a major part will occur because educational opportunities is more available to ethnic and racial groups and the opportunity will continue to increase. Elitism will be a major factor. Regardless of one's racial ethnic status, economic status will become the dominant factor. Ability to live in expensive homes, possession of expensive items will determine ones status. The philosophical warfare will be economic rather than racial/ethnic.

In past years social class was primarily based upon one's racial and ethnic status. To a large extent regardless of one's financial status, unless one was extremely wealthy, his or her social status was attached to his/her ethnic and/or racial background. Stated in other terms, you may have been monetarily wealthy; however, you were considered a wealthy black person or wealthy Mexican person. On the surface this does not seem bad, however, the implications were your wealth was qualified by your race and/or ethnicity, thus your influence was limited by your racial and/or ethnic background. Your status as a wealthy person was not as important and meaningful, and did not carry as much power as a wealthy white person. To further make a point, wealthy alliances which is where the power structure is made, most often consisted of white to white alliances. However, today we are beginning to see changes occur, in that wealth is wealth regardless of race and ethnicity. Stated in other terms the ethnic and/or race of a wealthy person does not matter as much as in past years. Wealthy ethnic and racial persons are more and more being accepted into the clubs of wealthy persons. The important thing today, and will continue to increase, is what the person can bring to the "table" with his/her wealth. Again stated in other terms, wealthy ethnic and racial minorities are being welcomed to the wealthy and influential clubs without much reservations. This opening of the doors to influential clubs and decision-making groups will set wealthy ethnic and racial minority persons apart from their less influential racial and minority group members. This is the beginning of lessening the classification of persons by race and ethnicity and replacing this with social class status. The important question will be what you can bring to the table of influence.

The United States is an economically-based society, and economics determines many aspects of persons' lives. What kind of education one receives, what type of home one has, what kind of employment one has, and to a great extent, what kind of social life one has. This is not intended as a "knock" on American society, but is discussed to point out how social class status impacts one's life. While ethnic and racial classification is not likely to disappear in the immediate future, over time the emphasis will be on one's social classification. Also, many ethnic and racial minority as well as nonethnic racial minority persons will continue to work to eliminate discrimination based upon race and ethnicity. However, as time elapses and as ethnic and racial persons become acquainted with and accustomed to the perks and privileges of upper social class status, the divide between social classes will consist of the wealthy class composed of persons from various backgrounds versus poor and middle-class persons.

Persons with excellent financial support will be able to, regardless of race, ethnicity and gender, become part of the elite classes. These groups, as is the current situation, will have power because money euphemistically talks thus they will have the attention of policymakers. Unlike the financially elite classes the economically lower class will not have many of the resources needed to lift themselves from subsistence living levels. These persons will need help from professional helpers who are sensitive to their needs. Professional helpers including teachers and education counselors can be of assistance by encouraging academic achievement beginning at an early age. The helpers should encourage innovation and being leaders rather than followers, thus becoming part of the policymakers. Additionally and foremost, encourage self-respect and belief in their abilities to be successful.

ROLE OF POLITICS

One of the major and perhaps most important roles politics should play in American society is to establish rules, regulations, and laws which promote and protect the rights of its citizens, as well as help develop situations where all persons have opportunities to be lawfully successful. In ideal situations all inhabitants would be treated equally and fairly, regardless of race, color, creed, gender, and lawful beliefs. This author is cognizant of the fact that what has just been stated is a naive dreamer's view of society as it is currently conducted. In today's political society money trumps the majority will of the people. Stated in other terms, who has the most money has the most influence, thus what he/she or they want too often takes priority over the needs and desires of the majority of people. Perhaps to be fair with my statement, too often money, to a significant degree, determines the "wants" of the people. To be more specific, persons with large amounts of money are able, through propaganda and financial support of political candidates as well as others who establish policy, to determine by which rules and regulations a society must live.

The relationship of influential policymakers and the financial elite persons is an interesting one in that there is a symbiotic relationship, the policymakers need money and influential backing to maintain their power positions and the financial elite need the policymaker's positions to support their efforts which maintain their wealth, power and influence. The truth is the previously mentioned connections are so beneficial to both groups that neither dare to disconnect and consider the needs of the public. In fact, the idea that both groups keep in their minds is that their decisions and actions benefit the public at large and it is this type of thinking which justifies their symbiotic relationship. To be more specific, the rationale is that what is being done is for the good of the majority.

This fact, stated in simple terms, means that those with significant financial resources influence the rules by which society must live and those without significant financial influence have little input into the establishment and enforcement of said rules. To further point out the impact of who has the most influence with regard to rules and regulations, persons with minimum financial resources have and will continue to have minimal input into the establishment of policies and laws. Succinctly stated this means that influence in the very near future will primarily be based upon socioeconomic status rather than racial, ethnic and gender status. A point that is being made is the poor and less influential persons in the not too distant future will become the majority population and will be composed of all races and ethnicity. Social discrimination will be directed at the poor regardless of ethnic and/or racial background. Therefore the issue will be social class status.

SOCIAL CLASS STATUS

A reality is that for some people, particularly the wealthy, this symbiotic relationship is good and ideal for maintaining and expanding their wealth and influence. This, to a large extent, is what motivates some to seek wealth, because often with wealth comes significant influence. As previously stated, in the not too distant future (in this author's opinion, within the next twenty years), an increased number of persons of ethnic, and racial backgrounds as well as women will join the upper middle and upper economic classes. The reasons why there will be increased numbers of the previously mentioned groups becoming members of the upper classes are: 1. Increased education, especially college and professional education and training. The overall American society has become less prejudiced and more open to accepting persons who in the past were not allowed access to higher levels of education and training. 2. When previously discriminated and excluded groups receive the necessary qualification, more are being hired and promoted to jobs and positions that pay good salaries which affords them the opportunities to obtain the benefits of upper class status. 3. Money talks, in those instances where some may be opposed to certain groups moving up the economic ladder, there are not many who will refuse the financial resources that come with accepting persons whom they view as less than they are. The idea is that "I will take their money but I don't have to like them," or "I am willing to allow them into the social club but I will limit my association with them." 4. Laws which prohibit discrimination often carry substantial punishment for those who break the laws. 5. Perhaps, most importantly is the fact that overall the American society is much more open-minded with regard to the rights of previously disenfranchised persons.

The previously mentioned facts has help open the doors to upper social class membership to ethnic, racial, and female persons. This cultural shift is good for the American society and those that benefit from the liberalization of human relationships in America. With this new degree of access comes power, and the question becomes how will the new upper-class, ethnic, racial and females handle same. Will they work toward helping others reach this newly opened door of opportunities, or will they become new members of the old club of wealth and privilege and carry on the same traditions of exclusion that have kept the poor on the outside wishfully looking inward? Herein is a significant and important role for helping professionals which is to advocate for equal opportunities for lower socioeconomic persons, women, poor persons, and racial minorities. Stated more succinctly, helping professionals will need to advocate with and for the less affluent in American society.

FROM WHERE WILL HELP COME?

There are numerous organizations as well as state and federal agencies whose primary goals is to assist persons with various needs that are necessary to have a productive and meaningful life. Most if not all of these organizations do excellent work in providing assistance to persons needing their help; however, often their assistance is limited by lack of financial resources. This fact becomes a challenge of which helping professionals are currently aware, and many are creative and resourceful in finding ways to assist those in need.

It is this author's belief that it is human nature to want to be of assistance to others, especially in cases where someone appears to be in need. I realize when viewing the actions of some persons one can wonder where is the humanity and feelings of compassion these persons have for their fellow humans. That being said I think that one would agree these are the actions of a minority of persons rather than the action of the majority of persons. The majority of persons realize that no one is capable of meeting all of his/her needs, thus everyone, more often than we may realize, need assistance from our fellow human beings. As humans we all need support in many of our efforts to succeed in attempting to achieve goals and feel as though we are contributing to society. Being compassionate is part of our DNA composition. Stated in other terms, for most persons who are not totally self-centered, helping our fellow humans is a natural and inborn reaction. Certainly, there are persons who become so selfish that they develop a "me first" attitude; however, this is the exception.

As previously stated, the majority of humans prefer to be of assistance rather than take advantage of one's weaknesses. Therefore, helping professionals in the not too distant future will be needed to step forward and increase their advocacy for persons who are socially disadvantaged.

Role of Helping Professionals

There is significant and challenging roles for helping professionals as we see the demographics shift from race and gender discrimination to social class discrimination in the United States. As previously stated race, ethnicity and gender in the very near future will not be as much of factors leading to discrimination as social background. Economically poor and less affluent Caucasians will be considered as less valuable to society similar to poor blacks, other minorities, and women. The discrimination will not be a result of pigmentation or gender, but will be based in significant ways on an economic basis. This is not saying that the socially economically poor will be totally neglected. In fairness to this society, America is much better than that even with the social changes, and services will continue to be available to persons considered to be of a lower social class. Therein is a major role for the helping professional to advocate for fair and equitable services for socially neglected groups.

SUMMARY

As have previously stated, in this world change is a constant action. Many times we feel that change takes too long to occur, especially when the change relates to somethings that we want to be modified or completely removed. In the arena of human relationships when change occurs there are those that are in favor as well as those that are opposed to change. As changes occur, often many of those that are impacted are significantly involved in the impact of the changes so much so that they often are unable to think rationally about what is happening. In these types of situations it is important for helping professionals be involved in assisting those that are affected. The roles of helping professionals will vary, some will be for the changes, others will be against the changes, and others will be neutral with regard to the changes. Regardless of the role the helping professional takes in the evolution of issues and actions, the helping professional should above all be professional.

As discussed in this chapter, the United States is going through cultural evolutions with regard to several significant issues and the results of the evolutions will have significant impact upon the American societies for many years into the future. Significant emotions will be expended in the debates for and against some of the significant issues before us, and in many cases when emotions are elevated rational thinking become the causality. Helping professionals are human thus they will have strong feelings with regard to some of the cultural evolutions and certainly they have the right to express their opinions. Their professional mannerism and knowledge can be the voice of reason that help make the situations better understood and acceptable to those which oppose same.

Mental Exercise

1. What are some of your views with regard to same-sex marriages?
2. How can you assist persons with disabilities?

3. What are some of your views with regard to persons immigrating to the United States?
4. Should there be a mandatory retirement age? If yes, explain the age and why. If no, explain why not.
5. Are there any disadvantages in older workers remaining on the job? If yes, what are some?
6. What does the term social equality mean to you?
7. Will there ever be social equality in the United States? Defend your position.
8. Can poverty in the United States be eliminated? If yes, how? If no, why not?

References

Bryan, W. V. (2014). *Multicultural aspects of human behavior* (3rd Ed.). Springfield IL. Charles C Thomas.

Kornblum, W., & Julian, J. (2007) *Social Problems* (12th Ed.). New Jersey. Pearson Prentice Hall.

Lovett, D. (2013). Gay marriage: It matters. Unpublished paper, University of Oklahoma.

Chapter 10

FUTURE CHALLENGES FOR HELPERS

Chapter Outline
- Introduction
- Race Relations
- American Indians
  - Assimilation
- Social Issues
- Progress Made
- African Americans
  - Slavery
  - Reconstruction
  - Segregation
  - Black Nationalism
  - Integration
- Social Issues of the Day
- Asian Americans
- Hispanic Latino Americans
- Sexism
- Disabilities
- Elderly
- Immigration
- Marriage
  - Interracial Marriage
  - LGBT Rights Including Same-Sex Marriages
- Summary
  - References

INTRODUCTION

The history of the United States is replete with progress, errors, setbacks, more progress, more errors and the context of this sentence could continue with the setbacks and progress. However, one thing with which the United States can be credited is as a nation it has recognized its mistakes and has made valid attempts to correct them. Some of the efforts have taken considerable time, efforts, and human emotions to correct mistakes and develop a balance where a majority of its population can be relatively comfortable with the results. In some respects one could refer to the United States efforts as an attempt to strike a reasonable human relationship balance for the majority of its citizens and human inhabitants.

The United States of America, like all countries, is not a perfect union and in some respects it is a living experiment with attempts to develop a society that is as perfect as human beings can create perfection. To accomplish this difficult task (if possible of reaching a perfect society), the United States and its citizens and others are constantly evaluating life to determine if its societies are treating its inhabitants in ways that are fair, and in manners where hopefully the majority (if not all), of its inhabitants can live peaceful, happy and productive lives.

In this experiment of life the United States of America, as well as other countries which allow and encourage its citizens to freely express themselves, through the years have made some decisions that please some people and displeased others. In some cases this is understandable; however, with closer examination of some of the decisions, it becomes clear that mistakes were made. In a democracy the majority rules, and in some instances significant portions of the population affected by decisions were not allowed equal representation and contributions of their views. In fairness, in most instances as a result of the population's efforts to be fair, the United States has recognized many of its mistakes and made corrections which have given disenfranchised populations greater access to opportunities to which they previously were excluded.

The United States (as is true for most if not all free and progressive societies), is constantly involved in issues which those on one side believe certain actions will make the nation a more equal, fair and progressive society in which to live. Other members of the populace believe that some of the issues, if they become legal and/or accepted, will

lower the nation's integrity and negatively affect the country's standard of living.

In this chapter of *The Professional Helper*, I will discuss some of the
problems that inhabitants of the United States have experienced and
what has been done to correct wrongs. Additionally, I will present to
the readers of this text what this author believes are some of the major
issues that the United States of America will have to address and/or
continue to address, and make significant decisions with regard to
those issues. Stated in more succinct terms, what will the future of the
United States look like as a result of the ways certain questions and issues are addressed? In the discussion it will become clear that professional helpers will be involved in analyzing issues and promoting responses as well as helping guide actions that will provide solutions to
these issues.

It is the contention of this author that there will be numerous professionals involved in helping evaluate and guide the nation though issues such as immigrations, women's rights, same sex marriages, working with persons who have a disability, race relations, mental health,
unemployment, obesity, ageism, poverty, and a variety of other social
issues, to mention only a few. Regardless of the educational background of the professional helper all will have to be trained and sensitive to the needs of those with whom they are attempting to help.
While this part of the second edition is primarily devoted to discussion
of the social and psychologically trained professional helper, the author recognizes that many other types of professionally trained helpers
will, and most likely be involved in the helping process. As previously stated this text concentrates on professionally trained social and psychologically trained professionals. However, many of the characteristics discussed will apply to other professionally trained persons. Additionally, while speaking of professionally trained persons, this does not
mean the helper has to be trained at a master's and/or doctoral degree
level. Advanced degrees do not guarantee competence, and because
professional education is important and very helpful, certain other
skills are equally important and several will be discussed. What is discussed with regard to being an effective professional helper can apply
to various levels of professional training.

As the United States makes transitions in various human relationships, the professional helper should be center stage in assisting with
insuring that we as a country have learned from past mistakes and

apply that knowledge to better managing current and upcoming relationships. Wise helping professionals will have learned from past relations and utilize the wisdom gained from these past actions and events, thus avoiding making similar mistakes in helping develop progressive and positive human relations that will help society develop and manage more equitable relationships among the populous.

In any society (the United States being no exception), people group together based upon like interests and develop common goals, and too often some of those goals have components of selfishness designed to promote narrow interests which cause exclusion of others whom they view as not advancing their interests and ideas. A major role of helping professionals will be to assist in bringing together the goals and needs of various interest groups so that the majority benefit rather than a selected few. This bringing together approach requires helping professionals to understand many of the needs and motivations of stakeholders concerns, and skillfully bring together opposing views "to the discussion table" so that each group better understands each others motivations and motives. This type of "meeting of the minds," realistically will not solve all problems, however, it will provide for better understanding of each groups motivations and if not able to get all parties to agree, they will have better understanding of why there are disagreements.

It is this author's opinion that helping professions will and should play major roles in helping shape future human relationships in the twenty-first century. If we do not assume those roles, selfish interest groups will continue to dominate human relationships in the United States, and as in past history, some groups will not have equal input into the development of the nation. If this continues to be the case, the majority of the population will be negatively affected by actions put forth by a minority of the population.

The following topics: race relations, sexism, persons with disabilities, elderly, immigration, marriage and sexual preferences (LGBT) will be briefly discussed. In these discussions a brief historical view will be presented to display past views and actions, which will be followed by suggestions of what needs to be done, and how helping professionals fit into helping develop solutions to these issues as well as be of assistance to those that are impacted by actions both overt and covert.

RACE RELATIONS

No country and/or government has a perfect human relations record with all of its inhabitants, and certainly this is the case with regard to the United States government. In past years there was separation of various races which was supported by laws. African Americans were legally not allowed in many states to eat in the same facilities as Caucasian, they were not allowed to attend the same public schools, and they were only allowed to ride in the back of public transportation, which was in part or completely supported by taxpayer monies of which African Americans contributed to paying these taxes. American Indians who owned America before European settlement were driven from their lands and restricted to where they could live and to a large extent how they could live. Women of all races were treated as second class citizens and women of color were treated as less than second-class citizens. Treatment of American Indians, the enslavement of Africans, and the disregard of civil rights for African Americans, and the exploration of immigrants are a few of the disregards of fair and equal treatment that some minorities have encountered in the United States.

A fair question to be asked is why I discuss these and other issues, and the answer is: 1. Not everyone is aware of the depth of discrimination that existed in the United States. Many persons, especially younger Americans never experienced discrimination and second-class citizenship, however, they see some of the effects such as high unemployment, poverty, gang violence, etc., and they wonder where does this anger originate? 2. The hurt is deep. To be more specific, many people continue to be impacted by discrimination which occurred many years ago, as well as discrimination that is occurring today that stems from past behaviors and beliefs.

Therefore, a brief history of past race relations with some of the American ethnic minorities will be discussed. Past human relations is being discussed to establish a baseline for identifying where we were so we can discuss where we presently are, and project where we will be in the short-term future if certain actions are taken. Hopefully, by providing this information, current and future helping professionals will better understand the need for their assistance in helping insure equal opportunities for all Americans. I will begin with America's first people, the American Indians, next will be African Americans, followed by Asian Americans, and Hispanic Latinos.

AMERICAN INDIANS

When the first European made contact with a portion of what is now the United States of America, there were more than 300 tribes of Indians, each having its own form of government, living as what we might consider independent nations. As a result of this contact, the independence was to come to an end for most Native tribes. Richardson (1981) correctly points out that the Native population has been dramatically decreased as a result of two things—disease and wars.

A major percentage of the decrease in population can be attributed to the European introduction of diseases such as diphtheria, smallpox, measles, chickenpox, influenza, scarlet fever, malaria, typhus and typhoid fever. All of which Indians has no immunity. The death toll from these diseases and others was so great that American Indian historian Susan Harjo (1988) has labeled it as one of the greatest natural catastrophes of all times. Her assessment, at least for the American Indian's as well as this author's standpoint is accurate.

The other major event that added to the decimation of the Indian population was wars which generally speaking were fought as a result of the Europeans attempting to seize the Native's land. Susan Harjo (1988) provides an excellent overview of what has happened to the Native Americans' land base:

> The Indian land base has gone from 138 million acres in 1887 to approximately 50 million acres today. There are many reasons for land loss, including flooding for Corps of Engineer projects, creation of national monuments, taking of land for tax defaults and welfare payment, invalidation of wills, and Bureau of Indian Affairs (BIA) forced sales on the open market. The 1917 Allotment Act or Dawes Act alone resulted in the loss of more than half the Indian land. Of the 48 million acres left after the Allotment Act took its toll, 20 million acres were desert or semiarid and not suitable for cultivation. The federal government promised to irrigate these lands and "to make the deserts bloom." For most of these arid reservations, this promise remains unfulfilled.

The Allotment Act allocated land on reservations that had been guaranteed by treaties. Every family head was to receive 160 acres and a single person 80 acres. The idea was that Indians should become farmers and thereby become more civilized. This notion of farming was not well received by many tribes and was particularly onerous to many Indians in the Great Plains. The land was to be held in trust for 25 years. Indians deemed "competent" by the federal government could end the trust status, own the land in fee simple, and become U.S. Citizens. Any land outside the allotted acreage was declared to be "excess' and sold to non-Indian settlers.

The relocation of Native Americans is without a doubt one of the most shameful acts forced upon any group of people. Thousands of people were removed from places and ways of living that were familiar to them and forced to adjust to environments and surroundings that were unfamiliar. Additionally, many were required to adopt a new lifestyle that was foreign to them. Perhaps the most familiar acts of relocation to Americans is the "Trail of Tears" where several Indian tribes were moved from the Southeast area of the United States to Oklahoma. During this move, thousands of Indians died and many more suffered debilitating illness.

Assimilation

Susan Harjo, identifies what she considers two major ways in which the goals of assimilation were to be programmed with Native Americans: (1) Allowing Christian groups to establish their denominations on Indian land to convert Indians to Christianity, thus getting them to forsake their religious beliefs and practices and various religious ceremonies which to many of the Euro-Americans were paganistic; (2) Imposing an educational system upon the children that had as its primary objective to instill non-Indian values. This was done through a boarding school system which required the children to be separated from their parents for up to twelve years. The children were forbidden to speak their tribal language or practice any of the tribal traditions. Parents and relatives were not allowed to visit the children during the school year. The boarding school staff impressed upon the children that their tribal traditions were savage. Blanchard (1983) says these deplorable efforts were attempts to "civilize" the children. Scholars Lowrey (1983), Josephy (1982, Blanchard (1983), and Kleinfeld and Bloom (1977) feel that this experience along with others, had a definite impact upon weakening the various Native American cultures. Federal efforts were made to break-up tribal land holdings and turn Indians into individual land owners, imposing taxes on their lands.

SOCIAL ISSUES

A major social issue for most Native American tribes has been and continues to be the regaining and/or maintenance of their cultures. If there is one common thread which weaves its way through all Native American tribes, it is a belief in harmony with mind, body, spirit, and mother earth. Most Native Americans view the earth as a living entity which has a spirit, thus, land is an important part of their cultural ways of life, as is their spiritual and religious ceremonies.

While there are other issues such as education, health care, living conditions and social discrimination to mention only four, these are some of the major issues that this author believes will be of significant concerns with regard to future treatment of American Indians. Stated in more succinct terms these are some of the major issues the United States will have to address within the next ten to fifteen years to provide American Indians their rights as full citizens of the United States of America. A major need is improvement in the health of many American Indians and Alaskan Natives. The following provides a very brief overview of health needs of American Indians and Alaskan Natives. As of this writing there are approximately four and one-half million American Indians and Alaskan Natives. Of these two groups 7.5% of births are considered low birth weight, this to some extent occur as a result of poor dietary habits often resulting from lack of sufficient foods and dietary education. Additional statistics indicate an estimate of 14.3% of American Indians and Alaskan Natives is in fair or poor health condition. Twenty-four percent of this ethnic group 18 years or older smoke cigarettes, both male and females. The death rate per 100, 00 is 382.5 percent, significantly higher than the average for other ethnic groups. The leading causes of death for the two previously mentioned groups are heart disease, cancer, and accidents. Other statistics of interest are: Injuries 94.5 per 100.000 compared to the United States all races 39.2%. Diabetes 61.0 per 100. 000 compared to United States all races 22.0%. Suicide, 18.5% per 100.000 compared to United States all races. Tuberculosis, 11.6%. Five time higher than for non-Hispanic whites.

PROGRESS MADE

In this author's opinion there is a need for many, if not most non-American Indians to have a better and more realistic understanding of American Indians rights and needs. There is a perception that all American Indians receive "free money," to be more specific, the belief is they receive checks from the United States government. The reality is some do receive money from the United States government, however, often the money they receive from the government is payment for royalty for minerals, and/or oil extracted from their land. Another myth is that most, if not all, American Indians receive considerable money from gaming operations. It is true that in some parts of the United States some American Indian tribes own and operate gaming operations, but what many do not know is that part, if not a considerable amount of the proceeds is used to repair and upkeep of roads, bridges and other infrastructure that benefits all citizens in that area. Additionally, some of the proceeds from gaming is used by tribes to provide education, health care and other resources needed by their tribal members. Finally, it is this authors opinion that if all of the money, which it does not, goes directly to tribal member and/or investors, that is the American way. Fortune five hundred companies use their proceeds as they choose, and very little if any discussion is made with regard to the way they utilize their resources.

One of the most significant progress that has been made by some tribes is the recognition that they are the masters of their fate, stated in other terms, many tribes have diligently worked to improve tribal schools, health services and their overall identity. These and other efforts have instilled increased pride in their lives, and ways of living their lives. They (as some other ethnic minorities) have looked at the struggles of their ancestors and realize the physical, mental and emotional strengths of their forefathers and mothers. This realization has built additional strength and pride in their ways of life, and is providing additional encouragement to continue to leave a legacy for future generations.

With regard to helping professionals, a major need is for more trained helping professionals with American Indian backgrounds. As American Indians are increasingly taking control of their daily lives and future prospects, there is a need for helping professionals who are very sensitive to the needs and potentials of American Indian tribes and American Indian individuals. To be more specific, more teachers, counselors, researchers, and other professionals sensitive to the needs and desires of American Indian people are needed to continue the progress that has occurred. Additionally, there is a need for persons of Native American origin and others to help keep young generations of American Indians motivated to maintain Indian pride and serve as motivating forces to make all people of the United States more aware of the contributions of American Indians, and the tremendous potential of American's first people.

AFRICAN AMERICANS

From a historical perspective this author (in previous publications) has divided African American's issues into the following areas: Slavery (1619-1865), Reconstruction (1865-1877), Segregation (1877-1964), Black Nationalism (1930-1964), Integration (1964 to present). Therefore, a brief overview of each will be provided to identify a historical perspectives of issues that will serve as background information for needed changes in the near future of human relations with African Americans.

Slavery

The purpose of slavery in America is clear, that being to provide inexpensive and steady, controlled labor forces to work the fields, shops, and homes of the owners. Meager as the efforts were, questions can be raised as to the cheapness of feeding, clothing, housing, and the occasional medical care of slaves. Slavery to their owners had one major advantage that made the institution more desirable than employing persons for wages–the ability to control the work force. Slavery did not allow for demands of higher wages and work stoppage if the demands were not met. Slavery was never intended to be an on-the-job training program; therefore, the impact was as emotionally and psychologically devastating as the practice was cruel. The emotional and psychological cost to the slaves were so severe that the impact has been felt by generations of their offspring. Additionally, the impact has affected the entire nation of American citizens in various ways. Some of the major impacts upon the slaves and their generations to follow are: (a) labeled as inferior, (b) branded as immoral, (c) stereotyped as unable to be educated, and (d) deprived of normal family relationships.

Reconstruction

With the end of slavery in 1865, persons who had been enslaved were legally free. While freedom had long been the dream of African Americans who were not free, it was unfortunate that most were not prepared to live as free individuals. They knew how to farm but most were not knowledgeable of the ways of economically managing a farm, and if they had possessed the management tools they would have had difficulty implementing them, because (as result of the Civil War) much of the infrastructure of the Southern states had been destroyed. In short, if they were able to raise crops, how would they market them? These were some of the conditions that the period of reconstruction began for persons who had been considered slaves. It is true that promises of land and livestock had been made, but very few saw those promises become reality. Instead of being a period of time when the Southern states were rebuilt and persons who had previously been enslaved were being prepared to live lives free from discrimination and intimidation, selfish intentions and greedy-minded persons chose to use the situation for their benefits.

Instead of being helped to develop property management skills, selfish and violent groups such as the Ku Klux Klan (KKK) as well as other white supremacy groups, killed, maimed, and intimidated former slaves and anyone who chose to help them. These and other activities to a large extent brought to an end the experiment of reconstruction of the South.

Segregation

As the southern politics and other day-to-day activities returned to the control of the former land owners, two things high on their agendas were to insure that the ex-slaves were powerless, and that there was complete separation of the black and white races as much as possible. The impact of these decision was to last for many years and to a considerable extent continues to play a role in the daily lives of many African Americans today. Some of the measures taken were: (a) denial of the right of African Americans to vote in the former Confederate states: (b) segregated public school systems with the black schools inadequately funded; (c) segregated public and private facilities such as denying African Americans the right to dine in facilities where whites dined and separate restroom facilities to mention a couple; (d) the denial of African Americans the right to purchase homes wherever they could afford; (e) the denial of the right to worship wherever one desired; (f) the basic denial of free speech; and (g) relegation to menial tasks and receiving lower salaries than their white counterparts.

In fairness to the southern states, it must be noted that African Americans were to some degree denied these same right in virtually every state of the Union. It was the Southern states that most vigorously and aggressively promoted and practiced these discrimination.

Black Nationalism

The idea that some African Americans had was to separate themselves from America, escape racial prejudice, and racial violence by removing themselves from American soil. The thought was if they were not going to be accepted into American society and be treated as first-class citizens, they should separate themselves from mainstream America. It is important to note that the idea of separating from the United States was only one of the approaches, and perhaps represented the most extreme effort to extricate themselves from prejudice and bigotry. The approaches were put forth by Marcus Garvey, and he promoted the idea of African Americans returning to Africa. Mr. Garvey had very limited success with his concept in that he had very few persons that bought into his ideas. The period of Black Nationalism occurred during a portion of the period of segregation where there were attempts—and most were successful—with regard to keeping

African Americans and Caucasians separated in the school systems, including colleges and universities, churches, recreational facilities, housing, eating establishments, and medical facilities to mention only a few.

Integration

A major reason the National philosophy and law of racial segregation was defeated, as the social policy of the United States, was because socially enlighten Caucasians and strong-willed African Americans took strong publically visible stands denouncing racial segregation.

The National Association for the Advancement of Colored People (NAACP) legal defense fund led by Thurgood Marshall was successful in winning the *Brown vs. Topeka Board of Education* decision which was the beginning of the end of segregated school systems. Through marches, sit-ins, demonstrations, work stoppages, and refusing to shop at the segregated facilities and ride city buses, segregated facilities were integrated.

SOCIAL ISSUES OF THE DAY

Certainly much has been accomplished toward reducing the inequality that exists between African Americans and Euro-Americans. Laws and attitudinal changes have accounted for much of the progress. However, despite this progress inclusion and equality remains a major social issue.

Equality struggles have been a hallmark of African American existence in America. While the efforts have met with some degree of success, such as access to improved educational opportunities, advancements in employment and personal security, the difficulties of the struggles coupled with the slow pace of progression, has been attributed as a reason for some of the unresolved social issues. Issues such as inequality in employment opportunities, and inequality in salary, to mention only two inequalities related to employment.

Additional social needs which helping professionals must continue to be involved are: violence, some of which comes from frustration regarding lack of adequate employment that provides sufficient income to support legal attempts at improving one's life. In this regard, helping professionals are needed to assist youth and additional age groups of African Americans with appropriate training and education that will qualify them for higher paying jobs. Education is one of the keys to some, if not many, of the problems African Americans encounter. Education, whether it is trade school or college/university education is one of the keys to improving one's life situation. This author is not unmindful of the fact that advanced trade school or college diplomas are of little use to the prospective employee if they will not be hired, or if they are hired and their pay is not equal to others with similar training and experience. To be more specific, if the persons is not hired at levels for which he/she is prepared, one of the things that occur is frustration and distrust in society and its promises of good education and training that led to good employment. Therefore, helping professionals must go beyond encouraging African Americans to seek exemplary training and education, they must help those persons who need such help, in obtaining some of their dreams. Stated in other terms, employers and American society in general have to be educated with the fact that if we want a better American society we must be fair and honest with regard to employing African Americans and after employment being fair with regard to salary and promotions.

ASIAN AMERICANS

A major concept that many Americans have with regard to Asian Americans is: (a) they are well educated, (b) they have significant monetary resources, and (c). Most Asian's are all alike. With regard to being well educated, this is similar to saying that all African Americans are good athletes and/or good singers. There is no question that many, if not most Asian's value education and this value is instilled in the youth at an early age. This value for education does in many cases translate into doing well in school including college, which often lead to good jobs. This is particularly true for some Japanese, Chinese, and Korean Americans. The problem with this broad brush stroke classifying all Asian Americans as well educated assumes that all Asian Americans are well educated and have lucrative paying jobs. This is not the case. Asian Americans are similar to other ethnic groups with regard to education and types of jobs they attain, some have good educational backgrounds and are employed in well-paying jobs, however, this is not true for all Asian Americans. Two points need to be made, first, there are more Asian American people than Japanese, Chinese and Korean who may not be as fortunate as the previously mentioned three Asian American groups to have educational degrees from prestigious colleges and universities as well as degrees in educational fields that pay significantly higher wages than what some may consider average income. The second point to be made is that many well educated and trained Asian Americans do not receive income that coincided with their education and training.

The previous point of income not coinciding with level of education and training is one of the reasons some Asian Americans are not as wealthy as many may think. The question becomes, are they being discriminated because of their ethnicity, some will argue that this is a realistic assumption.

The final misperception with regard to Asian Americans this author will discuss is that all Asians are alike. The true fact is that there are numerous Asian Americans other than Japanese, Chinese and Korean and I will mention only a few: Vietnamese Americans, Filipino Americans, Cambodian Americans, Hmong Americans, Thai Americans, and Laotian Americans. These and other Asian Americans are similar to other ethnic groups in America in that some are well educated and financially successful, and others within their groups are not.

With regard to some roles for helping professionals begin with developing a better understanding of the cultures of each Asian American group with which they have contact. Each Asian American group are individual groups which may have very little in common with other Asian Americans specifically with regard to cultural issues, such as lifestyles, religious beliefs, educational standards, and beliefs with regard to family relationships to mention only four cultural issues. Another factor helping professionals must be aware is level of acculturation with regard to American lifestyles. Many Asian Americans have been born and reared in the United States, thus their level of acculturation may be comparable to most persons, regardless of ethnicity, who are born in the United States and have lived their entire life in this environment. Likewise, some may have been born and reared in the United States, but through their parents and other relatives and friends been taught the values of family members such as grandparents who either live in and have maintained "old country" traditions and beliefs.

With regard to acculturation and belief systems, helping professionals must be aware of religious beliefs, if any, that some Asian Americans have. Even though they may have lived in America all of their lives or a significant portion of their lives, they may have maintained and adhered to religious doctrines and beliefs of their native country or the native country, of their ancestors. These and other beliefs, especially social beliefs, health beliefs and respect for authority figures, to mention only three, may differ from what some skilled helping professionals have been taught and believe. Therefore, helping professionals must educate themselves with regard to belief systems, and lifestyles among others rather than always expecting the client to totally conform to American belief systems.

As a summary statement with regard to Asian Americans, I use the comments of Lee and Nolan (1998) with regard to the psychology of Asian Americans.

> Today's generation of young Asian Americans represents a wide spectrum of experiences and social classes. The Asian American identity of the 1960s and 1970s has been supplanted by a diverse collage of dramatically different philosophies and approaches to American life. With new ethnic groups and communities joining the fray, the Asian American narrative has become much more rich and complicated than ever before. p. 17

Although dated, this brief but succinct explanation remains true and perhaps more so than when it was written.

HISPANIC LATINO AMERICANS

Similar to Asian Americans there are several Hispanic Latino American groups in the United States; however, I will only discuss the three largest population groups: Mexican Americans, Puerto Rican Americans and Cuban Americans.

With the possible exception of Cubans, the migration of Hispanic Latinos to the United States has been an ebb and flow conditioned by the United States' need for cheap labor. For decades, Mexicans have been welcomed and encouraged to come to the states to help meet the labor demands of the country, only to find that they were equally unwelcome when the demand for their labor diminished. Similarly, Puerto Ricans have been attracted to the United States to meet some of the labor needs, especially in times when the Puerto Rican economy has had problems providing work for its willing population. Thus, poverty and discrimination have been major social problems at least for Mexicans and Puerto Ricans. According to the United States Commission on Civil rights, "Both Mexicans and Puerto Ricans have been victims of economic and social discrimination and prejudice, it appears that Puerto Ricans have suffered even more intensely than any other group."

With regard to Cubans, since much of their entry into the United States has been in waves, there are considerable economic and social differences among the United States' Cuban population. The group of Cuban immigrants who came to America fleeing the Castro government were more affluent and well educated, therefore, they experienced fewer problems integrating into Euro-American society. Experiencing less discrimination and prejudice than many of the groups to follow has meant their social plight has been less traumatic.

The proximity of the Mexican American border makes for relatively easy access to the United States thus frequently resulting in considerable discussion with Mexican nationals who attempt to enter the United States seeking increased opportunities for themselves and their families. A variety of opinions among United States citizens exist with regard to the entry of undocumented Mexicans. Some feel that they are taking jobs and resources that should be reserved for United States citizens, and others believe the United States should be compassionate and offer opportunities to those seeking to improve their lives.

With regard to the issues that helping professionals must be made aware: the first and perhaps most important is that many Hispanic Latino persons (even though they are grouped into one category), in many instances, the only thing (other than being human beings) they have in common is the Spanish language. Even the Spanish language is not always a common thread because some Hispanic persons, especially younger generations, who have lived in the United States all their lives may not speak or read Spanish. The point being made is that each of the three groups previously mentioned as well as other

Hispanic Latino persons must be viewed as individuals and treated as such.

Several things that helping professionals who work with or plan to work with Hispanic Latino persons must be aware are: (a). As previously mentioned being aware of level of acculturation. According to Casas and Vasquez (1996) "Depending on level of acculturation, Hispanics often display a great concern for immediacy and the "here and now" (as opposed to a more teleological orientation in Anglo-American cultures) p. 164. (b). Understand their belief systems. Frequently attribute control to an external locus (causality replaced by luck, supernatural power and acts of God); favor an extended family support system rather than a basic adherence to the nuclear family; often take a concrete tangible approach to life, rather than an abstract, long-term outlook, p. 164. (c). Understand societal forces which influence them. Casas and Vasquez address this point with the following comment, "There is no way to understand and counsel a Hispanic client, or any client, without assessing cultural factors as well as the individual's experience of oppression, p. 165.

SEXISM

Sexism can refer to male or female; however, I am referring to women's rights. Throughout the history of the United States, women have been treated as the lesser gender, however, the facts are that women have been as much a part of the development of the United States as men. In early American history most women may not have been on the battlefield with men; however, they have played many roles, such as keeping home and hearth functioning, and working in industries when there were shortages of men because of wars. Additionally, during the agrarian period of the United States many women worked long and strenuous hours in fields to keep the farms going and profitable, and to help feed the nation. This fact remains true today in areas of the United States where farming and ranching are strong standards of living. There are many other contributions both large and small that could be discussed, however, the point has been made that women have made significant contributions to building the United States as a world leader and the most powerful nation in the world.

Despite their contributions to the building of the nation, women have (in past years) been treated, at best, as second-class citizens, and denied the right to vote until 1920. For decades women, if they were married, were not allowed to own property and most everything they had and could have was legally dependent upon their husband.

Regardless of their accomplishments and contributions to the building of America as it currently exists, women were, and continue to be considered the weaker sex. In this context, early American society, as well as most other nations, have treated women as not being equal to men. In addition to the perceived inherent weakness, women were and to a major extent today considered fragile, unable not only to match the physical prowess of men, but also overly sensitive and unable to withstand the pressures of leadership. Given the fact women are the childbearers, it is often felt and believed that their natural role in life is nurturing. Nurturing not only consists of caring for the children, it includes caring for the home and husband. Therefore, the pedestal upon which many women (particularly Euro-American women), were placed, some social scientists as well as feminists have described it as being built to help the males, maintain their dominance over women. Stated in other terms, by characterizing women as the ones who must have the protection of males and by describing the nurturing role as one that could only be done by or at least best be accomplished by females, women have been kept in an inferior and dependent condition with relationship to men.

In the work environment women, as of this writing, earn approximately seventy-seven cents to each dollar a male earns. Women are beginning to gradually crack the euphemistic glass ceiling, which means more and more women are being hired in positions of significant authority. Although this improvement in human relations is long overdue the fact remains, women in many parts of American society continue to not be treated on an equal basis of men. However, domestic relations are gradually changing, men in the United States are beginning to assume home domestic responsibilities with their wives, such as assisting with child care. This is opening opportunities for women to not only secure meaningful employment, but also giving them opportunities to advance in their chosen careers.

The roles that helping professionals can and should be involved with regard to assisting women:

1. Advocate with women. I have phrased this as advocate with women, not for women because they are able to take on this task themselves; however, they can, and will enjoy the assistance. Some of the advocacies relates to wages that commensurate with their abilities, training, and performance. I state this in such a manner because I don't think the advocacy should be for wages equal to men, rather the wages should be based upon skills, training, and motivation which means their wages could be beyond the average wage of males.
2. Advocate with women for control of their bodies. It is this author's opinion that in situations of abortions, and health issues (to mention only two), if the woman is mentally and emotionally capable of making decisions she should have the last word on such actions. This does not mean that a husband, or significant other male figure should not be consulted; however, the woman should have the final word.
3. Assist women in making decisions with regard to child care. This point has several dimensions such as adoptions, previously mentioned abortions, and sexual procedures which may impact childbearing.
4. Counseling with regard to career choices and how to attain same.
5. Marriage and family issues.
6. Religious issues, if the helper is qualified in this area. In fact, being appropriately qualified is a prerequisite for assisting in any of the previously mentioned areas.

DISABILITIES

Persons with disabilities are the most diverse group of humans on this planet. They are represented in every ethnic racial group as well as persons of both genders and all sexual persuasion. Persons with disabilities are members of every economic strata that exist. In summary, persons with disabilities is part of every aspect of societies that exist. It is estimated that in the United States persons with disabilities make up one-fifth of the population and worldwide no one knows the percentage. It is this author's contention that everyone has some disability, it is a matter of how one defines a disability. Certainly, part of any definition of disability is limitations and everyone has some limitations; therefore whether one has a disability is dependent upon how one defines disability.

Treatment of persons with disabilities range from overprotection designed to protect them from harm to extermination. Because of the range of emotions with regard to persons with disabilities perceived worth to society, many persons with disabilities are often confused with regard to how they fit into societies. Too often they are treated with pity rather than offered opportunities to be as self-sufficient as their physical, emotional and/or psychological situation will allow.

Throughout human history persons with disabilities had to endure a variety of treatments ranging from being treated as persons to be protected to persons to be eliminated. Some of the first persons eliminated in Adolph Hitler's attempt of cultural cleansing were persons with disabilities. Although his efforts did take the lives of many persons with disabilities in Germany, his murderous efforts to eliminate all persons did not succeed. However, what he attempted along with other efforts such as Eugenics, is a reminder how disabilities are viewed by some.

There are numerous things persons with disabilities need; however, one is not sympathy and paternalism. What many persons with disabilities need is advocacy. To be more specific what persons with disabilities need is persons to advocate with them. The following, by no means, is a complete list of advocacy needs, but they are listed to make the point of some of the ways helping professionals can be of assistance to persons with disabilities:

1. More and better employment.
2. Better understanding of capabilities of persons with disabilities.
3. Better education and understanding of children with intellectual disabilities.
4. Adequate public transportation so they can secure and reach employment sites.
5. Better understanding of persons with emotional disabilities. This one includes more research into some of the causes of emotional problems.
6. Better understanding of children with intellectual disabilities. It is this author's belief that the identification of intellectual disabilities

is not the child or adult's problem, the problem is psychology and education has not identified and learned the full range of how humans learn. Therefore, there is a significant need for more research with regard to the many dimensions of learning.

7. More empathic treatment of persons diagnosed with mental and emotional disabilities which includes housing for persons with mental and emotional disabilities.

At this point I think it is appropriate to have a note from this author, who has a disability, and the note is that persons with disabilities have to step forward, as they did in the development and push for the Americans with Disabilities Act of 1990 and demand more opportunities. The following comments by Eisenberg (1982) succinctly captures the essences of persons with disabilities taking charge of their lives and being the leading advocate for their rights.

> Disabled people have in part bought into our society's value system of pronouncing everything young, beautiful, healthy, and vigorous as being "good" and everything at variance to this norm as being "bad." They are, therefore, partially responsible for the current situation in which they find themselves. There are, however, a number of things they can do to help remediate the problem. Certainly they can continue to agitate for additional enforceable legal proscriptions to combat the discrimination they face. Although the Rehabilitation Act of 1973 has provided a foundation on which meaningful progress can be made in the fight for equality, there has been a marked reluctance on the part of both individuals and city, county, state, and indeed federal legislators and bureaucrats to live up to the intended spirit of the law. Another way the disabled can achieve equality is through increased contact with the able-bodied and by providing them with information about disability. p. 9–10.

Some of what has been stated is dated, given some of the Federal legislation that has been enacted since the previously mentioned writing. The fact remains that if further progress is to be made it is, to a large degree, the responsibility of persons with disabilities to make society aware of their needs. Who better to do this than the persons most affected?

These are only a few of the needs of persons with disabilities. The listing and many others not listed is an indication that helping professionals with appropriate training and education can help make a significant difference in the lives of many persons with disabilities.

ELDERLY

When is a person considered elderly? What are the conditions that causes a person to be elderly? As the life expectancy of persons in the United States continues to increase and many of these persons remain active, the question of when is a person elderly becomes a valid point of discussion. The lack of agreement with regard to what constitutes an elderly person emphasizes that in many instances aging is a state of mind. There cannot be any questions that aging involves physiological and psychological changes; however, there are persons who have lived over sixty years and have fewer physiological deficits than someone half their age. Relatedly, it is not difficult to identify persons who are sixty years of age who have been rendered physically and/or mentally incapable of carrying out normal activities of daily living by the aging process.

According to the U. S. Census Bureau, the United States' population sixty-five years and older is over 40 million and is projected to increase to over 72 million by the year 2030. It is further projected by senior citizens research groups that by year 2030 the number of citizens over the age of 85 will experience a dramatic increase and 40% of the United State population will be over the age of 50. An obvious conclusion that can be extracted from the previously mentioned statistics is that Americans are living longer and this trend will continue for a significant period of time.

One of the cultural impacts of Americans living longer and hopefully productive lives is the desire and quite likely the need to be employed longer. Stated in other terms, senior persons in the United States will want to and expect to continue to be employed beyond the age of sixty-five. This need of senior citizens and quite likely demands of the same group will have a double-edge impact upon the American society. The first impact will be that the United States workforce will benefit from the years of experience that the seniors have developed as productive members of the workforce. The second impact will be because the seniors are working several and/or many more years than past generations of workers, fewer higher paying jobs will not be available to younger workers, employees under the age of forty, and an additional impact is that possibly few higher level management positions will be available to younger workers. This last fact could be considered reverse ageism.

The fact that the lifespan in the United States has increased and likely will continue to increase, does not diminish roles of helping professionals. Financial helping professionals' roles will increase because workers will need expert advice on preparing financially for eventual retirement. One may say that this has always been a role for financial helping professionals, this is true, but a major difference will be that the role will increase. In past years as well as currently, many, if not most financial helping professionals worked with high income earners, and a difference and a benefit of being able to work longer is that many of the average workers will, with good professional advice, be able to pay off mortgages and other debts, therefore, they could have additional money to invest for retirement. This is the area where professional financial advisers will be able to be of valuable assistance.

Another role for helping professionals with regard to the elderly is assisting them with regard to planning for meaningful retirement. This goes beyond having enough money to retire, this role involves assisting the retirees with having a meaningful life beyond work. For many persons, when one works thirty or forty years one's employment often becomes a major part of his/her life, if not the center of life. One's day-to-day activities often are influenced by his/her employment. Stated in other terms, one's life is centered on employment. Vacations are dictated by when you can take same as well as how long one can have vacation time. Often where one lives and how one lives is, in large part, determined by employment. When one retires, this will change. One is no longer inhibited by the employment clock. Therefore, professional helpers can be of great assistance with regard to assisting the retiree with making decisions relevant to the rest of his/her life. Part of this decision will include living arrangements. To be more specific, assistance with making decisions such as, "since we no longer have children at home and we no longer have employment concerns do we need the type of home we have? What are we going to do with the extra free time? What will we do to maintain a feeling of being useful?" These are only a few areas of concern that helping professionals can be of assistance.

Schlossberg (1984) provides some valuable advice to helping professionals with regard to assisting adults in transition:

> Adults in transition are often confused and in need of assistance. Adults can identify the issues which concern them—for example, being "burned out," divorced, having to change jobs. These issues often relate to the ability to love, work, and play. If these adults can explore the issue more fully, understanding its underlying meaning, and develop a plan, they will eventually be able to cope effectively and resolve the problem.
>
> Friends, coworkers, and professional and paraprofessional helpers can learn about issues of major concern to most adults, listen to the adult in transition in a way that facilitates exploration, provide a framework so that the adult in transition can better understand his or her situation, and, finally, influence the adult to cope more creatively. Basically, the helper, friend, or colleague can approach any issue which is brought up by thinking, can I help him or her explore the problem more fully, understand the issue in all its complexity, and resolve it creatively?
>
> To help adults explore, understand, and cope, helpers need to increase their knowledge of communications skills, counseling skills, and adult development. Further, they need to integrate this knowledge. That is, helpers need to be able to weave in skills and knowledge at each phase of helping—whether it is exploring why the individual can or cannot love, work, or play; understanding the underlying reason for the issue; or developing strategies to cope more effectively with life. p. 2.

Doctor Schlossberg has provided some excellent advice to helping professionals as they work with adults making life transitions. Transitions, if handled properly, can mean the differences between being happy or in a state of despair.

IMMIGRATION

A review of American history will document that in part the development of American society has been built as a result of persons immigrating to the United States. History will also document that various foreign groups have played significant roles in development of the United States economy and physical structure. Japanese, Chinese and Korean immigrants were responsible for helping develop the agricultural structure of the United States. Although African slaves did not come to the United States as willing immigrants, there can be no argument or doubt that they were significant contributors to the development of Southern states. For many past years as well as currently, Mexicans and South Americans have come to the United States to better their lives and in the process have significantly contributed to the economic development of the United States. Therefore, immigration has been a vital force in developing the United States as a world leader in many areas from agriculture to outer space development.

Currently, there is significant discussion, debate and disgust with regard to immigration coming, primarily from Mexico and South America. There is no question that some of the disgust relate to the fact that some of the illegal immigrants coming to America for less than honorable reasons. However, there also is no question that a significant number of persons from the previously mentioned countries come seeking better lives for themselves and their families. This added to the fact that to a significant degree much of America was aided by the efforts and ingenuity of immigrants.

The purpose of this discussion is not to debate the rights and wrongs of immigration, the purpose is to discuss some roles helping professionals can assume with regard to assisting immigrants, the following are only a few: (a). Understanding of United States laws. (b). Securing employment. (c). Assisting with English, when and if needed. (d). Assisting with housing. (e). Advocating for fair and just employment. To be more specific, assisting with avoiding exploration. (f). Securing appropriate education. (g). Advocates for their legal rights.

MARRIAGE

Interracial Marriage

Marriage for many years in the United States has been defined as a legal union between a male and female. For a significant number of years there was an exception to the previous mentioned definition that being for a number of states it was illegal for Caucasian and African American to marry. For many years in the United States there were taboos with regard to what was called "race mixing." This meant interracial dating and marriage primarily between African Americans and Caucasians, and to a lesser degree American Indians and Caucasians was viewed with disdain. In fact, it was not until 1967 that the United States Supreme Court ruled in *Loving v. Virginia* that state's bans on interracial marriage violated the Fourteenth Amendment of the U. S. Constitution. The following is a brief background with regard to actions which precipitated the *Loving v. Virginia case.* Richard Loving, a Caucasian male, and Mildred Jeter, an African American female, were reared in the state of Virginia, they fell in love, went to Washington, DC and married. After their marriage, they returned to Virginia to carry forward their lives as husband and wife, however, the state of Virginia had different plans and arrested them for breaking the state law against interracial marriage. They were found guilty and were given jail sentences, but the sentence was suspended upon the condition that they leave the state of Virginia for twenty-five years. These conditions were accepted by Mr. and Mrs. Loving and they moved to Washington, DC. At some point in their exile from the state of Virginia, they returned to the state for a visit and they were again arrested. This led to a lawsuit against the State of Virginia which eventually resulted in the previously mentioned Supreme Court decision that declared the ban on interracial marriage violated the United States' Constitution's Fourteenth Amendment. This ruling overturned an 1883 Supreme Court ruling, *Pace v. Alabama*, which stated that state's bans on interracial marriages did not violate the Fourteenth Amendment.

Although not all states had bans on interracial marriages, the reality is until the late 1960s, and through most, if not all, of the 1980s, there were considerable resentment toward what was called race mixing, which is evident in the civil rights struggles of the 1970s and 1980s where considerable resentment occurred with regard to African American students attending school with Caucasian students as well as African Americans eating in, and resting in establishments that were considered for "whites only."

Lesbian, Gay, Bisexual and Transgender Rights Including Same-Sex Marriages

Some have identified the rights of lesbian, gay, bisexual and transgender persons as the civil rights struggle of the twenty-first century.

Lovett (2013) in the following comments succulently frames this rights issue as a civil rights struggle.

> Throughout history in the United States there have been many struggles of individual's rights who are by someone's definition not as equal. The struggles have been tragic in so many ways and in all ways they were unnecessary because these struggles were for each individual living here in the United States to have the basic human rights that should be given to all; the right of life, liberty and the pursuit of happiness. This sentence does not have a 'but' or 'only' if you believe like the majority or act like the majority. It is a right that should be given to all. It seems that over the many years of struggles and horrible tragedies as a nation we still have not learned anything.

Much of the objections to gay rights are based on religious/moral grounds. Some objections are based upon belief that having sexual relations with someone of the same gender is simply immoral and many of those that make this proclamation use the Christian Holy Bible as their main source as documentation of the inappropriateness of this behavior. Whether one subscribes to this type of objection is a personal belief and those that disagree with using the Bible as justification for their belief can point to the fact that in years past some persons justified enslaving and separating persons based upon their racial classification on words in the Bible. Additionally, some may point out the fact that the Holy Bible speaks against strong drink, commonly referred to as intake of alcohol beverages, however, the sale of and consumption of alcohol is legal in the United States. Others justify objection of gay rights based upon what they believe–nature never intended for persons of the same gender to marry and/or have intimate sexual relations.

The issue of same-sex marriage in the United States is one of the major civil rights issues of the twenty-first century. Therefore, as helping professionals were involved in helping solve some of the civil rights issues of the twentieth century which included interracial marriage, they should and will be involved in helping solve the current issue of same-sex marriage. As was the case in interracial marriage, helping professionals were on both sides of the debate, and I am sure there will be similar stances taken in this twenty-first century debate.

SUMMARY

Just as the United States has made cultural evolutions in areas of race relations, rights of women, and disabilities (to mention only three), the nation is involved in or will soon be involved in cultural evolutions of several social issues. As with the cases for previous evolutions, helping professionals and their expertise in understanding human nature will need to be at the forefront of helping the nation navigate through difficult issues.

Chapter Review Questions

1. Why were African Americans not allowed to eat in same facilities as Caucasians? Why is it important for helping professionals to know about this period in American history?
2. Who are considered the original Americans? What has been some of the impacts of this group's loss of land and other possessions, and how can this impact the helping relationship?
3. How can helping professionals assist minorities as they attempt to migrate to the United States to improve their lives?
4. How can helping professionals assist American women as they attempt to receive equal rights similar to American men?
5. What are some of the needs of persons with disabilities and how can helping professionals assist them in attaining same?
6. What are some of the major issues facing elderly Americans, and what can helping professional do to assist?
7. What are some of the major issues facing LGBT persons, and what roles and what environment should helping professionals play in those issues?

Mental Exercise

1. List, in your opinion, at least five current needs of some American Indians and what you as a helping professional can do to assist this group?
2. List, in your opinion, at least five current needs of African Americans and what you as a helping professional can do to assist this group?

3. List, in your opinion, at least five current needs of Asian Americans and what you as a helping professional can do to assist this group?

4. List, in your opinion, at least five current needs of Hispanic Latino Americans and what you as a helping professional can do to assist this group?

5. What does the term sexism mean to you, and what can you do to help eliminate discrimination based upon one's gender?

6. List, in your opinion, the top five needs of persons with disabilities, and what you as a helping professional can do to assist this group?

7. What does the term elderly mean to you?

8. List at least five things for persons you consider elderly that will need your assistance.

References

Blanchard, E. L. (1983). In D. W. Sue and D. Sue, Counseling the culturally different (2nd ed.). New York: John Wiley and Sons.

Casas, M. J., & Vasquez, M. J. T. (1996) in Pedersen, P. B. et al. (Eds.) Counseling Across Cultures (4th Ed) Thousand Oaks. Sage.

Eisenberg, M. G. (1982). *Disabled people as second-class citizens.* New York: Springer   Publishing Co.

Harjo, S. S. (1993). The American Indian experience. In H. P. McAdoo (Ed.), *Family ethnicity.* Newbury Park, CA: Sage.

Josephy, A. M. (1982). *Now that the buffalo's gone: A study of today's American Indians.* New York: Knopf.

Kleinfield, J., & Bloom, J. (1977). Boarding schools: Effects on the mental health of Eskimo adolescents. *American Journal of Psychiatry, 134*:411-147.

Lee, C., and Nolan, W. S. Z. (1998). *Handbook of Asian American psychology.* Thousand Oaks, CA: Sage.

Lowrey, L. (1983). Bridging a culture in counseling. *Journal of Applied Rehabilitation Counseling. 14*:69-73.

Richardson, E. H. (1981). In D. W. Sue and D. Sue (Eds), Counseling the culturally different (2nd ed.). New York: John Wiley and Sons.

Schlossberg, N. K. (1984). *Counseling adults in transition.* New York: Springer Publishing

Part III

UNDERSTANDING PSYCHOSOCIAL DYNAMICS OF HELPING

Chapter 11

ANALYSIS OF A PROFESSIONAL HELPING RELATIONSHIP

Chapter Outline
- Introduction
- Establish Rapport
- Identify major problems clients are encountering
- Identify resources available to clients
- Identify clients' definition of events
- Identify possible solutions
- Assist clients with acknowledging that problems exist
- Assist clients establish goals
- Get all concerned persons involved in treatment
- March to Resolution
- Identify Cultural Issues
- Identify Acculturation Issues
- Identify Religious Issues
- Additional information with regard to working with families
- Assisting families with regard to behavioral changes
- Termination of the Helping Relationship

INTRODUCTION

As previously stated in this book, there are numerous types of help-ing relationships, ranging from friends helping friends to profes-sional counseling therapy sessions. The emphasis of this chapter relates to professional helping relationships; however, regardless of the emphasis of the helping relationship there are some components that apply to most helping relationships. Therefore some of what is discussed with regard to analysis of a helping relationship will apply to friend helping friend as well as professional helper assisting a client.

The underlying goal of most, if not all, helping relationships is to assist someone achieve a goal, whether that goal is to assist a friend with tidying a room or assisting a married couple with understanding why they are unhappy with their marriage, and the options they may have to resolve their unhappiness. Certainly there are significantly different roles in a helping relationship depending upon what is expected of the helping relationship. Likewise, depending upon the helping setting as well as goals of the helping relationship, there are certain steps to be taken to increase the chances of success. The following are several steps that this author has found useful and effective in helping clients solve their problems. Note that I have said helping clients solve their problems–this author strongly believe that unless a person or persons have serious mental and/or emotional problems which prohibits him from implementing rational thinking, then everyone has the potential and capability to understand his problems and with competent assistance solve his problem or problems. The professional helper is on the scene to help guide the person toward understanding the problem(s), understanding his/her options and applying those options in ways that remove the problem rather than increase the problem.

A major goal of this chapter is to discuss ways to analyze the information one has about the client or clients with the intent of using the information obtained from the analysis to aid in working with the clients in helping them solve the problems or issues that have brought you and the clients together. The analysis is essential for you to provide well-thought-through advice and directions to your clients.

ESTABLISH RAPPORT

The preamble to effectively analyzing the helping relationship is to make the clients aware that it is your, the helper's, firm belief that there are answers to their problems and they have the answers, and it is your goal to get them to the point that they understand they are the masters of their fate. Some may title this first step as establishing rapport with the client(s). To some extent this is true in that establishing rapport is designed to make the clients feel comfortable with you as the helper and believe that you have their best interest at heart, and will do nothing to harm them psychologically. Whereas informing and hopefully making them believe that you as the helper will do no harm certainly is designed to both make the clients comfortable with you as their helper, and also believe you are capable to assist them in dealing with their situations. A major part of the helper's role is to assist the clients in believing in themselves to the point they feel empowered and capable, with assistance, to solve their problems which is different than having the clients feeling comfortable with you and believing that you are capable of solving their problems. The psychological differences is learning to believe in themselves.

Lack of belief in self, generally speaking, is a major part of clients' inability to move forward with implementing solutions to their problems. Often the problems have existed for quite some time and attempts to solve the problems, or in many cases lack of sufficient attempts, have caused the problem to not only continue to be a problem, but also has been the cause of the problem escalating. The following discussions which this author calls Analysis of a Helping Relationship is designed to help guide the professional helper in working with individual clients as well as families to secure solutions to their problems. As previously stated, this author believes most everyone has the ability to solve their problems. Unless the person has severe brain damage and/or emotional and mental problems that are hampering him/her from rational thinking, the person is capable of developing solutions to his problems. It is a matter of willing to do so and confidence in one's abilities to do so, and this is where the helping professional can play an important role by encouraging the client or clients who have rational intellectual abilities to construct solutions to said problems. Again, it is this authors opinion that the helping professional should not create answers to the clients problems, unless for reasons previously mentioned the client is unable to put together reasonable thinking and actions to solve the problem or problems that are affecting his life. If the helping professional creates solutions to the clients problems and, hands the solution to him or her, this does very little for the client to successfully handle the next problem or set of problems. A goal of the helping professional should be to assist the clients in developing logical and reasonable steps in recognizing and solving problems so she, the client, can utilize this approach to solving current and future problems. I am mindful of the fact that all issues are not the same, and one approach will not fit all situations. However, what the helper is doing by guiding the client to developing solutions to his problems is building the client's confidence in his abilities to resolve many of his issues through his own efforts. The following are some questions the helping professional should consider with regard to assisting the clients in solving their issues and problems.

IDENTIFY MAJOR PROBLEMS CLIENTS ARE ENCOUNTERING?

At first glance the issue of determining the major problem or problems appear to be relative easy. There are a number of ways clients come to you for your services; agency referral and self-referrals are perhaps the most common methods. Therefore, how the client or clients come to you will, to a large extent, determine the depth of information you will receive with regard to the problem or problems identified to you. Any experienced helping professional will readily point out that referral information often is lacking in details with regard to issue or issues that have caused the person to be in your office. Agency referrals often do not contain in-depth background information that would be helpful for you to have a good understanding of the client's life situation. In some situations this may be good because it helps eliminate preconceptions that may create helper bias. On the other side of the referral issue, persons who are self-referrals initially provide limited information. Many times the reason for the limited information is they do not know themselves the extent of their problem, they simply know that they are not satisfied with life as it currently exists. In some instances, the client will be reluctant to provide much information. This is a normal reaction to discussing sensitive problems to a stranger who has some level of authority over him. Occasionally, with regard to self-referrals, the person will overwhelm you with information, which creates other issues for the helping professional, namely trying to determine what the major issue or issues are.

As a helping professional there are times when you must use your best Sherlock Holmes detective skills to determine either the real psychological problems the person is encountering and/or the issues which are contributing to the problems. The best way to determine the major problems and the extent they are having on the individual and/or family is to ask the major players. The major player or players are the clients you are attempting to help. Referral information provides generalized information, which is helpful but does not always contain the detailed information you, the helper, need to assist the clients with developing effective strategies to deal with the problems. As previously stated, the best and most effective source of information are the persons directly involved. Certainly, there may be problems obtaining the in-depth information needed to get to the heart of the problems, however, this is where the helper earns his stripes as an effective helper. In most instances the major players in the helping relationship drama have the answer to what are the key issues that need to be resolved to have a successful ending to the individual and/or family drama. Oftentimes the solution to the problem or problems have not been applied because key players are not willing to admit there are problems, and also not willing to apply the needed efforts to resolve the problem. Sometimes this is the actual reason the problems have continued to exist. In most cases this is the exception rather than the rule. The major reason the individual or family members are not effectively responding to applying effective solutions to the problems is because they are so close to the problems they are unable to see an effective solution. Therefore, the role for the helping professional is to make the actors in the life drama aware of their involvement in the problems and guide them to possible solutions. Note, that I have said "guide them to possible solutions" rather than telling them what the solutions are. A longer lasting or permanent solution will occur when the players in the life drama see and understand their involvement and accept their roles in both the problems and the solutions to the problems. Stated in other terms, this can be referred to as identifying the individual and/or family dynamics associated with the problems. There are a variety of helping tools the helper can use to get the clients moving in the direction of better understanding the extent of the problems and its impacts upon the individual and/or family.

One of the techniques that can be used is role playing. If you are working with a family, you can have each person discuss the problem as they view same and how it impacts him/her and how he/she believe it impacts the family. You can have them switch roles and assume another person's role and perceptions as he/she perceives the situation. This approach can be used in individual counseling, where the client assumes the role of himself and discusses how the issues are impacting himself, and then reverse by assuming the roles of others who are impacted by the issues being discussed. Hopefully, the role reversals will help the client or clients obtain an understanding of not only the impact upon himself, but also the impact upon others.

Taibbi (2007) provides some very good advice with regard to getting a handle on what are the problems to be addressed in a helping relationship.

> People come to you because of problems, therefore it is vital that you know exactly what the problems are. This means having a clear understanding of just what the client is talking about and struggling with: What does 'not feeling myself,' 'acting up in class,' or 'a problem with attitude' mean? At face value, these are not solvable problems because the behaviors, emotions, and symptoms indicated are vague, undefined. By helping clients become clearer and more precise about what they are saying, you help them become clearer and more precise about what they are thinking and feeling. This not only begins to bring the problem into the room and to create a clearer picture of what is wrong, but it also helps you begin formulating a clear, positive vision of what can be.
>
> You also need to be clear about who has the problem. Sometimes, especially when the client is a self-referred adult, the client in the room and the client with the problem are one and the same, and it's all pretty simple: 'I feel depressed: I'm here so you can help me': 'My kids are running all over me; I need to learn how to handle them better.' Other times, however, it's not quite so easy. Often the only person with the problem is the person who is seeing a problem in someone else: the mother who thinks her son should find new friends, but the son thinks his friends are just fine; the father who thinks the mother should be tougher, but the mother feels she has a close relationship with her daughter and the father is just jealous: the wife who wants her husband to stop drinking so much, but he says that he only has a beer now and then and it isn't a problem for anyone but her. If only this other person would change, each says, I would be happy. p. 28
>
> When the problem behaviors seem so obvious–the husband is falling down drunk every night; the little boy is fighting everyone in the neighborhood; the teenager is refusing to go to school–it's easy for you to get caught up in everyone's concern and to join forces with them in trying to convince, the identified patient (I.P.), that a problem really does exist.

It's an awkward role that you need to avoid. You're stepping out of the service role, rapidly becoming an enforcer, and the I.P. generally starts to respond to you with more and more resistance. From his or her point of view, he or she simply doesn't have a problem, at least not the problem that everyone is so concerned about, and your siding with the others only makes you more quickly dismissed. p. 29

As one can see, it is often difficult to determine what the real problems are and who or what is causing the problems. However, as a helping professional it is your job to be objective in determining the root of the problems. In many instances there are more than one reason for the problem likewise more than one person involved in keeping the problem alive. Therefore, a wise helping professional will work with the client(s) with regard to exploring various options with regard to solving the problem. One way of helping the client(s) deal with solving the problem is to assist the individual(s) with regard to identifying the available resources to use in resolution of the problem(s).

IDENTIFY RESOURCES AVAILABLE TO CLIENTS

As a helping professional if you view one of your roles as a helper in finding a solution to the problem or problems rather than the architect of the solution to the problem, a major role you will play will be to help guide the individual or family to an acceptable solution. Therefore, an effective way of implementing this role is to help the clients identify the resources necessary to help solve the problem. It is this author's belief that unless persons have some severe mental or emotional problems that prohibit their abilities to think and respond in a rational manner, they are able to develop solutions to their problems. In many instances developing a solution to life's problems is not the lack of intellect, rather it is the lack of motivation and/or being so involved with the problem that the person either no longer has hope or has become so beaten down by the perceived weight of the problem that he has given up on finding and implementing a solution. From the standpoint of the helping professional, the major problem of getting the person and/or family involved in identifying and utilizing resources often becomes one of helping the persons believe in their abilities to successfully deal with the problems. In reality, sometimes the helping professional becomes a major stumbling block in that the helper becomes so involved that he attempts to solve the client's problem for him. This may work for the immediate moments; however a major loss will be the opportunities for the clients to learn about understanding the true meanings of the situation and the ability to develop self-confidence with regard to managing and solving some of their life problems. Egan (1994) provides his assessment of the importance of identifying resources:

> Unskilled or new helpers concentrate on clients' deficits. Skilled, experienced helpers, as they listen to and observe clients, do not blind themselves to deficits, but they are quick to spot clients' resources, whether used, unused, or even abused. These resources can become the building blocks for the future. p. 145–146

Egan, concludes his comments with regard to the value of assisting clients with identifying resources with the following:

> For some clients the very fact that they approach someone for help may be sufficient to help them begin to pull together the resources needed to manage their problem situations more effectively. For these clients, going to a helper is a declaration, not of helplessness, but of intent: 'I'm going to do something about this problem.' p. 154.

IDENTIFY CLIENT'S CRISIS MEETING RESOURCES

As the helping professional, once you have subscribed to the concept that the best resource for solving the problem or problems is the individual and/or the family, you must help them identify the crisis meeting resources the individual and/or family has. As previously stated, the best resources for helping solve problems are the resources that the clients currently have or to which they have access. This author believes the helper should (as much as possible) limit the number of new things that are introduced in the helping relationship. Clients are more likely to accept and utilize things of which they are familiar rather than unfamiliar resources. It is true that there are times when it is appropriate to help the individual or family learn new resources and ways of dealing with sensitive issues. When attempting to get clients to utilize resources with which they are familiar, sometimes you have to either sell them on the benefits of the resources or "dress the resource in a new package." When attempting to get the client to utilize resources that the person or family has available, generally speaking, one of two things will occur. One is the person will reject the suggestion by saying, "I have tried that and it has not worked," or be positive and say "I never thought about doing it that way." If the client rejects the suggestion, your job is to either convince her to try the potential solution or modify the potential solution so that it is acceptable to the client.

With regard to working toward an effective and acceptable solution, the benefit of utilizing things with which the clients are familiar is the possible solution and is either nonthreatening or less threatening to them than having to accept and utilize something that is new. However, there is another side to consider, some clients want to feel that they are turning their life around, thus they are more acceptable to utilizing something which they consider to be new to them. The approach to utilize becomes a judgment call on the part of the helper. A frank discussion with the clients with regard to the pros and cons of either approach is the best way to help the clients make their decision. Certainly, the helper one does not want to trick the clients or be viewed by the clients as having been tricked.

Another approach that can help the professional successfully work with clients that are dealing with stressful situations, is to learn about other problems the clients have had and were successful in resolving same. Everyone has had difficult situations to handle, sometimes they are successful, and other times they are unsuccessful. The helping profession can utilize both the successful and unsuccessful attempts to assist the clients in their current need for help. With regard to previous successful efforts, the professional helper can have the clients trace the steps they used in solving that situation or situations and extract from that information ways of utilizing the procedures they used and apply them to the current situation. With regard to the unsuccessful efforts, as the helper you can assist the clients examine why they were unsuccessful, and perhaps that knowledge added to what they could have done will help them modify their approaches to solving the current problem.

IDENTIFY CLIENT'S DEFINITION OF EVENTS

Definition of events means how the client and/or family view the situation. Do they consider it as one of the worse things that have or could happen to them, or do they consider it a problem they can overcome? No helper is all-knowing nor do they always have the correct views or perceptions with regard to a client's emotional state of mind and view of the problems he believes the clients are encountering. Therefore, it is important to check your views of the events in comparison to the client's views of the events. A major reason there are problems with the helper successfully assisting the clients occurs because there are disconnects between the helper's views of how the client or clients view the problems. This is where a difference in cultural views also come into play. Because of difference in cultural views, the helper may view the situation from a "middle-class" vantage point, whereas the client's view may be from a different socioeconomic standpoint. Because of this perception disconnect, the problem may not be as serious as the helper's view, or it may be more serious than the client's view. Therefore, it becomes of paramount importance that (as much as possible) the helper has a clear concept of the feelings of what this situation means to all concerned persons.

It is important for the helper to check his perceptions of how he thinks the client feels with regard to the issue or issues for which they are seeking help, or have been referred for help. The helper should encourage the clients to discuss how they would like for their lives to be in the here-and-now as well as in the future. Another way of approaching this conversation is to ask the clients to project their views of an ideal life situation. Next, have the client discuss her current views of her life situation. This will provide the helper with a prospective of the disconnection and distance between what the client desires and what she considers is her current life situation. Assuming that the disconnection is reasonable, the helper should work with the client with regard to reaching a reasonable approach to an acceptable life situation.

IDENTIFY POSSIBLE SOLUTIONS

In most life situations there are more than one solution to most problems. The helping professional must work with the client to recognize what solutions are available, and of those, which ones are best for her situation. Most every professional helper will agree that when selecting solutions it is of paramount importance that the solution will work to help eliminate the clients problems, or reduce the problems to a manageable level, but also be a solution with which the clients can feel comfortable on a daily basis. The helper may see solutions which she feels would be best for the client. However, regardless of how well the solution works, if the client does not feel comfortable with the solution she, in most cases, will not put forth the necessary efforts to make the solution the success it could be.

ASSIST CLIENT'S WITH ACKNOWLEDGING PROBLEMS EXIST

There are at least two problems with regard to acknowledgment of the existence of a problem or problems: (1) the persons involved are in denial, or (2) they have lived with the situation for such a long time thus they view or have accepted the situation as a normal way for them to live. In reality they know that how they are living is not the norm; however, they are surviving, thus they have accepted that this is the way life will be. Unfortunately, this is often the way spouses of substance abusers begin to feel. This does not mean they are totally satisfied with the situation, but they continue to live with the situations rather than deal with the unknown which is something that change often brings. In some instances, clients in situations where law enforcement, courts, or other influential sources mandate that they obtain help, clients will seek help; however, this does not mean that they acknowledge that they need help. In those cases where the clients seek help without being forced to do so it may seem that these would be the clients most easily helped because of their actions–they have acknowledged there is a problem and they need help. These types of clients are ones that the helper does not have to work with them to accept the fact they need help, the fact they acknowledge there are problems does not mean all parties concerned agree with regard to what the problems are. In the case of families, quite often some members may view certain members of the family as the one(s) creating the problem thus their part in the family drama is as the recipient of their actions.

In other cases everyone involved recognizes there are problems, and, everyone is blaming each other. Regardless of whether persons are denying the existence of problems and are blaming others, it is the responsibility of the helper to make all persons involved recognize that they have some ownership in the problems. A successful resolution will best occur when everyone becomes involved in developing a solution to the problems.

ASSIST CLIENT'S ESTABLISH GOALS

Goals should be established in measurable terms. Too often we establish goals with vague and general terminology such as "I want to be happy," "I want to be respected." A problem with these types of goals is how do you measure happiness and how do you measure respect. In most instances if you are unable to measure goals, then it is difficult to determine if the goals have been achieved. Certainly, some clients will state that "they know when they are happy and when they are being respected." There is some validity in these statements in the sense they are often based upon feelings, but feelings change and generally speaking not measurable. Feelings often are based upon moods, some days very minor things may cause one to be happy or sad, and the next day the same or very similar actions may cause the opposite of yesterday's feeling.

Therefore, when assisting clients to establish their goals for the helping relationship, encourage them to form the goals in terminology that is reasonable and measurable. Reasonable means to establish a goal that one can reasonably expect can happen. Measurable means to establish goals in quantifiable terms.

GET ALL CONCERNED PERSONS INVOLVED IN TREATMENT

When problems arise in families or groups, it is not uncommon that the blame for the cause and continuation of the problem is directed to one or more members of the family or organization. However, it is quite rare that any one person will admit, to or accept responsibility for the disharmony. In reality, while one person may have initiated the problem, several persons have contributed to the expansion of the problem. A task confronting the professional helper is twofold: (1) is to get those responsible for the discontent to accept responsibility for their actions, and (2) get all concerned, regardless of whether they were directly involved in the creation of the problem, to accept their responsibilities as possible solutions to resolving the issues. Without acknowledging responsibility for the problem, and/or responsibility for helping solve the problem, progress on reaching a solution will be either very slow or nonexistent.

> What keeps people stuck is their great difficulty in seeing their own participation in the problems that plague them. With eyes fixed firmly on what those recalcitrant others are doing, it's hard for most people to see the patterns that bind them together. Nichols & Schwartz (2001)

MARCH TO RESOLUTION

To begin the march to resolution of the problem, step one is to get those involved to acknowledge there is a problem. Step two, after acknowledging there is a problem, you must get them to realize the impact the problem is having on the person and/or the family or group involved. The third step is to get all concerned to begin discussing the problem. A good way to get the individual and/or persons involved is to go back to what they consider the beginning of the problem to identify how and when the problem began. One may be surprised to find that discussing the origin of the problem those involved will acknowledge the issue that began the problem was not as complicated as the problem has become. The problem began as a minor issue, however, over time the issue has grown and become more complex. Persons involved may began to realize they have allowed a minor misunderstanding to become an untamed monster.

The untamed monster, generally speaking, is that those involved have taken uncompromising stances with regard to the issue, thus making the issue much more of a problem than it had to be. The fourth step is to have those involved discuss what steps they have taken to resolve the problem. Most persons will have, at some point in the life of the problem, initiated solutions to end the problem. It is important to determine what those steps were, what were the responses to those steps, and what became of the efforts. After analyzing these steps hopefully the participant will realize that there are solutions to the problem, and with cooperation the positive solutions will be forthcoming. This lead to the fifth step, have those involved discuss solutions to the problem. In most cases persons involved in problem situations have ideas of how to resolve problems. The job of the professional helper is to make the discussion environment comfortable enough to get them to discuss their thoughts. By helping the persons involved believe that their thoughts count and that they are capable of helping resolve the problem, they will become more willing to express their opinions with regard to the solutions. In the case of group or family counseling, it is important to stress to them that they must keep their discussion of solutions positive. Step six is to get the individual or group to devise a method of determining whether the solutions are being followed.

IDENTIFY CULTURAL ISSUES

I begin this discussion with analyzing cultural issues because I firmly believe that the basis for most of our thoughts and actions are related to the cultures that influence our lives. Our belief systems, things which we value, and our ethics are developed and significantly influenced by the cultures of which we are members, whether willing or unwilling members. Regardless of whether we are willing or unwilling members, many of our beliefs and actions will be influenced; therefore, knowledge of the cultural environments will help better understand some of the actions or lack thereof that clients take.

Corsini and Wedding (2005) in their book *Current Psychotherapies* quote Prochaska and Norcross and Giordano and Carini-Giordano (1995) with regard to the importance of helping professionals being cultural sensitive.

Developing a culturally sensitive therapy calls for moving beyond the white middle-class outlook from which many therapists operate (prizing self-sufficiency, independence, and individual development) and recognizing that such values are not necessarily embraced by all ethnic groups. For example, many clients from traditional Asian backgrounds are socialized to subordinate their individual needs to those of their families or society in general. In developing a multicultural frame work, the family therapist must recognize that acculturation is an ongoing process that occurs over generations, and that ethnic values continue to influence a client family's child-rearing practices, intergenerational relationships, family boundaries, and so forth.

A culturally competent family therapist remains alert to the fact that how he or she access or counsels a family is influenced not only by professional knowledge, but also by his or her own 'cultural filters'—values, attitudes, customs, religious beliefs and practices, and especially, beliefs regarding what constitutes normal behavior that stem largely from the therapist's own cultural background. p. 376

This preamble having been presented, I will move forward and discuss how culture will impact the helping relationship, also see **Chapter 5** of this text.

Depending upon how clients are referred or sent to you will determine the extent of information you have about the client or clients. In some cases referral information sheets will have significant background information with regard to the clients. However, in some referrals the information may be somewhat limited, and often in-depth cultural information is lacking. Frequently, the extent of cultural information that is provided is race, gender, age, marital status, possibly economic status, maximum educational level, and type of employment.

One's cultures and their impact and influence they have upon the client's belief system and actions, as a result of the belief system, are very important pieces of information of which a helping professional should be aware. As previously implied, too often referral information that a helping professional receives is quite limited regarding to cultural information which may be and often is, beneficial to know. As discussed in **Chapter 5**, one's cultures have significant influences not only upon ones daily actions, but also upon how one interprets his life and his place within his immediate surroundings. It is impossible for a helping professional, and in fact for anyone, to be knowledgeable of all cultures and their beliefs. However, it is not an impossibility for a helping professional to become knowledgeable with regard to major cultures which impacts the helper's life.

When a helping professional begins an analysis of the client's background, too often the helper falls into the common trap of only seeing and developing an understanding of the basic cultural backgrounds of the client i.e. race, ethnicity, gender, and economic status. Too often it is from this limited background search that strategies for helping the client are developed. Because culture is so broad its impact is felt with regard to how and why a client makes many of his/her life decisions. The professional helper must take a broad and in-depth analysis of various cultural components which are impacting the client's life as well as other cultural components which have the potential of impacting the decisions the clients will make. As the helper makes an analysis of various cultural aspects of the person's life, she perhaps will uncover new avenues to explore with regard to factors impacting the person's decision making and actions taken. By understanding cultural components of a client's life, helpers will find they have found a key to help unlock the doors of understanding information with regard to why clients feel the way they do, understanding why they have certain feelings, and understanding why they have been reluctant to change some of their behaviors. Understanding cultural influences will assist the helping professional explain the behavior and thought processes the client is experiencing.

As is the case with regard to the helping professional initially not comprehending the many cultural factors that have the possibility of impacting the actions and decisions made by the client, the same often is true for the client. As human beings we do not daily think about various factors which impact and influence our behaviors, therefore, it is imperative that as helping professionals we do a comprehensive review in searching and analyzing the client's background. It is a reality, as previously stated, that referral background information with regard to client's cultures are often brief and limited, likewise clients' views of their cultural backgrounds are equally brief. This is why the helping professional must become adept at looking deep into a client's cultural background. To do this the helping professional when initially interviewing the client must ask some deep probing questions with regard to the client's background, as well as factors that could have an influence on the person's beliefs and actions. Offered as an example, health professionals when seeking background information from a patient ask probing questions which go much beyond the basics, age, marital status, children, and so forth. The health professional may ask additional questions with regard to one's social background, religious background, and educational background to mention only three. These questions may at first glance appear to be nonrelevant when the patient is initially being seen because of inability to get eight hours sleep at night. The answers to the seemly irrelevant questions may, in fact, provide valuable information with regard to the problem of lack of sleep or additional problems that may occur as a result of lack of sleep. Likewise, the helping professional must think beyond the initial problem and explore background information which will provide insight into deeper issues than the ones being initially discussed.

As previously stated, information with regard to clients' cultures are often limited; therefore, do not make quick judgments with regard to the person's culture, i.e., race, gender and ethnicity. In reality often this will be the extent of the person's cultural information. You as the helping professional must be cognizant of the fact that the person's cultural influences go much deeper than that. As an example of more depth than race, gender and ethnicity, are other cultural factors such as religious beliefs or lack thereof, physical conditions, i.e., disabilities including hidden disabilities and social affiliations, to mention only three.

IDENTIFY ACCULTURATION ISSUES

To answer the question with regard to whether there are issues of acculturation that may impact the helping relationship, I will provide a brief discussion of what acculturation is. Within a given society, of all the cultural groups which exist, in most cases, one will become the dominant culture and many of that society's activities, belief systems, values and standards are determined by the dominant culture. In an attempt to be accepted by and be considered part of the society, subordinate cultures attempt to emulate the dominant culture. This is considered a form of acculturation. Some social scientists say that acculturation, within the context of American society, refers to the degree to which an individual identifies with the attitudes, lifestyles, and values of the dominant culture. In American society, there are numerous dominant cultural characteristics and the extent to which individuals and groups of individuals deviate from those characteristics and standards determine how much they are devalued. Likewise, the closer they mimic and/or incorporate them in their lifestyles, the more they are valued. Many of Euro-American cultural standards are so well woven into the fabric of American society that not only do members of the dominant culture accept them as the correct standards by which to live, also in many instances persons of subordinate cultures also make this same judgment.

Unless carried to an extreme, there is generally speaking, nothing wrong with Euro-American standards. The major problem in American society has been the extent to which the dominant culture has suppressed the subordinate cultures. The lack of consideration given to other points of view and ways of doing things as well as lifestyles is what has been questioned, not the right or wrong of Euro-American cultural standards. One might correctly observe and point out German culture in Germany is dominant and serves as a benchmark by which societal standards are judged in that country. Also in some countries, societal standards are based upon religious orientation and one religious sect dominates all other groups, religious and nonreligious oriented. Appropriate responses to these observations are: (a) the fact that one culture completely dominates another in any part of the world is no justification for such occurrences in other parts. This would be similar to justifying oppression by pointing to country X and saying that it has a high standard of living for the majority of its people despite a restrictive society. (b) America is composed of many different groups of people who have worked together to develop the country and society into a world leader; therefore, each cultural group should be valued. (c) The uniqueness and greatness of America has, to a large extent, been based upon the diversity of ideas. The freedom to think, dream and work toward moving those dreams into realities has been a hallmark of American society. Therefore, one fact that has distinguished America from many other societies has been its diversity.

A summarization of what is acculturation can succulently be explained as the act of adopting the standards of the dominant culture. In cases where the client is of a culture other than the dominant culture, acculturation does not mean that the person totally abandons the cultural values and beliefs of the culture in which he was reared. What the helping professional should examine is to what extent, if any, the client has taken on the cultural ways and values of the dominant society and if he has, to what extent has he accepted the cultural values of the dominant society. As a result of totally accepting the dominant culture, has he abandoned his culture and to what extent? This assessment becomes very important with regard to the helping professional determining some of the following. In the case of the client being acculturated: How much of the client's culture in which he was reared has he retained? If the person has a family are the family members acculturated? If the person has a low level of acculturation, what is the impact on the person and his family? If the person has a high level of acculturation, what are some of the impacts of same.

Everyone is acculturated to some extent. Given the broad range of human activity that culture covers, everyone moves in and out of cultures during his/her daily activities. In most instances differences in cultures present very few problems; however, where problems occur is when persons have been reared in a country other than the one he/she is now calling home. To a lesser degree acculturation does occur when a person relocates from one part of a nation to another part of the same nation. As an example, persons born and reared in the Southern part of the United States and relocates to the Northeastern part of the United States will experience some acculturation issues. However, the acculturation becomes much easier for this person because there are only a few language issues with which to become accustomed. However, if English is not his native language, acculturation can become a major issue. From a helping relationship standpoint being aware of acculturation is very important because you exceedingly become aware of the fact that the person or persons are often mentally functioning in two different worlds. The helping professional must take this fact into consideration as he evaluates the reactions the client presents in the helping relationship.

A helper has to evaluate his acculturation levels, because his acculturation level will impact how he views some of the client's actions and reactions or lack thereof. As hard as most helping professionals try to be objective, quite often without us being aware some of our biases enter into how we work with clients.

IDENTIFY RELIGIOUS ISSUES

It is this author's opinion that most persons are influenced by some religious precepts. This does not mean that the person has to be religious, in the sense of being a member of a specific religious denomination or organization, nor does it mean that the person has to believe in a supreme being. What is being stated is that most countries' "does and don'ts, rights and wrongs have some basis in religious philosophies.

The United States of America and many other countries are not countries that promote any one religion or religion in general; however, many of the laws that emphasize what is considered right or wrong in the society has as its foundation religious precepts. Additionally, persons living within these countries are expected and are mandated to conduct themselves according to the laws of the country, which as previously stated have some basis in religious beliefs. See Chapter 7 for discussion of the five major world religions. Even many, if not most, persons who commit criminal acts and others who perform less than noble acts often are reared in religious surroundings and will acknowledge the fact that they know "right from wrong" based upon religious precepts.

Beyond the point that has been made that most persons are aware of religious precepts regardless of whether they obey same, there are millions of persons who believe in religion and conduct their lives according to religious teachings and precepts. From a helping relationship standpoint if the helper knows that the client or clients have strong religious beliefs, it is important that the helper know something about those beliefs so that he can be sensitive to the beliefs and needs of the client as those beliefs relate to religion. This knowledge can be helpful in assisting the person being helped in a number of areas such as schooling, medical issues, dietary issues, discipline of children, and marriage issues, just to mention a few. Often when actions of a client is based upon religious beliefs, and those that are opposed to the action do not understand those beliefs or regardless if the authorities understand, the fact remains the actions are against regulation thus those are some of the most difficult situations for the helping professional to handle.

The following scenario will illustrate how a helping professional may become involved with a clients' religious beliefs and a medical procedure. The client may be of a religious faith that do not believe in blood transfusions. The client's underaged child has an accident and loses considerable blood and is taken to a hospital where the medical staff state that the child must have a blood transfusion. The parents refuse to allow the transfusion and the hospital seeks advice from legal staff. The helping profession is placed into a difficult situation, i. e., the rights of the parents versus perhaps the law. Does the helping professional advocate for the rights of the parents to make the decision by asking for an exception to any laws that apply which require the parents to consent to a blood transfusion, or does the helping professional–after explaining to the parents the medical decision and possible laws–try to convince the parents to waive their religious beliefs to possibly save the child's life? Stated in other terms the helping professional's assistance will be needed to either advocate for a client and/or help explain to the client what the issues are, and how their actions are viewed by the authorities that are questioning their actions. Additionally, the helping professional's expertise will be needed to help the client understand the point of view of the authorities who are questioning the client's actions or lack thereof.

ADDITIONAL INFORMATION WITH REGARD TO WORKING WITH FAMILIES

In most cases of being a helper, even though you may be working with one person, there are more people involved or at least significantly concerned and impacted by the issues of the person being helped. In many situations some of those persons affected by the issues are family members, therefore (whenever possible), a wise move may be to get family members involved. With regard to involving family an important question is which members should be involved? Often this becomes a major issue, first does the individual want any family members involved? Second, do family members want to be involved?

Family therapists teach us that the family is more than a collection of separate individuals; it is a system, an organic whole whose parts function in a way that transcends their separate characteristics. But even as members of family systems, we don't cease being individuals, with hearts, minds, and wills of our own. Although it isn't possible to understand people without taking into account their social context, notably the family, it is misleading to limit the focus to the surface of interactions–to social behavior divorced from inner experience.

The point is this: To provide effective and lasting psychological help, a therapist needs to understand and motivate individuals and influence their interactions. Nichols & Schwartz (2001, p. 7)

Certainly, there are concerns with regard to whether the entire family should be involved and if family therapy is appropriate. The fact that the issue or issues relate to the family does not guarantee that all family members will cooperate or will be happy to be involved in the helping process. Despite the reality that often family members are reluctant to be formally part of the helping process, it is the professional helper's responsibility to encourage those that are reluctant to participate. The professional helper should encourage participation by pointing out that while it may not appear that they are part of the problem, their cooperation and input will be important with regard to arriving at a solution or solutions to the problems to be discussed.

The major question becomes what will you do to get the entire family involved in the treatment? The reality is that in some, if not many, cases you will not be able to get all family member involved; however, you must try. Arriving at solutions that have lasting results will significantly be increased if all concerned becomes involved. As human beings, to a large degree, we are concerned with what is important to us. Stated in other terms, while we most often will not verbalize this, but "what is in this for me" is in our thought process as we decide whether to participate. Therefore, as the helping professional your chances of obtaining reluctant member's participation to some extent will depend upon how good you are at convincing them that participation is important and needed, because it is in their best interest that they participate. If this does not work you must conduct your helping with those that are willing to participate. This does not mean that you as the helper and the family members that are participating disregard the nonparticipating member. No solution at which the family arrives will be complete without taking into consideration how the missing member(s) will be impacted by decisions that are made.

How do you carry forward without the participation of the member or members who are not participating? There is a technique called the empty chair. This is a technique where an empty chair is placed before the individual or individuals. Ask them to act as though the missing person is sitting in the chair and address conversation to the missing person. During this procedure, the person talking to the missing person can think of what the person's responses would likely be. As the person identifies what she thinks the person's response will be, the helper can ask questions such as why she thinks the response will be as she has indicated, and what is your response to his/her responses?

ASSISTING FAMILIES WITH REGARD TO BEHAVIORAL CHANGES

With regard to analyzing a situation, especially in family situations, the helping professional hears from those involved that they are not happy or satisfied with the ways things are transpiring in their lives. However, in careful analysis of the family environment, the helper is able to identify the major issues the family or individual is encountering. Upon in closer examination, the helper also discovers there are one or more persons serving as an enabler. As the term enabler implies, others are helping the person or persons with their unhealthy psychological or physical behavior. Often the enablers do not intend to support the inappropriate behavior; however, they have lived with the situation for a long period of time and they have become accustomed to the behavior and results of the behavior. This does not mean that the enabler likes this approach, but rather than continue to confront the person, the enabler gives in to the behavior for the sake of what he or she views as "keeping a peaceful environment." This often happens in family situations where one or more persons are substance abusers. Offered as an example, the husband is a functioning alcoholic that spends all or most of his salary on gambling and drinking, and because of his behavior he contributes very little to paying family bills. The wife, even though she does not condone his behavior, pays all of the family's expenses from her salary. In this situation she is being an enabler in that she is helping support the husband's week-end drinking and gambling habits.

The previously mentioned scenario is an example of a problem that helping professionals may encounter. The question becomes what kind of behavioral changes will you encourage the client or clients to pursue? Certainly, one of the problems in helping the clients decide behavioral changes is if the person or persons are ready and willing to invest energy and efforts into behavioral change. Often the person or persons have lived with a problem for considerable time, and even though they do not like the environment, they have become accustomed to same. From their vantage point it is easier to live with certain behavior than to advocate change which will possibly create disharmony in the household.

As the helping professional you are on the outside looking in, and it is easy for you to see the problems and possibly know and/or have a solution for the situation. However, as a veteran helping professional you are aware that the chances for the solution being implemented and followed through in a manner where the solutions have a chance to be successful, they must be accepted by the clients as their solutions, not your solutions. This does not mean that your solutions should not be applied, however, what should be done is to carefully introduce possible solutions and help the clients embrace them as though they were the author of them. They have to believe the solutions will work and put forth the efforts necessary to make them work.

In summary, with regard to selecting behavior changes, the professional helper should help the client(s) select the solutions to be implemented. Also as much as possible, the helper must encourage the client(s) if necessary, and modify the solutions so that they view them as their own and believe in the solutions. Often it is necessary to help the clients develop several alternatives, because in reality many times the first solution may not meet with success; therefore, you the helper must help the clients have alternate solutions.

TERMINATION OF THE HELPING RELATIONSHIP

The helping professional's work is not complete until the individual and/or family has applied the solutions and tested them outside the helping environment, without your (the professional helper's) environment. This, therefore means a well-planned ending to the helping relationship. There are various approaches for establishing termination with regard to the helping relations. Each professional helper should establish his/her termination procedure. The following are some suggested steps to follow: (1). Begin discussing termination at the first session. This begins the process of establishing some structure to the helping relationship in that the helpee/client is made aware that there will be an end to the formal helping relation. (2). At each session discuss progress or lack thereof. (3). Each session discuss things to be done to enhance the chances of the helping relationship being successful. (4). Once termination time has arrived, provide the client or clients with information the necessary if additional contact is required. (5). Provide the client with other resources that can be utilized. This will help avoid the clients becoming dependent upon you. This does not mean that regardless of the circumstances you will not begin working with the client again. Certain circumstances may require additional contact. (6). Follow-up to determine how the client is progressing.

Summary

A key to helping professionals conducting psychological counseling is to effectively analyze the many components of the issue or issues involved in the problems that the clients are encountering. The helping professional (in this author's opinion) is not part of the helping relationship to dictate to the clients a solution or solutions. The helping professional is involved to help the clients discover solutions which they are willing to implement and work toward making the solutions a success. It is this author's opinion that everyone, unless they have significant brain damage or psychological problems which prohibit them from rational thinking, have the capacity to develop workable solutions to their problems. Therefore, the helping professional's major role is to assist the clients with regard to discovering solutions with which they can feel comfortable as they conduct their daily activities.

Mental Exercise

1. In your opinion, what constitutes a family?
2. List five types of family issues you believe, as a helper, you will have difficulty helping a family overcome and why.
3. Which family therapy or therapies do you like best?
4. In your opinion are there any times, as a helper, you should make decisions for the client or clients? Defend your answer.

5. In your opinion are there any justifications for a helper to make decisions for the client or clients and manipulate the client into believing the decision was his/her own? If yes, explain.

References

Corsini, R. J., & Wedding, D. (2005). *Current psychotherapies.* (5th Ed.). United States. Brooks/Cole.

Egan, G. (1994). *The skilled helper.* (5th Ed.). CA: Brooks/Cole.

Nichols, M. P., & Schwartz, R. C. (2001). *Family therapy: Concepts and methods.* (5th Ed.). Boston: Allyn & Bacon

Taibbi, R. (2007). *Doing Family Therapy.* (2nd Ed.). New York: Guilford Press.

Chapter 12

UNDERSTANDING INDIVIDUAL COUNSELING

Chapter Outline
- Introduction
- Psychoanalytical Therapy
  - Major Contributor
  - Major Concepts
  - Psychosexual Stages of Development
  - Psychoanalytical Therapy Goals
  - Psychoanalytical Therapy Techniques
- Gestalt Therapy
  - Major Contributor
  - Major Concepts
- Adlerian Therapy
  - Major Contributors
  - Major Concepts
- Behavioral Therapies
  - Major Contributor
  - Summary of Behavioral Therapies
- Person-Centered Therapy
  - Major Contributor
  - Summary of Person-Centered Therapy
- Summary
  - References

Chapter Objectives
- Present information with regard to selected individual counseling psychological therapies

• Present psychological therapy information to assist the professional helper develop his or her approaches to helping

INTRODUCTION

As previously discussed, various dimensions of being a successful helper exist: understanding oneself, understanding one's beliefs, understanding one's attitudes, understanding of resources, and understanding of human behavior. In Chapter 4 I stressed the need for the helper to be aware of his or her beliefs about the impact of human behavior on the helpee's actions. Paramount to this effort is the need to have reasonable and rationale understanding of the motivating forces of human behavior.

In this chapter, I begin by discussing some psychological theorists' beliefs about human behavior. Next I discuss the counseling approaches of individual counseling/psychotherapy.

Beginning helpers, in their attempts to understand psychological helping theories and possible identify with one or more of them with the intent of incorporating them as part of their helping tools, often look at the goals and techniques of the therapies to determine whether they fit with their helping style. Certainly, goals and techniques are key ingredients of a helping technique. However, the key component that is often overlooked and the component on which the goals and methods are based are the theorist's beliefs about human behavior – to be more specific, the motivation for human behavior. Taibbi (2007) underscores the importance of understanding and developing a helping theory with the following remarks:

> An effective therapist needs to be grounded in some kind of theory. Too many theories can overwhelm you, the wrong kind can constrict you, but have none and you are set adrift in a vast ocean of facts and observations. A theory of therapy gives you something to hold onto. It can be as simple or complex as you like, because what a theory says is less important than what it can give to you and allow you to do. (p. 7)

Considering Taibbi's remarks, one may conclude that the theory or theories of what motivates human behavior is the foundation on which goals and techniques are developed.

Before I discuss some psychological theories of helping, I identify the three schools of thought with regard to psychological therapies. Today, there are numerous psychological helping theories; however, most fit within one of three categories: **humanistic, psychodynamic,** or **behavioral**.

Humanistic therapies are grounded in existentialism and phenomenological concepts. Therefore, humanistic therapies promote the concepts of the growth potential of humans. Stated in other terms, each person has the potential to understand and solve his or her problems. Emphasis is on conscious awareness. Helpers of the humanist school of thought also emphasize the understanding of one's perceptions of events and situations. Examples of humanistic therapies are Adlerian therapy, person-centered therapy, gestalt therapy, and existential therapy.

The **behavioral** school of thought promotes the belief in assessing conscious behavior and applying treatment so that outcome can be measured. Operant and classical conditioning are the foundation of behavioral therapy; however, there have been several significant contributions to behavioral therapy, such as rational emotive behavior therapy and cognitive therapy.

The **psychodynamic** psychological school of thought promotes the concept of the importance of understanding the unconscious and how it impacts current behavior. Psychodynamic belief underscores the idea that unconscious material provides the primary influence on current behavior. The classic example of a psychodynamic psychological therapy is psychoanalytic therapy.

At this point, let us look at some of the current psychological theories of helping–psychoanalytical, behavioral therapies, person-centered, Adlerian, and gestalt–from the standpoint of understanding human behavior, some of the goals and techniques, and how they impact behavior.

PSYCHOANALYTICAL THERAPY

Major Contributor

Sigmund Freud was born in Vienna in 1856. He was educated and trained as a physician and is the originator and major contributor to the psychological therapy called psychoanalysis. Sigmund Freud was the most influential psychotherapist of his time and arguably the most influential of all times. His ideas and work have influenced almost every major therapy in existence today. Some theorists have incorporated some of his ideas into their theories, whereas others disagree with his theoretical conclusions and have developed their theories in opposition to Freud's beliefs. Regardless of the directions these theorists have taken, it is difficult to deny Freud's influence.

Major Concepts

With regard to psychoanalytical therapy and human behavior, Sigmund Freud postulated four forces that motivate human behavior: **pleasure principle, anxiety, defense mechanisms,** and **psychosexual development**. With regard to the **pleasure principle**, Freud identifies this principle as the most basic of human needs, and that the instinctual human behavior motivation is the desire to experience pleasure and avoid pain. Arlow (2005) explains Freud's ideas in the following manner:

> Freud believed there were a number of general principles of human behavior. Foremost among these was the pleasure principle, namely, the idea that human psychology is governed by a tendency to seek pleasure and avoid pain. Such response derives from the biological inheritance of human beings and must have been of evolutionary significance in the struggle of the species to survive. (p. 17)

To further elaborate on our basic human behavior, Freud postulated that the human personality exists in three distinct and separate states: **conscious, preconscious,** and **unconscious**. The conscious state is our day-to-day personality, which interacts with others. Stated in other terms, our conscious state is the part of our lives of which we are aware.

Freud's core belief about personality development is that the **unconscious** stores all of our experiences and memories, thus, when we repress material in our unconscious, the information influences our present behavior. Therefore, it is imperative when emotional and/or psychological problems occur, the helper must assist the helpee with regard to understanding the connection between the unconscious and current behavior. The **preconscious state**, according to Freud, is represented by the dreams we have. Arlow (2005) informs us that "Freud attempted to elaborate a theory of the human mind that would encompass dreaming, psychopathology, and normal functioning." Arlow further points out that "the central principle of this theory is that mental life represents an unrelenting conflict between the conscious and unconscious parts of the mind" (p. 22). Thus, dream analysis is an important tool for some helpers because, from their perspectives, dreams represent an expression of unconscious material; therefore, an understanding of this material can identify unresolved psychological problems in a helpee's life. This does not mean that all helpers who use or subscribe to psychoanalysis therapy have to be an expert at dream analysis. What this does mean is that some helpers use dream analysis as a tool for understanding human behavior.

Our subconscious state is represented by what Freud named **id, ego,** and **superego**. The **id** represents our basic human motivation and instinctual need, which is to avoid pain and/or unpleasant events and act in a manner that increases our chances of experiencing pleasure. The id may be referred to as the biological element of human personality. As we look at human development, we recognize that when a child is born, his or her primary instinct is survival, such as receiving food when hungry, relief of pain when hurting, and becoming warm when cold. A result of meeting these survival needs, the infant experiences a sensation of satisfaction that one can translate into happiness. When the infant's security and satisfaction needs are not met, the child experiences distress or unhappiness. As we grow older, the id continues to expand as we identify things that bring us pleasure; thus, the id continues to seek pleasure and attempts to avoid painful or unpleasant things. According to Freud, the id's primary goal is to satisfy instinctual needs. On the other end of the personality spectrum is the **superego**. The superego represents the moralistic side of our personality. The superego is developed from the morals we extract from the societies in which we live. The problem with the superego is that it is based on perfection; from the view point of the superego, things are either right or wrong, black or white, and often no shades in between. The superego represents the ideal rather than the realistic.

The **ego** is the balance between the primal instinct of the id and the perfectionist superego. To further explain the three components of the personality that impact human behavior, we can look at human personality on a continuum–the id on one end and the superego on the other end, with the ego in the middle giving a sense of balance to our personality. When we examine the id and the superego, it becomes quite clear that it would be difficult to constantly live at either end of the continuum. In a civilized society, we cannot constantly do only those things that make us feel good; we have to consider the laws of the society in which we live as well as have concerns with regard to the rights of others. On the other end of the continuum, life events do not always provide a perfectly clear path of correctness, as our superego prefers. There are generally more than one rightness, thus the ego mediates between the two extremes and helps us function appropriately within societal guidelines as well as helps maintain our sanity. Although Freud did not state the importance of the ego in this manner, one can see how an unchecked id can lead to antisocial behavior and an unmediated superego could cause emotional mental problems trying to live with an uncompromising belief system.

Anxiety: Corey (2005) points out that "anxiety is a state of tension that motivates us to do something. It develops out of a conflict among the id, ego, and superego over control of the available psychic energy. The function of anxiety is to warn of impending danger" (p. 58). Sigmund Freud recognized the obvious, which is that everyone throughout life experience anxiety, and anxiety affects human behavior. Sigmund Freud realized that there are different types of anxiety, and the type of anxiety experienced impacts the extent of our behavior or reaction to the anxiety. Freud identified three types of anxiety: **reality anxiety**, which is the fear of danger from the external world; **neurotic anxiety**, which is the fear that our instincts will get out of control and cause us to do things for which we will be punished; and **moral anxiety**, which is the fear of our own conscious, which means we develop feelings of anxiety when we act contrary to our moral beliefs (Corey, 2005).

Ego defense mechanisms: Freud postulated that when anxieties get out of control, our human behavioral reaction is to develop defenses. Some of the ego defenses he identified are denial, rationalization, repression, projection, and regression, to mention only five. The previously mentioned defense mechanisms are only a few defensive actions we take to protect ourselves from pain. Some may be conscious reactions and others are unconscious reactions; however, most, if not all, are in some ways distortion of reality. One can see that

Freud's introduction of defense mechanisms relates back to his seminal theory that our most primitive behavior is to decrease pain and enhance pleasure.

Psychosexual Stages of Development

Freud identified what he considered to be five stages of personality development all having an impact on human behavior. The stages are: **oral, anal, phallic, latency,** and **genital**.

Oral stage (first year of life): The oral stage centers on the child's relationship with the mother. To be more specific, the closeness (or lack thereof) that develops between the mother and the child during the first years of the child's life has an impact on how the personality develops. Inadequate adjustment at this stage may, according to psychoanalytic theory, set into motion later-life personality problems, such as mistrust of others and fear of intimate relationships (Corey, 1994).

Anal stage (ages 1–3): Arlow (2005) explains the anal phase in the following manner:

> During the anal phase, interest in the bodily processes with regard to smelling, touching, and playing with feces is paramount. The disgust displayed by those who train the child and the shame the child is made to feel may contribute to a lowered sense of self-esteem. In reaction, the child may respond by stubborn assertiveness, contrary rebelliousness, and the determination to be in control. (p. 28)

A logical inference with regard to this stage of personality development is that the manner in which parents discipline their children can have an impact on personality development (Corey, 2005).

Phallic stage (ages 3–6): This stage is characterized by incestuous desires of the child toward the parent of the opposite sex. The reaction of the child's significant others toward these desires may set the tone for later-life attitudes with regard to the person's sexual attitudes (Corey, 2005).

Latency stage (ages 6–12): Previous to this stage of development, the child has directed most of his or her attention to family members; however, during this stage, the child begins to show interest in socialization and forming interests outside of the home. The psychological implications for this stage relates to how the significant others in the child's life react to these efforts of independence. At this stage, the child wants more independence; however, at the same time, he needs the reassurance of the safety and comforts of the home and his significant others. How this attempt at semi-independence is handled by significant others can have an impact, in the present and future, on the child's ability to interact socially.

Genital stage (ages 12 to death): Freud believed that from adolescent through the rest of our lives, we seek loving and satisfactory relationships; therefore, he did not develop additional stages. This stage of development begins with our attempts to establish independence, preparing for adulthood, and the stage carries through to the various stages of adulthood, where we begin to establish careers, families, social interests, and other life patterns that give meaning to life. From the Freudian standpoint, the ability or lack thereof to have handled the previously mentioned stages will have an impact on how successful we are in life.

Psychoanalytical Therapy Goals

This therapy's goals are designed to strengthen the helpee's ability to deal with life situations. In an attempt to consolidate the goals, I discuss two broad categories that will encompass several of the major goals of this helping therapy. One is to **modify the helpee's behavior** by bringing the unconscious to consciousness. As previously discussed, one of the basic beliefs of psychoanalytical therapy is that memories stored in the unconscious mind have a major impact on current behavior. Therefore, by getting the helpee in touch with these memories, the helper and helpee are better able to effect or improve behavior.

The second major goal is to **strengthen the ego**. Also as previously stated, the ego serves as an arbitrator or balance between the id and the superego. The helper, in this regard, is attempting to assist the helpee to understand his desires to increase pleasure and decrease pain while dealing with the moralistic side of his life. Stated in other terms, the professional helper is working with the helpee to realize the consequences of his behavior with regard to satisfying his ego desires. Juxtaposed with this effort, the helper assists the helpee to understand that in dealing with the moral issues of his behavior there will have to be compromises. The helper assists the helpee to understand that life is not always black or white–there are shades of gray that can add balance to his life, therefore, meeting some of his basic desires while satisfying his and societal moral standards. In some instances, strengthening the ego may mean that the helper assists the helpee to live with the fact that his basic desires are too far removed from the prevailing society's willingness to accept the behavior. He must learn to accept and implement more acceptable behavior.

Psychoanalytical Therapy Techniques

Some of the classic techniques of this therapy are **discussion, interpretation, dream analysis,** and **free association**. **Discussion** is a key element in psychoanalytical therapy, as is the case in most talk therapies. However, with psychoanalytical therapy, discussion is often used to uncover childhood experiences. From the psychoanalytical perspective, some childhood experiences may provide some clues to motivation of current behavior.

Interpretation of childhood experiences and interpretation of dreams can provide valuable information with regard to motivation of current behavior. As previously stated, from the perspective of psychoanalytical therapy, dreams represent the preconscious mind; therefore, analysis of dreams also provides valuable information with regard to motivation of behavior.

Free association is a technique where the professional helper says a word or makes a statement and the helpee is asked to state what immediately comes to his mind with regard to the word or statement. Psychoanalytical helpers believe that by the helpee giving an immediate response without giving considerable thought to the response reveals valuable psychological information that can be used to assist the helpee with understanding his personality and behavior.

Next, let us examine gestalt therapy.

GESTALT THERAPY

Major Contributors

The originators and early major contributors of gestalt therapy are Fredrick (Fritz) Perls and his wife, Laura Perls. Fritz Perls was a physician by education and training, and Laura Perls was a psychotherapist. Fritz began his psychotherapist career as a follower of the psychoanalytic approach, but in the process of developing gestalt therapy, he broke away from the psychoanalytical view of the unconscious being the primary motivation for human behavior.

Major Concepts

The Perls developed gestalt therapy on the following foundations: phenomenology, awareness, existentialism, holism, and field theory. They interpreted human behavior as being more influenced by one's perceptions of what is occurring in the here and now than the Freudian belief of the unconscious impact on current behavior. The gestalt followers do not deny that past behavior impacts current behavior; however, they believe that, by concentrating on what is happening in the present, one has a better chance of improving psychological health for the client's future. Corey (2005) makes the following observation with regard to how a gestalt therapist deals with the past: "When the past seems to have a significant bearing on clients' present attitudes and behavior, it is dealt with by bringing it into the present as much as possible" (p. 197). This can be done by asking a question such as, "How do you feel about this (the situation) at the present time?"

Continuing with the theme of understanding the motivation for human behavior as being critical to developing therapeutic goals and techniques, from a gestalt viewpoint, recognizing current behavior is important. However, equally, if not more, important to understanding the motivation is comprehending the **phenomenological** or **perceptions** of the client with regard to the behavior. How does the client perceive her current circumstances and behavior? What are the client's present feelings about her life situations? These and other **here and now** questions and the answers to those questions are critical from a gestalt standpoint.

Perception is a key component of gestalt therapy. As individuals, we too frequently overlook the fact that we can view and/or experience an event numerous times, and each time we will have a different perspective of the event. Sometimes the differences in perspective are slight, and other times they are significant. One can read a book or a chapter in a book several times and each time have different perceptions of what was read. Additionally, each time one walks into a room, although the room setting does not change, he will have a slightly, and sometimes significantly, different perception of the room and its contents. The difference in perception is not because the room has changed, but the perceiver has changed. To be more specific, each time the perceiver walks into the room, she has had different experiences that are affecting her views of life, and it is the frame of mind in which the perceiver is that impacts her perceptions of her surroundings.

From the viewpoint of the gestalt faithful, a result of the phenomenological exploration is **awareness** or **insight**–being aware of one's feeling and reactions to those feelings. This awareness is critical to understanding motivation of behavior. Behavior is not a random and isolated act; behavior occurs as a result of some stimulus. Therefore, becoming aware of factors that stimulate this behavior is essential to adequately living with or dealing with the behavior.

Field theory promotes the idea that one's experiences are part of a larger whole (field), and what one is experiencing interrelates to that whole, which has an impact on the behavior. Therefore, behavior is not an isolated event and must be viewed in its context of being part of the field. Thus, one must be aware of the client's field (environment) to better understand her behavior and the impact of that behavior. Field theory emphasizes the fact that a person's action and beliefs must be viewed in the context of his or her environment.

Gestalt therapy is part of the humanistic psychological school of thought and, as is the case for all humanistic therapies, is based on **existentialism**. Existentialism promotes the idea that all humans have psychological and affective growth potential. To be more specific, existentialism views humans as continually remaking and rediscovering themselves. This idea of one continual restructuring of oneself has meaning for both understanding motivation of behavior as well as understanding a human's abilities to correct or change behavior.

In a quest to understand normal and abnormal human behavior, gestalt therapy concepts can prove to be helpful. Whether behavior is considered normal or abnormal, one has to view the behavior from a contextual standpoint. As an example, in many environments, moving around with few clothes covering one's body is considered inappropriate behavior; however, in some environments, especially tropical or very hot climates, the fewer clothes one wears, the better. In fact, being fully dressed may be considered abnormal in that environment. In various countries, including the United States, behavior may vary from region to region. Thus, understanding one's field or environment is necessary to make judgments about appropriateness or inappropriateness. Additionally, with regard to perception, understanding helpees' perceptions of what is correct or incorrect behavior is also essential. Although sometimes difficult to understand, by some people, behavior that may appear to be widely accepted as inappropriate may be acceptable or tolerated by some. Therefore, if a child is reared in an environment that tolerates behavior widely condemned, that child, because the behavior is accepted or tolerated, may not view engaging in that behavior as something to avoid. Certainly, this does not make the engagement of that type of behavior acceptable to the masses, nor should the behavior be accepted. However, one's perception of one's environment can have a major impact on behavior.

Gestalt therapy goals and techniques: Yontef and Jacobs (2005) and Corey (2005) agree that the primary goal of gestalt therapy is **awareness**. Yontef and Jacobs feel that the *only* goal of gestalt therapy is awareness. They point out that "awareness requires self-knowledge, knowledge of the environment, responsibility for choices, self-acceptance, and the ability to contact (p. 217). Corey agrees with the previous authors' assessment of gestalt goals as he made the following statements: "The basic goal of gestalt therapy is attaining awareness and, with it, greater choice. Awareness includes knowing the environment, knowing oneself, accepting oneself, and being able to make contact" (p. 199).

Zinker (1978) (as quoted in Corey, 2005) provides an excellent summary of some expectation of the outcomes of the goals of gestalt therapy:

- Move toward increased awareness of themselves.
- Assume ownership of their experiences.

• Become aware of all of their senses.
• Learn to accept responsibility of what they do.
• Move from outside support to increased internal support. (p. 200)

The helper using gestalt therapy is free to use any techniques she can develop as long as she keeps the helpee focused on the here and now, concentrating on being aware of self, feelings, and thoughts.

ADLERIAN THERAPY

Major Contributor

Adlerian therapy, or individual therapy as it was called by its creator, Alfred Adler, is also part of the humanistic therapy school of thought. Alfred Adler was born in Austria, completed medical school, and became a physician. He later devoted his professional energy to psychotherapy. Adler was a colleague of Sigmund Freud and, at one point in his career, was a follower of psychoanalytic therapy. Adler disagreed with the deterministic philosophy of psychoanalytic therapy, which promoted the idea that humans are driven by their instinctual urges and desires, and behavior is basically controlled by unconscious material. Because of his disillusionment with the psychoanalytical philosophy, Adler began to promote the idea that humans have choices and make life choices; thus, he developed Adlerian therapy as a present- and future-oriented therapy.

Major Concepts

Adlerian Therapy and Human Behavior: To understand Adlerian therapy's viewpoints of human behavior and what motivates that behavior, we must look at several of the basic concepts of the therapy: **ideal self, inferiority, superiority, goal oriented, choices, present** and **future oriented**, and **social oriented**. As previously stated, Adlerian therapy is a humanistic therapy that champions the philosophy that behavior occurs in a social context. As a helper influenced by the Adlerian therapy philosophy, one must understand the behavior of humans from the helpee's phenomenological viewpoints and believe in the helpee's potential for self-growth. Adler believed that a basic desire of humans is to become part of a social order and make contributions to society. According to Adlerian theory, early in life, around age six (6), humans begin to develop a personal view of their **ideal self**. To be more specific, the young child begins to formulate in his mind what an ideal world would be when he is grown. In this process of developing a mental image of an **ideal self**, the person realizes that he is not the person he would like to become. This realization in Adlerian terminology is called a state of **inferiority**. In Adlerian terminology, inferiority does not denote a negative condition, which is generally how we think this term is used. Rather, the term identifies a state of realization that one is not what one wants to be; therefore, one has to develop as a human entity to become the ideal self. Stated more succulently, inferiority means an opportunity to grow and become creative. Because the person recognizes that he is in an inferior position, the person begins to develop life goals that hopefully will lead to a position of **superiority**. Again, with regard to Adlerian terminology, it should be noted that superiority is not used to denote being better than another person; rather, this term identifies the fact that the person is striving toward the ideal self.

The movement toward the ideal self is an indication that, from the Adlerian point of view, human behavior is goal oriented. As Adlerian followers state, the person is moving from a **felt minus** (inferior) to a **felt plus** (superior).

Adler posited that children's behavioral development is based, in part, on their birth order within the family. Stated in other expressions, the experiences that one has based on the relationship with siblings and parents have an impact on their psychological development and behavior, and these relationships are affected by the birth order within the family.

Adlerian therapy goals and techniques: As previously discussed, a major theme of Adlerian therapy with regard to emotionally healthy individuals is that we are socially oriented. Stated in other terms, we want to be an integral part of a community, society, and so on. Corey (2005) makes us aware that Adlerian helpers do not see helpees as being sick and in need of being cured; rather, they view helpees as being discouraged. Therefore, two of the **primary goals** are to assist helpees to **clarify their life goals** and **assist helpees in moving toward their ideal self**.

A major technique is **reeducating** helpees to understand their life goals and how to move positively toward being an integral part of a social order. Stated in other terms, the helper assists the helpee to become a contributor to his community and to society.

BEHAVIORAL THERAPIES

Major Contributors

The behavioral therapies discussed next are part of the psychological behavioral school of thought and, as the name implies, reveal the impact of human behavior on one's daily life more than any of the other therapies previously discussed. There are several types of behavioral therapies, including **rational emotive behavioral therapy (REBT), social learning theory**, and **cognitive behavioral therapy (CBT)**.

For a psychological therapeutic tool to remain viable, it must adjust its theory and techniques to incorporate the latest discoveries relevant to the understanding of what motivates human behavior. Behavioral therapy is an excellent example of this adjustment because there have been several psychological therapy branches developed from the original thoughts of human behavior. The foundation for behavioral therapy is **classical conditioning** and **operant conditioning**. Ivan Pavlov, a Russian physiologist, is credited with being the first to demonstrate classical conditioning. Pavlov demonstrated, in his experiments with dogs, that in classical conditioning, when an unconditioned stimulus such as food produces an unconditioned response such as salivation and is associated with a conditioned stimulus such as the ring of a bell, if the pairing is repeated often enough, the conditioned stimulus will alone produce the unconditioned response. Pavlov built his classical conditioning and resulting impact on behavior on a **relationship of association**. As discussed, in Pavlov's experiments, the dog associated the ring of the bell with food, and thus salivation began just as salivation occurred when food was present. Although Pavlov's experiment was conducted with animals, if one extrapolates the finding to human behavior, one can see one of the weaknesses or criticisms of classical behavior therapy, which is that behavior is devoid of cognition. Pavlov's experiments were not based on reward and punishment, or what is commonly referred to as reinforcement theory.

John B. Watson, an American psychologist, carried Pavlov's experimental results into human behavior. His belief was that human behavior is based on reflex and conditioning. Watson's beliefs are not much different than Pavlov's results, except they are applied to human behavior. Again, the criticism is that this line of thinking does not consider human behavior as being motivated by thinking. B. F. Skinner, another American psychologist, is considered the most influential proponent of behaviorism. Skinner believed that humans do not have free choice; thus, his view of human personality and behavior is one of determinism. To be more specific, he viewed human behavior as being determined by environmental factors. Skinner introduced the concept of reinforcement to behavior. Skinner's contribution to behaviorism is called **operant conditioning**. Skinner postulated that behavior that is positively reinforced will be repeated; conversely, behavior that is punished or ignored will be eliminated. B. F. Skinner posits that learning cannot occur without some kind of reinforcement, either positive or negative.

Nichols and Schwartz (1995) provide an explanation of how operant conditioning works in a clinical setting:

> The operant conditioner carefully observes target behavior and then quantifies its frequency and rate. Then to complete a functional analysis of the behavior, the experimenter or clinician notes the consequences of the behavior to determine the contingencies of reinforcement. For example, someone interested in a child's temper tantrums would begin by observing when they occurred and what the consequences were. A typical finding might be that the parents gave in if the tantrums were prolonged. Thus the parents would be discovered to have been reinforcing the very behavior they least wanted. To eliminate the tantrums, they would be taught to ignore or punish them. Moreover they would be told that giving in even occasionally would maintain the tantrum because behavior that is partially or intermittently reinforced is the most difficult to extinguish. (p. 322)

Classical and operant conditioning theories are similar with regard to the fact that neither models of behavior identify the thinking process, attitudes, and values as influencing behavior. Although the roots of the behavioral tree (classical and operant conditioning) did not recognize cognition as influencing behavior, several of the branches—rational emotive behavioral therapy, social learning behavioral therapy, and cognitive behavioral therapy—have added thinking as a major determinant of human behavior.

Albert Bandura's theory of social learning has made a significant contribution to the concept of what affects human behavior. Bandura utilized principles of cognition to help explain how behavior is changed. According to Corey (2005), Bandura posited that "behavior is influenced by stimulus events, by external reinforcement and by cognitive mediational experiences" (p. 230). Wilson (2005) further explains Bandura's contribution in the following way:

> In the social cognitive approach, the influence of environmental events on behavior is largely determined by the cognitive process governing how environmental influences are perceived and how the individual interpreted them. Psychological functioning, according to this view, involves a reciprocal interaction among three interlocking sets of influences; behavior, cognitive processes and environmental factors. (p. 203)

Bandura recognized that the environment causes human behavior; however, he also believed that human behavior causes our environment. Stated in other terms, our environment influences us and we influence our environment. This concept is called **reciprocal determinism**.

Albert Ellis, an American-born psychologist, initially was a strong believer of psychoanalytical therapy. He later moved away from the deterministic views of psychoanalytical theory and developed what is called rational emotive behavioral therapy (**REBT**). Ellis believed that, as humans, our behavior is predicated on how we think about events that impact our lives. Therefore, abnormal behavior is the product of irrational thinking. If abnormal behavior is the result of irrational thinking, then it is reasonable to assume that acceptable behavior emanates from rational thinking. Ellis believed that it is not so much the events of our lives that cause us to react in ways that we react, but it is the interpretation of those events that propel our behavior. For example, if a student receives a poor grade on an examination and she becomes depressed, Ellis' theory is that the depression is not caused by receiving the poor marks, but rather the interpretation the student has placed on the grade. The irrational thinking that may be occurring could go as follows: "I have devoted considerable number of hours preparing for this examination and I failed therefore I must not be as intelligent as I thought I am." A rational emotive therapist would work with the helpee to have more rational thoughts with regard to this subject. First, the helpee may be encouraged to realize that she is intelligent because she was able to meet all of the requirements for entry into college; and second, the helpee may be encouraged to explore how she had studied for the examination to discover any flaws in her preparation. Through these types of exploratory exercises, the helpee is moved away from irrational thinking and encouraged to think more rationally. Corey (2005) has pointed out that rational emotive behavioral therapy is based on the assumption that cognition, emotions, and behavior interact significantly and have a reciprocal cause-and-effect relation. Corey, provides a more in-depth discussion of rational emotive therapy with the following comments:

> We originally learn irrational beliefs from significant others during childhood. Additionally, we create irrational dogmas and superstitions by ourselves. Then we actively reinforce self-defeating beliefs by the process of auto suggestion and self-repetition and by behaving as if they are useful. Hence, it is largely our own repetition of early indoctrinated irrational thoughts, rather than a parent's repetition that keeps dysfunctional attitudes alive and operative within us. (p. 273)

Behavioral Therapy Goals and Techniques: Because of the various types of behavioral therapy, it is difficult to provide a complete list of the goals of the different concepts of behavioral therapy. In fact, the intent of this discussion is to give a general overview of the goals, not an all-inclusive discussion. Also, one can view the goals and techniques as woven together. Given the stated disclaimer, I point out that there are three goals and techniques that fit into most, if not all, forms of behavioral therapy: **collaborative empiricism, guided discover,** and **self-therapy**.

With regard to **collaborative empiricism**, by examining each word, we get an idea of the meaning of the phrase. *Collaborative* means working together, and *empiricism* means testing ideas or experiences. Therefore, collaborative empiricism is referring to the helper and the helpee working together to understand the possible meaning to the helpee's life situation.

Beck and Weishaar (2005) provide the following explanation of collaborative empiricism:

> In a collaborative process, the therapist and patient examine the patient's beliefs about himself, other people, and the world. The patient's maladaptive conclusions are treated as testable hypotheses. Behavioral experiments and verbal procedures are used to examine alternative interpretations and to generate contradictory evidence that supports more adaptive beliefs and lead to therapeutic change. (p. 238)

As the title implies, **guided discovery** indicates collaboration between the helper and the helpee with regard to identifying and applying appropriate treatment to the issues at hand. The helper plays a significant role in assisting the helpee; however, it is the helpee's responsibility to carry through with the treatment. Beck and Weishaar (2005) explains the process in the following way: "guided discover implies that the therapist does not exhort or cajole the patient to adopt a new set of beliefs. Rather, the therapist encourages the patient's use of information, facts, and probabilities to obtain a realistic perspective" (p. 253).

Summary of Behavioral Therapies

A major goal/technique of most behavior therapies is for the helpee to eventually conduct his own therapy (**self-therapy**). As discussed in collaborative empiricism and guided discovery, the helper assists the helpee to identify causes of issues and helps explore alternative behaviors. Additionally, the helper works with the helpee with regard to conducting her own therapy in her own environment.

PERSON-CENTERED THERAPY

Major Contributor

One of the best-known therapies of the humanistic school of thought is person centered, and the major contributor is the American psychologist, Carl Rogers. This therapy has gone through an evolution of name changes as the therapy has expanded its therapeutic reach to additional helpees. Initially, the therapy was called nondirective primarily because of the manner in which the therapy was conducted. Later the name was changed to client-centered therapy to, in part, denote the fact that the therapy is driven by the client rather than being therapist dominated. The current name of person centered reflects that the therapy is still centered on the helpee and also indicates that the clientele has expanded to other fields, such as business and education.

As the name person centered implies, this therapy places considerable emphasis on what the helpee can do rather than on what the helper should or can do. Carl Rogers promoted the idea that the counselor does not have all the answers, and a major role of the counselor is to establish an environment that is conducive to cognition and emotional growth by the helpee. With regard to assisting the helpee with her psychological self-growth, the qualities of the professional helper is a key ingredient in the helper/helpee relationship. According to Carl Rogers, three of the key ingredients are: **empathy, congruence,** and **unconditional positive regard**.

With regard to empathy, no one can fully understand how another person feels; therefore, it is imperative that the helper become an astute listener and observer of body language. The professional helper has to not only have heard the words being spoken but also must feel, as much as humanly possible, the underlying tone and meaning of those spoken words. The helper must, again as much as humanly possible, feel the feelings that the helpee is feeling as she expresses herself. Obviously, this is not an easy task for most helpers, but it is essential so that the helper can reflect back to the helpee what she is saying and, more important, feeling. A great deal of writing has occurred with regard to the attending skill of the helper reflecting back to the helpee what he, the helpee, has said. Often beginning helpers using the Rogerian approach tend to think that simply repeating or rephrasing the helpee's words is sufficient to show empathy. However, a skilled person-centered helper will not only reflect words that the helpee has said, but will also reflect meaning or understanding of the underlying meaning of what has been said.

Being congruent is another of the cornerstones of the professional helper's relationship with the helpee. The helper must be honest with the helpee, and that honesty must show with respect to congruence between the helper's verbal communication and her body posture and other forms of nonverbal communication. If the professional helper expects the helpee to be honest with her, she must be honest with the helpee. Through congruence, the helper models honesty to the helpee and engenders trust.

Rogers emphasized unconditional positive regard as a necessary trait of the helper. Unconditional positive regard means that, although the helper may not agree with the helpee's actions or behaviors, she is accepting of the helpee as a worthwhile human being who has the capacity to change his behavior. This means that the helper does not wait until the helpee changes his behavior before she is willing to provide positive regard to the helpee; rather she accepts him as he is and assists him to become the person he has the potential to become.

Unconditional positive regard often is one of the concepts many beginning and some seasoned helpers find difficult to accept. It has been my experience that when beginning and aspiring helpers are asked to list and discuss types of helpees whom they believe they will have difficulties assisting, and they are asked whether they think they can provide unconditional positive regard to those helpees, most indicate that they do not think that they will be able to do so. Although this is an important concept, the fact remains that it is a difficult action to carry through. This is why it is important for all professional helpers to periodically conduct a self-analysis of personal attitudes and beliefs.

With regard to human behavior and personality, person-centered therapy does not discuss as directly the motivation of behavior as some of the previously mentioned therapies. Person-centered therapy takes a phenomenological approach to human behavior and personality development, in that this therapy emphasizes that the helpee's perception is his reality. Stated in other terms, the helpee's behavior is based on how he interrupts his environment. Because how the helpee sees the world determines his behavior, the goal of behavior is to satisfy the helpee's needs as he or she perceives them. Therefore, part of what the helpee perceives becomes incorporated into his self-esteem and self-concept. Thus, the helpee behaves in ways that are consistent with his self.

Person-centered therapy is also grounded in existentialism, which promotes the idea that humans have the ability of self-psychological growth. To be more precise, humans have the potential to solve their own problems. Therefore, one of the roles of the professional helper, from the person-centered viewpoint, is to establish an environment that is conducive to the helpee utilizing those resources that are necessary to apply to the situation in which he is encountering. Oltmanns and Emery (2004) point out that people who subscribe to this theory also believe in humans as innately good and, therefore, blame abnormalities in human behavior on people's frustrations to society and claim that people are responsible for changing their own behavior.

Person-Centered Goals and Techniques: One of the goals is to assist the helpee in his or her psychological growth by listening to the helpee and giving undivided attention to what the helpee is saying and feeling. Additionally, the helper is to view the world as the helpee views the world and assist the helpee in knowing him or herself. With regard to techniques, Rogers did not emphasize techniques; he emphasized the counselor/helper qualities. Succinctly stated, the counselor/helper is the technique. Therefore, one can state that some of the techniques are effective listener, accepting, positive regard, and empathy.

Summary of Person-Centered Therapy

Person-centered therapy is based, in part, on the existential philosophy of viewing the helpee as someone in a constant state of growth, thus being able to solve his or her own problems. Therefore, one of the important roles the helper can assume is to develop an environment that is conducive to the helpee tapping into his or her inner strengths and developing solutions to the issues being encountered. In essence, the helper, from the standpoint of person-centered therapy, is the technique.

SUMMARY

The overview of the previously discussed individual counseling therapies was not intended to be a comprehensive view of any of the therapies. Rather, the intent is to provide some general information with regard to these therapies so the reader can use these therapies as well as others not discussed as guides to helping develop his or her own therapy. As previously mentioned, few, if any, current professional helpers follow any particular therapy as the originator(s) developed. The professional helper will study the various therapies and decide which one or ones best fit his or her professional psychological belief system and use the therapy or therapies as a foundation for developing his or her approach that works best in his or her situation. Additionally, there are other therapies not discussed that the helper is encouraged to review.

Chapter Review Questions

1. What are the three schools of thought to which most psychological helping therapies fit into?
2. What are the some of the major concepts of psychoanalytical therapy?
3. What are some of the major concepts of Adlerian therapy?
4. What are some of the major concepts of gestalt therapy?
5. What are some of the major concepts of person-centered therapy?
6. What are some of the major concepts of behavioral therapies?
7. Who were the major contributors to gestalt therapy?
8. Who was the major contributor to person-centered therapy?
9. Who was the major contributor to Adlerian therapy?
10. Who are some of the major contributors to behavioral therapy?

Mental Exercise

Instructions: Read the following case study and answer the questions listed at the end of the case study.

Mark

Mark is a 29-year-old African-American male. Mark is single and graduated from high school when he was 19 years of age. Mark is the middle child of seven children. His father is a factory worker, and his mother is a teacher's aide at one of the local elementary schools. Two of his sisters who are older than he have graduated from junior college and are currently employees of the state in which they live and where Mark and his family also live and have lived all of his life. Two of Mark's brothers completed college on basketball scholarships, and one is playing semi-professional basketball in a northeastern state. Another brother is playing professional basketball in Italy. All of the previously mentioned siblings are older than Mark. The remaining two siblings, a brother and sister, are younger than he. Both have finished high school but did not go to college. Both are gainfully employed.

Mark currently works for a temporary employment service agency because he has had difficulty securing and maintaining jobs in the past. Before working for the temporary service agency, which places him on various jobs depending on the request the agency receives, Mark had worked as a plumber's helper. Prior to that job, he worked for an auto parts company delivering parts, but was fired after the company discovered that he did not have a valid driver's license. Also, Mark was very slow on making his deliveries; his time of delivery took almost twice as long as other drivers.

Mark's parents have stressed education to their children, and both parents at various times have worked two jobs to send those whom chose to go, to college, as well as to provide the daily needs of the family. Mark currently lives at home with his parents but periodically moves out on his own, but seems to have difficulty paying his bills on time; thus, his utilities are often disconnected.

Mark has a learning disability and had a diagnosis in school as ADHD. Therefore, he graduated from public school having attended what has been commonly called "special education" format after repeating the 9th and 12th grades.

Mark has a pleasing personality and makes friends easily, thus he always seems to have an active social life. He is not married but dates frequently; however, he seems to have difficulties maintaining a close relationship.

Mark interacts well with all of his siblings, but has a younger brother with whom he seems to have the best relationship. This brother seems to help him with daily activities same as he appeared to help him with school work when he was in school. The younger brother is 2 years Mark's junior.

Mark works with several youth groups in the community; he helps with sports activities because he was very good in high school in both basketball and baseball. He was recruited to several colleges, but did not attend because he could not make sufficient scores on the entrance examinations.

Mark is concerned with his inability to secure a substantial job. He realizes that his work for the temporary agency does not provide him with benefits, and the older he gets, the more he realizes that he needs steady employment that has a full range of benefits. Mark also realizes that his inability to read beyond an eighth-grade level is a problem.

Mark has discussed his concerns with his parents and his brother, and they have suggested he seek help.

Answer the following questions:

1. Which psychological therapy or therapies will you use in your helping relationship with Mark? Explain why you have chosen this therapy or the therapies.
2. What are the major problems with regard to Mark's situation?
3. Are there cultural and/or ethnic/racial issues to consider? Defend your answer.
4. How will you attempt to establish rapport, trust, and so on?
5. Identify the crisis meeting resources. (Crisis meeting resources means the resources Mark and/or the family has that he/they can use to help resolve problems. Examples are good communication, money, strong family, and/or community support.)
6. What is your perception of Mark's definition of the event(s)? (Definition of events means how the family and/or individual view the situation—do they consider it as one of the worse things that have happened, or could happen to them, or do they consider it a problem but something that they can overcome?)
7. Are there other family members who should be involved in the treatment? Defend your answer.
8. What type of behavioral changes will you attempt to get Mark to work toward?
9. What are the goals you will encourage Mark to establish for the helping relationship?
10. How will you terminate the helping relationship?

References

Arlow, J. A. (2005). Psychoanalysis. In R. J. Corsini, & D. Wedding (Eds.). *Current psychotherapies* (7th ed.), Monterey, CA: Thomson/Brooks/Cole.

Beck, A. T., & Weishaar, M. E. (2005). Cognitive therapy. In R. J. Corsini, & D. Wedding (Eds.), *Current psychotherapies* (7th ed.). Monterey, CA: Thomson/Brooks/Cole.

Corey, G. (1994). *Theory and practice of counseling and psychotherapy* Monterey, CA: Brooks/Cole.

Corey, G. (2005). *Theory and practice of counseling and psychotherapy* (7th ed.). Monterey, CA: Thomson/Brooks/Cole.

Nichols, M. P., & Schwartz, R. C. (1995). *Family therapy* (3rd ed.). Boston: Allyn & Bacon.

Oltmanns, T. F., & Emery, R. E. (2004). *Abnormal psychology* (4th ed.). Upper Saddle River, NJ: Pearson Prentice Hall.

Taibbi, R. (2007). *Doing family therapy: Craft and creativity in clinical practice* (2nd ed.). New York: Guilford Press.

Wilson, G. T. (2005). Behavior therapy. In R. J. Corsini, & D. Wedding (Eds.), *Current psychotherapies* (7th ed.). Monterey, CA: Thomson/Brooks/Cole.

Yontef, G., & Jacobs, L. (2005). In R. J. Corsini, & D. Wedding (Eds.), *Current psychotherapies* (7th ed.). Monterey, CA: Thomson/Brooks/Cole.

Zinker, J. (1978). Quoted in Corey, G. (2005). *Theory and practice of counseling and psychotherapy* (7th ed.). Monterey, CA: Thomson/Brooks/Cole.

Suggested Readings

Barlow, D. H. (Ed.). (2008). *Clinical handbook of psychological disorders: A step-by-step treatment manual* (4th ed.). New York: Guilford.

Cooper, M. (2007). *The handbook of person-centered psychotherapy and counseling.* New York: Palgrave Macmillan.

Corsini, R. J., & Wedding, D. (Eds.). (2005). *Current psychotherapies* (7th ed.) Monterey, CA: Thomson/Brooks/Cole.

Gazda, G. M. (1976). *Theories and methods of group counseling in the schools* (2nd ed.). Springfield, IL: Charles C Thomas.

Gilbert, P., & Leaher, R. L. (Eds.). (2007). *The therapeutic relationship in the cognitive behavioral psychotherapies.* London, New York: Routledge.

Hersen, M., & Gross, A. M. (Eds.). (2008). *Handbook of clinical psychology.* Hoboken, NJ: Wiley.

Lebow, J. (2008). *Twenty-first century psychotherapies: Contemporary approaches to theory and practice.* Hoboken, NJ: Wiley.

Ofer, Z. (2007). *Boundaries in psychotherapy: Ethical and clinical exploration.* Washington, DC: American Psychological Association.

Seligman, L., & Reechenberg, L. W. (2007). *Selecting effective treatment: A comprehensive systematic guide to treating mental disorders* (3rd ed.). San Francisco: Jossey-Bass.

Veague, H. B., & Collins, C. (2007). *Personality disorders.* New York: Chelsea House.

Young, M. E. (1992). *Counseling methods and techniques: An eclectic approach.* New York: Maxwell Macmillan International.

Chapter 13

UNDERSTANDING FAMILY COUNSELING

Chapter Outline

• Major Concepts
• Summary of Solution-Focused Therapy
• Conclusion of Family Therapy
• References

Course Objectives
• Provide information with regard to selected family therapies
• Provide information so that the professional helper can begin to develop his or her own therapy

INTRODUCTION

In most cases of being a helper, even though you may be working with one person there generally speaking are more people involved, or at least significantly concerned and impacted by the issues of which the person being helped is involved. In many situations some of those persons affected by the issues are family members; therefore, whenever possible a wise move maybe to get family members involved. With regard to getting family involved, an important question is which members should be involved? Often this becomes a major issue, first does the individual want any family members involved? Second, do family members want to be involved?

Certainly, there are concerns that the entire family are involved and family therapy is appropriate. The fact that the issue or issues relate to the family does not guarantee that all family members will cooperate or will be happy to be involved in the helping process. Despite the reality that often family members are reluctant to be formally part of the helping process, it is the professional helper's responsibility to encourage those that are reluctant to participate. The professional helper should encourage participation by pointing out that while it may not appear that they are part of the problem, their cooperation and input will be important with regard to arriving at a solution or solutions to the problems to be discussed.

The major question becomes what will you do to get the entire family involved in the treatment? The reality is that in some, if not many cases, you will not be able to get all family members involved; however, you must try. Because arriving at solutions that will be lasting solutions will significantly be increased if all concerned becomes involved. As human beings, to a large degree, we are concerned with what is important to us. Stated in other terms, while we most often will not verbalize this but what is in this for me is in our thought process as we decide whether to participate. Therefore, as the helping professional your chances of obtaining reluctant member's participation to some extent will depend upon how well you are at convincing them that not only is their participation important and needed, it is in their best interest that they participate. This does not mean that you as the helper and the family members that are participating disregard the nonparticipating member. No solution at which the family arrives will be complete without taking into consideration how the missing member(s) will be impacted by decisions that are made.

In some instances a question becomes, how do you carry forward without the participation of the member or members who are not participating? There is a technique called the empty chair. This is a technique where an empty chair is placed before the individual or individuals and ask them to act as though the missing person is sitting in the chair and address conversation to the missing person. An addition to that is the person talking to the missing person can think of what the person's responses would likely be. As the person identifies what she thinks the person's response will be, as the helper, you can ask questions such as why she thinks the response will be as she has indicated and what is her response to his/her responses?

The points being made is that in many instances family therapy is an important tool to use in assisting families deal with and solve some of their problems. As previously stated some family members will be reluctant to participate; however it is your responsibility to encourage participation and develop techniques that will help you be successful in helping families resolve many of their problems. However, before we get into techniques, lets learn about various family therapies and the theories that support them.

According to Nichols and Schwartz (2005), most family therapy theories have as its foundation system theory and cybernetics. System theory promotes the idea that, to understand an event, one must understand the impact that event has on the immediate environment. From the standpoint of family counseling, to understand the dynamics of the family, one must view the family as a system that is comprised of numerous subsystems. Each person within the family is a subsystem, and the interaction with other members of the family creates other subsystems. This combining of various family members together to create subsystems frequently changes as events and issues arise within the family. Offered as an example, father and son collaborate together, creating a subsystem to convince mother to agree to them going fishing for the weekend rather than helping clean the home. Later, mother and father become a subsystem, grounding the son for inappropriate behavior. Other than each individual family member being a subsystem of the family, various family members combining together for a common cause create other subsystems, and these subsystems are fluid, changing as the issues and events take place within the family. With regard to systems approach to family counseling, family counselors/therapists must look not only at the impact an event is having on the family, but how the other family members fit into the problem. A final point being made with regard to families and system theory is that the family as a unit is also a subsystem of a larger system, such as a community, civic club, and religious organization, to mention only three.

Becvar (2003) adds to our understanding of the foundations of family therapy by pointing out that "to understand behavior, one must consider it in context; systems are characterized by rules." She further elaborates by stating "each person has a personal belief system according to which reality is experienced and understood and which is that person's truth; and problems are maintained in the context of recurrent patterns of communication" (p. 10).

As previously mentioned, the second foundation on which family counseling is based is cybernetics, which refers to how the system maintains itself. Relating the concept of cybernetics to the family means viewing the communication patterns of family members: who communicates with whom and how this communication is done and maintained.

Family therapy, similar to individual therapy, has evolved over the years. As the practice of family therapy is evolving, some of the more contemporary therapies, such as narrative and solution focus, do not dissect families into subsystems.

With the following statement Sexton, Weeks, and Robbins (2003) affirm Nichols and Schwartz's pronouncement that system theory is one of the foundations of family therapy; however, they further point out that since the application of system theory as a foundation, significant advances have been made with regard to understanding family interactions.

Systems theory was the early foundation for family therapy, but we have made significant advances in our understanding of how families work since the application of this general theory to the family. The field has increasingly turned its attention to include a focus on successful 'functioning' of families. Thus, increasingly, the foundations of our practice have moved toward family strengths and resiliency and understanding problems with a consideration of social and ecological context, as well as an appreciation of the specific meanings of family members in their unique settings. (p. 1)

There is discussion of two of the contemporary family therapies – narrative and solution focus – in this chapter. However, first I discuss some of the ground-breaking therapies.

In this chapter on family counseling, I provide a brief discussion of the following therapies: **Bowen Family Systems Therapy, Psychoanalytic Family Therapy, Structural Family Therapy, Cognitive Behavioral Family Therapy, Narrative Family Therapy,** and **Solution Focus Family Therapy**.

In the previous discussion of individual counseling, I emphasized understanding human behavior because this understanding is one key to developing goals and techniques. With regard to family counseling, I am emphasizing understanding family behavior as a key component to constructing goals and techniques. In fact, understanding the dynamics of family behavior is essentially the same as analyzing human behavior with regard to individual counseling, with the added dimension of observing the interaction of several human behaviors.

BOWEN FAMILY SYSTEMS THERAPY

Major Contributor

Murray Bowen is the major contributor to this system of family therapy. Doctor Bowen as a psychiatrist had considerable mental health work experience, having worked at the Menninger clinic and at the National Institute of Mental Health. Doctor Bowen has made significant contributions to the field of family therapy with regard to how family interaction is viewed. He emphasized that, in working with families, one must recognize the unresolved emotional attachments to one's family of origin and work toward resolving those attachments. With regard to explaining an aspect of family interaction, he introduced the concept of family triangles, which are discussed later.

Understanding Family Behavior: The major concepts of this theory of therapy are: **Differentiation of Self, Triangles, Nuclear Family Emotional Process, Family Project Process, Multigenerational Transmission Process,** and **Sibling Position**. Each of these concepts represents some form of unresolved emotional attachment, and the following discussion provides a brief explanation of how they impact family relations.

Differentiation of Self: This concept emphasizes that there are two types of thought processes or interactions based on thoughts that family members possess. One is **differentiated**, which refers to the ability to separate thoughts from feelings. The second thought process is called **undifferentiated**, which refers to being unable to separate thoughts from feelings.

With regard to family interaction, persons who are differentiated are able to view situations and issues more objectively, keeping their emotions in check, and thus are able to understand and react to family issues rationally. In contrast, undifferentiated family members tend to react to issues with their emotions rather than intellectually, analyzing the issues and making decision and/or reacting accordingly. According to Nichols and Schwartz, 2005) undifferentiated family members find it difficult in family situations to stand alone; they need others to help support their positions or stances on issues.

Most persons who work with families in crisis or families facing problems will point out that a great deal of family discord and inability to correct the discord is a result of emotions–family members reacting emotionally rather than rationally. This theory of therapy refers to this as undifferentiation, and one goal is to help the family understand what is happening and the impact it is having on the family.

Triangles: This is a simple and accurate concept of family interaction. When observing family dynamics with regard to disagreement over a family issue, the conventional thinking has been that there will be two opposing sides formed; however, Bowen introduced the concept that triangles occur when two people within the family are having problems and one or both bring in a third person, which forms a triangle, primarily with the intent of the third person taking his or her side. This theory of family therapy talks about detrianglation, which simply means breaking up the triangles so that effective communication can flow.

Family Projection Process: This concept refers to how parents transfer their problems or issues onto their children. When parents are having problems relating to each other, too frequently, one of the parents may direct his or her attention to one or more of the children. This does not mean that the parent is projecting his or her frustration onto one or more of the children, but is devoting more attention to that child because of not being able to direct the attention to the unreceptive spouse. In this manner, the parent is unintentionally, and in some cases intentionally, involving the child or children into his or her frustrations.

Nuclear Family Emotional Process: Earlier, I discussed the concepts of differentiation and undifferentiation and their impact on family interaction. The theory is that the more undifferentiated the person is, the less likely he or she will be able to effectively interact with family members because he or she reacts more emotionally than rationally. The nuclear family emotional concept posits that the less differentiated a person is with the family of origin, the greater the chance he or she will project anxiety into the current family. The family of origin refers to one's birth family or family in which the person was reared. Nichols and Schwartz (2005) point out that this undifferentiation will produce one or more of the following: (a) overt marital conflict, (b) reactive emotional distance, (c) physical or emotional dysfunction in one of the spouses (usually the more accommodating one), or (d) projection of problems onto one or more of the children.

Multigenerational Transmission Process: This concept is basically stating that the undifferentiation is carried from generation to generation. This sounds somewhat like nuclear family emotional process, except this concept is implying that if the chain of undifferentiation is not broken, it will be passed on to the next generation and so on. Additionally, the concept points out that undifferentiated persons tend to marry the same type of person, thus this propensity to act out emotions is passed to offspring.

Sibling Position: Similar to Adlerian therapy theory, which is discussed in individual counseling, Bowen's family system theory promotes the idea that birth order has an impact on one's personality characteristics. Although children are members of the same family, have the same parents, and, as much as possible, are treated fairly, each has a tendency to interpret events, actions, and situation differently. For some, there may be a slight difference of interpretation, whereas others may have significantly different interpretations of events. Some therapists such as Adler and Bowen contribute this in part to sibling position within the family.

Emotional Cutoff: This concept discusses various ways that persons attempt to remove themselves from the bonds of their family of origin. Most people attempt to become independent of their parents; it is the manner in which this is done that can create problems. If there has been considerable unresolved anxiety with parents and/or siblings, the emotional cutoff can be unproductive.

The previously discussed concepts of Bowen Family Systems Therapy explain some of the philosophical foundation of the therapy. These concepts serve as the basis of the goals of the therapy.

Goals

- Teach family members about themselves and their relationships
- Work with family members about assuming responsibility for their problems
- Help family members recognize and break up family triangles (detriangulation)
- Increase parents' abilities to recognize, understand, and handle their children's behavior
- Increase the family's ability to function with less anxiety

Techniques

According to Nichols (2006), Bowenian therapy does not promote techniques; however, it asks questions, and the type of questions asked provides some idea of the technique. The questions are called **process questions**. Process questions are queries designed to identify what is occurring inside people and between them. Example process questions are "How do you feel about ____? How do you deal with ____?

Although the developer of this therapy did not list specific techniques, the professional helper should view the general goals of the therapy and view her goals for her specific helping relationship and develop techniques that she feels will be most successful in accomplishing the previously mentioned goals. It is this author's opinion that each helping professional should not feel welded to any set of techniques, including those identified by the developers of the therapy (if they promote specific techniques). Rather, the helper should use those techniques that she feels will produce the desired results and supplement those techniques with ones she develops on her own.

Summary of Bowen Family Systems Therapy

1. The central theme of this therapy is that unresolved emotional attachment to one's family must be resolved, rather than passively accepted or reactively rejected.
2. Major concepts of this theory are:
   - Differentiation of Self
   - Triangles
   - Nuclear Family Emotional Process
   - Family Projection Process
   - Multigenerational Transmission Process
   - Sibling Position

PSYCHOANALYTIC FAMILY THERAPY

Major Contributors

Sigmund Freud (Freudian Drive Psychology), Heinz Kohut (Self-Psychology), and Melanie Klein (Object Relations Theory). As previously discussed in individual therapy, Sigmund Freud is considered by many to be the most influential theorist of psychological therapy. His theories with regard to personality development and human behavior have influenced, in one way or another, most modern psychological treatment therapies.

Another contributor of the development of psychoanalytical family therapy is Heinz Kohut. Heinz Kohut was born in Vienna, Austria, and received his medical degree from the University of Vienna. As a result of anti-Semitic tensions in Austria, Dr. Kohut moved to the United States and became a faculty member at the University of Chicago. Kohut began his psychological work as a follower of Freud's psychoanalytical theoretical approach, but later began to make modifications to Freud's approach to therapy by introducing **self-psychology**, which is discussed later.

The third major contributor to psychoanalytical family therapy is Melanie Klein. She also was born in Vienna, Austria, and became a child analyst. Her psychological orientation was Freudian psychoanalytic therapy; however, she deviated from some of Freud's basic principles, particularly child development. One of her main deviations led to her contributions to **object relations theory**, which also is discussed later.

Freudian Drive Psychology: I provide a brief overview of Freudian drive psychology, in that it was previously discussed in the individual counseling section. In developing his theory of psychoanalysis, Sigmund Freud described several components that impact the development of human behavior and personality. These components were the id, ego, and superego; psychosexual development; defense mechanisms; and anxiety.

Children learn early in life the consequences of inappropriate expression of some of these building blocks of behavior and personality. Freud posited that emotional disorders may occur as a result of events being moved below one's conscious level of memory. The result is that, although we do not remember the events, they impact our behavior. Based on the classical psychoanalytical view, the helping profession must assist the helpee to understand the unconscious material and how it is impacting current behavior. In summary, Freudian drive psychology promotes the idea that human behavior is driven by instincts, and our basic instinct is to avoid pain and increase pleasure. However, in some instances, doing what is pleasurable goes against acceptable societal standards and/or what we have been socialized to believe is morally acceptable. This conflict between our instinctual drives and acceptable decorum may create frustration and repression of instincts.

Self-Psychology: A second component of psychoanalytical family therapy is what has been referred to as self-psychology. Self-psychology purports that healthy human emotional development is predicated on productive interaction with significant caregivers. This interaction is especially important in childhood. To be more specific, the quality of childhood relationships with significant caregivers will have important implications with regard to the near- and long-term emotional development of the child. In this regard, self-psychology advocates identify three significant psychological needs of children: (a) **alter ego needs**–appropriate emotional development requires that children have significant contact with others like themselves; (b) **idealizing needs**–to develop in an emotionally stable way, children need to have emotional attachment to emotionally stable caregivers; and (c) **mirroring needs**–to develop in an emotionally stable manner, children must feel loved. It is through these steps that a positive image of the child's self is built.

Another major contribution that self-psychology has made to psychoanalytical family therapy is introducing the concept of **empathy** into the helping relationship. One of the key techniques of classical psychoanalytical therapy is **analytical neutrality**, which means the helper does not express emotional opinions with regard to information presented by the helpee. In contrast to that view, self-psychology says the quality of the helping relationship is dependent on the helper expressing empathic understanding of the helpee's situation.

Object Relations Theory: Freud identified objects as anything that an infant directs his or her attention, and these objects are used with regard to helping satisfy needs. Other interpretations of objects such as Melanie Klein and others have led to the current theory of object relations view of objects. Klein and others essentially stated that, as an infant and a child, we develop expectations of others based on our interactions with them. Nichols (2006) points out that the residue of these early relationships leaves an internal object–mental images of self and others built from experience and expectation. The unconscious remnants of those internalized objects form the core of the person.

Classical psychoanalysis is designed for individual psychological intervention, and, as we are aware, family counseling involves more than one person. Therefore, to implement psychoanalysis as a family counseling tool of intervention, there had to be some adaptations. The developers of self-psychology and object relations theories were followers of psychoanalysis. However, they expanded Freud's interpretation of some concepts, such as the nature of instinctual drives, and thus they built a bridge from individual counseling to family counseling. Things that self-psychology and object relation theories add to psychoanalysis and allow the professional helper to do are: (a) move from analytical neutrality to being empathically engaged with the helpees;

(b) move from the helper viewing the client's behavior as being the result of deterministic action or stated in other terms driven by instincts; (c) recognizing the impact that internalized view of significant objects, particularly the mother, has on the development of oneself; and (d) recognize the need of children to have significant contact with empathic caregivers. All of these variables, as previously stated, allowed psychoanalytical therapy to navigate the bridge between individual counseling to family counseling.

Goals

The following are some of the goals of psychoanalytical family counseling:
1. Free family members of unconscious constraints so that they will be able to interact with one another as healthy individuals.
2. Personality change.
3. Help families learn how to discontinue constricting one another so that they can become independent.

Techniques

The following are some of the techniques of psychoanalytical family counseling: (a) listening, (b) empathy, and (c) interpretation. Listening is not a technique unique to psychoanalytical family therapy; all helping relationships, whether stated or implied, utilize effective listening to better understand the helpee's life situation. As discussed in this book with regard to effective characteristics, effective listening is considered one of the most important and useful characteristics a helper can possess.

The empathic understanding of the helpee's situation is critical to establishing rapport and instilling confidence in the helpee to take positive and constructive steps toward managing or eliminating the situation. Therefore, from the psychoanalytical perspective, being as nonjudgmental as possible is one key to a successful outcome.

Interpretation of the situation is another way of stating the need to assist the helpee with regard to understanding the issues with which he is concerned. In some cases, interpretation may be easy. Sometimes helpees cannot understand the magnitude of the problems and its impact because they are too close to the problem. Sometimes helpees may overestimate the magnitude of the problem, and at other times the helpee may underestimate the problem because they are either too intimately involved, or are in denial of the situation. In either scenario, an impartial set of eyes and values can be of significant assistance.

Summary of Psychoanalytic Family Therapy

The following components are the basis of Psychoanalytic Family Therapy:

• Freudian drive psychology
• Self-psychology
• Object relations theory

STRUCTURAL FAMILY THERAPY

Major Contributor

Salvador Minuchin, a child psychiatrist and at one point in his career director of the Philadelphia Child Guidance Center, is the major contributor to structural family therapy. He is considered a giant in the field of family counseling.

Major Concepts

Three concepts provide the essence of structural family therapy: **structure, subsystems,** and **boundaries**.

Structure: Salvador Minuchin postulated that, to understand any system, one must be aware of the structure that supports the system. This concept is true of families. Each family has a structure that serves as the guiding force of family functionality. The more family members function within the system, the stronger the structure becomes, thus patterns of behavior become fixed. Because family members become accustomed to functioning within certain structures, their behavior becomes predictable. Therefore, it is important that the helper become aware of and understand the family structure. Minuchin posits that families, generally speaking, function within a small range of the behavioral options they have available to them. Although family members do not utilize the several or many options they have, changes in their patterns of living (or, to be more precise, changes in the structures with which they are familiar) can cause disruptions in the functioning of the family.

Subsystems: Each family member represents a subsystem, and other subsystems are formed as various family members join together to address issues, accomplish tasks, and/or influence family interaction. Subsystems are not static, they are fluid. Stated more succinctly, as certain family members form alliances or subsystems to address whatever issue or event is prevalent, this does not represent a permanent alliance. This subsystem may disband and other subsystems may be developed with other family members to address different issues. In fact, subsystems may be formed with a family member to address an issue involving another family member, and once that issue has either been resolved or reached a stalemate, later a subsystem may be formed with a family member who had been on the opposite side of the previous issue. It also should be noted that subsystems within a family are not always developed to deal with internal issues; rather, subsystems are often developed to deal with issues or concerns outside of the family structure that may be affecting the family. Additionally, issues do not always mean negative confrontational situations; they can refer to anything that may be impacting the family.

Boundaries: Nichols (2006) reminds us that individuals, subsystems, and whole families are demarcated by interpersonal boundaries —invisible barriers that regulate the number and extent of contacts that family members have with each other. He further points out that boundaries protect the autonomy of the family and its subsystems by managing proximity and hierarchy. Stated in other terms, boundaries protect and maintain the structure of the family with regard to things such as how emotionally close members relate to each other and the power structure within the family.

In Structural Family Therapy, boundaries are thought of ranging from **rigid** to **diffuse.** Rigid boundaries are restrictive with regard to interaction outside of the subsystem, and this restriction creates disengagement. **Disengagement,** as the term implies, represents lack of or poor communication. Nichols reminds us that disengaged persons or subsystems are independent but isolated; this isolation limits affection and assistance. Diffused boundaries lead to enmeshed individuals or subsystems. **Enmeshment** means individuals and subsystems are closely connected. Enmeshment leads to dependency. A clear boundary represents fewer restrictions, allows communication to flow relatively unencumbered, and thus effective interaction and engagement is likely to occur.

Goals

The goals for each family are dictated by the problems or behavior they present and by the nature of their structural dysfunctions. However, some of the general goals are:

1. Alter family structure of dysfunctional families so the family can solve its problems. In our discussion of major concepts, I pointed out that the family structure directs family interaction; therefore, defective family structure can create dysfunctional family interaction within and outside of the family.
2. Alter boundaries of dysfunctional families. The types of boundaries, particularly communication boundaries, have a major impact on whether the family is functioning appropriately. The helper must evaluate the boundaries to determine whether they are rigid, enmeshed, or clear. If the boundaries are impeding appropriate family interaction, the helper should work toward altering the impacting boundaries.
3. Alter or realign family subsystems. As previously discussed, family subsystems occur for a variety of reasons, and some can contribute to dysfunctional family relations. Astute helpers should be familiar with the family structure as well as the various subsystems and how they impact family relations.
4. Modify family functioning to increase the chances of family members solving their own problems. A goal of any helping relationship, whether it is individual, group, or family counseling, should be to strengthen the members' abilities to solve their own problems. Empowerment is the key to success.
5. Create an effective family hierarchical structure. Within a family, there are numerous possibilities of how communication and power flow. In many instances, they flow from the parents to the children; however, that structure may be from one parent to the

other parent and relayed to the children. In another scenario, the power may flow from one parent, excluding the other parent (assuming a two-parent family), directly to the children. Dysfunction within the family can occur as a result of how power flows and how power is or is not shared. Helping professionals have to be aware of these dynamics.

6. Assist parents to function together as a cohesive executive subsystem. As discussed in Item 5, within most two-parent families, the executive structure is the mother and father. Disagreements between the parents can create a fracture within the executive structure. Certainly, this fracture can create marital problems and also open the door for manipulation by the children as well as confusion on their part with regard to whom they should seek assistance and under which circumstances.

7. Differentiate the boundaries around enmeshed family members. The helper should be able to identify enmeshment, in that it represents family members who are closely engaged or dependent. Clearly, closeness within a family can be an advantage; however, when the closeness creates dependency, problems can arise. The helper should be aware of the degree of closeness and whether the engagement is hindering psychological and emotional growth. If the closeness is limiting growth, appropriate action should be taken to open boundaries so that growth can occur.

8. Increase interaction in disengaged families by making boundaries more permeable. Disengaged family members tend to be overly independent of each other. A major problem is that each member may have his or her own boundaries that other members are reluctant to or cannot penetrate. The helping professional recognizing this type of family dynamic must engage the family in being able to more effectively interact with each other.

Techniques

There are several techniques used by structural family therapists, ranging from establishing rapport to shaking up the family structure. All of the techniques are designed to restructure dysfunctional family dynamics. Some of the more commonly used techniques are: **joining and accommodating, enactment, structural mapping, highlight-**

ing and modifying interactions, shaping competence, and **boundary making**.

Joining and Accommodating: Helpers working with helpees, whether they are engaged in individual or family counseling, face the issue of gaining the trust of their clients or more commonly called establishing rapport. Joining and accommodating in Structural Family Therapy refers to entering the family's psychological world with the intent of understanding the family dynamics. This is done by gaining the trust of the family. Gaining the trust of the family can be done by getting to know each member of the family. Stated in other terms, establish rapport with each family member. It is not uncommon for family members to be defensive when faced with a stranger becoming involved in their personal lives. Therefore, the family counseling helper may have to deal with anxiety and feelings of defensiveness. One of the methods to ease this feeling of invasion is to get to know each family member as an individual and learn about his or her views with regard to the family dynamics.

Enactment: This technique involves engaging the family members in discussing issues facing the family–getting them to identify their take on the impact the issues are having on themselves and the family as a whole. Nichols (2006) indicates that this is a way in which the family helper can identify who talks to whom, how long, and under which circumstances. This type of discussion also provides the family helper with ideas of whether enmeshment and/or disengagement are prevalent.

Structural Mapping: Assessing the family structure is the primary objective of this technique. Through discussion, questions, and observation, the structural family helper attempts to: (a) determine how various family members relate to each other, (b) understand family communication patterns, and (c) understand family members' emotional attachments.

Highlighting and Modifying Interactions: This technique refers to concentrating on certain behaviors, such as communication patterns, and, after understanding the communication patterns, assisting in modifying those patterns and behaviors. The family helper's first concern should be with the family process of communication, rather than the content. To be more specific, the helper is mostly interested in, as previously stated, who talks with whom, when, and under which conditions. Additionally, the helper is interested in observing the effect this communication process has on each family member and the family as a unit.

Once the previously mentioned observations are made, the helper attempts to modify the behavior that is hindering the family from functioning at a more appropriate level. To get her points across, the structural family helper will emphasize her findings with voice intensity. This is done to get the family's attention and emphasize the importance of the helper's recommendations.

Shaping Competence: With this technique, the structural family helper takes somewhat of a behavioral approach by reinforcing positive actions, concentrating on things that the family is doing that enhance positive family dynamics. Additionally, the helper encourages the family members to do things for themselves rather than depend on her to do them. The obvious benefit is increased confidence and improvement of self-esteem of family members.

Boundary Making: As was discussed in the major concepts section, boundaries create problems for the family with regard to appropriate family dynamics. Thus, the structural family helper may have to help realign family boundaries.

Unbalancing: This technique involves the structural family helper taking sides with some family members against other family members. The idea is to break up subsystems and thus unbalance the family. The helper may take sides with one faction of a family on one issue and later take the side of other family members with regard to other issues. This does not mean that the helper agrees with the sides he is taking. Rather, as previously stated, the intent is to break up unproductive subsystems. This may be a controversial technique for some helpers, especially those who believe in helper neutrality.

Summary of Structural Family Therapy

The following three concepts are the essence of Structural Family Therapy:

1. Structural
2. Subsystems
3. Boundaries

COGNITIVE BEHAVIORAL FAMILY THERAPY

Major Contributors

Behavioral Therapy is the umbrella term for several types of psychological behavioral therapies. Behavioral therapy is a classic example of how therapies evolve over time as various contributors add their intellectual and scientific contributions to the body of knowledge regarding a particular treatment modality.

Ivan Pavlov is credited with beginning the process with his contribution of classical conditioning. B. F. Skinner added to the building blocks of Behavioral Therapy with his explanation of operant conditioning. Albert Ellis, with his rational emotive therapy, began the process of considering cognition as a key factor in explaining behavior. Aaron Beck and others expanded the concept of cognition, which led to Cognitive Behavioral Therapy. The reader is directed to individual counseling for more information with regard to these contributors.

Major Concepts

If there is a central concept that would cover most of the major forms of Behavioral Therapy, including Cognitive Behavioral Therapy, it is that behavior is maintained by its consequences. The old axiom of "for every action there is a corresponding reaction" applies to behavior therapy–for every action (behavior), there is some reaction (another behavior). The reaction will be perceived as either positive, negative, or neutral. The most important perceiver of the reaction is the person responsible for the behavior. It is his perception of the reaction that determines the response.

Some of the initial contributors to behavioral therapy, such as Pavlov and Skinner, viewed behavior as being devoid of cognition, primarily responding to stimulus. Cognitive Behavioral Therapy has added the component of humans as having control of their behaviors through the power of thinking. For a more detailed discussion of Behavioral Therapy and Cognitive Behavioral Therapy concepts, the reader is directed to the Behavioral Therapy section of individual counseling.

Goals

The goals of Cognitive Behavior Family Therapy are straightforward:

1. modify specific patterns of behavior to alleviate the present problem(s)
2. identify distorted beliefs and assist in changing them
3. extinguish undesired behavior and reinforce desired behavior.

Techniques

The techniques of Cognitive Behavioral Therapy depend on the type of behavior therapy being conducted. Some of the common techniques used, particularly with children are token economics (rewards given for appropriate behavior and rewards removed for inappropriate behavior). The time-out method relates to children who are exhibiting inappropriate behavior–they are placed in a location away from and without contact with other children for specific periods of time. Some counselors who work with children no longer subscribe to the use of time-out because they view this method as more punitive than therapeutic.

There are three general techniques that apply to all Behavioral Therapy, including cognitive behavioral family therapy: (a) assessment of behavior to determine whether the behavior should be maintained, altered, or eliminated; (b) evaluating the changes that need to be made–this evaluation is done in a collaborative fashion with the family; and (c) implementation of the agreed-on plan of action.

Summary of Cognitive Behavioral Family Therapy

The central theme of Behavioral Therapy is that behavior is maintained by its consequences (results of the behavior). Therefore, behavior resists change unless more rewarding consequences result from new behavior (Nichols, 2006).

NARRATIVE THERAPY

Major Contributor

Michael White, an Australian, was trained as a social worker and his major professional activities involved family therapy. He is the founder of the Adelaide Narrative Therapy Center in Australia, and he has written several books on Narrative Therapy.

Major Concepts

Narrative Therapy is a relative new therapy. Additionally, this therapy takes a somewhat different approach to viewing problems than some of the other family therapies previously discussed. The therapy blames the impact the problem(s) is having on the client, rather than the client's contribution to the problem. Stated in other terms, narrative therapists contend that the event's impact on the client creates the problems, rather than the client's interpretation of the problem. Offered as an example, let us say that a helpee is experiencing anxiety attacks. The Narrative Therapy point of view is that the anxiety attacks are causing the helpee to act irrationally, rather than the helpee's behavior causing the irrational behavior. The blame is placed on the problem or event, rather than the helpee.

Narrative Therapy contends that we develop stories of our lives based on experiences we have had. These experiences create expectations, which develop our story line.

Expanding on the central concept of this therapy, Narrative Therapy promotes the idea that events which occur in our lives help determine our behavior, and our perceptions of these events help form our opinions of ourselves, and we use these opinions to form a story of our life. Obviously, as humans, we experience many events; thus, we are selective with regard to which parts we select to become part of our life narrative. Thus, our interpretation of experiences determines how we view our immediate world. As we continue to construct our story line, we interpret events in ways that fit the story line we have developed for ourselves. This relates to the helping profession in this way: The story line that some helpees develop is one of discouragement and negative thoughts and views of oneself. Unfortunately, as the helpee develops the negative story line, he reinforces this story by viewing future events from a negative standpoint, thus continually building and expanding a discouraging story line of his life.

Nichols (2006) reminds us that the narrative metaphor focuses on clients' understanding and experience, expanding their attention to allow them to consider alternative ways of looking at themselves and their problems. Pointing out differences among most family therapists interpretation of issues and the manner in which narrative therapist view them, Nichols said the following: "Family therapists were interested in the family's impact on the problem, narrative therapists are interested in the problem's impact on the family" (p. 388). This reinforces the fact that has been identified earlier regarding the uniqueness of this form of therapy, which blames the problem for the behavior rather than the person's reaction to the problem. Nichols indicates that Narrative Therapy rescues families and blames society. Neither the patient nor the family is the problem—the problem is the problem. A unique approach indeed!

Goals

Once again, drawing from Nichols' excellent understanding of Narrative Therapy, the theory associated with this therapy is for the therapists to:

1. take a collaborative, empathic position with regard to the helpees story
2. observe the helpee's history to find times when he or she was able to resist the negative story line
3. use questions to better understand the story line
4. never label the helpee
5. assist the helpee to externalize his story.

Summarizations of the goals are: (a) **reconstruct his life**—assist the helpees to develop new and more positive stories of their lives, (b) **deconstruct lives**—assist the helpee to discontinue the negative perception of events that has led to the development of discouraging story lines; and (c) **externalize problems**—assist the helpee to remove the blame and shame that has been built with regard to the negative story lines developed by the helpee. Helpees are asked to identify times when he or she resisted the problem.

Techniques

The major techniques are the type of questions that the therapist asks. Questions should be designed to: (a) get the helpee to externalize the problem(s); (b) determine the effect of the problem; (c) identify the problem as the cause of the behavior, rather than the behavior as the cause; (d) identify how the problem has influenced the family; and (e) identify a time when the family was able to avoid or overcome the problem.

Another unique feature of this therapy is, once a new story line is written, the therapist and/or family members are encouraged to contact family and friends as well as anyone concerned with the actions of the helpee to inform them of the new story line. The narrative therapist often refers to this approach as authenticating the new story line.

Summary of Narrative Therapy

Narrative Therapy blames the impact of the problem(s) on the client rather than the client's contribution to the problem. The blame is placed on the problem or event rather than the helpee. Narrative Therapy contends that we develop stories of our lives based on experiences we have had. These experiences create expectations that develop our story line.

SOLUTION-FOCUSED THERAPY

Major Contributors

There are several contributors worthy of recognition for their contributions to this therapeutic approach. Two of the major contributors are a husband and wife team, Steve de Shazer and Insoo Kim Berg. Both contributors received a masters of Social Work and were mentored by the same person, John Weakland. Both were prolific writers and conducted workshops around the world promoting and teaching the philosophy of Solution-Focused Brief Therapy.

Major Concepts

Solution-Focused Brief Therapy takes a different philosophical approach to helping than the other therapies discussed in this chapter, with the possible exception of narrative therapy. Most of the other therapies are problem oriented. To be more specific, many of the other family therapies concentrate on problems that the helpee is experiencing and look for the root causes of the problems. Through the identification of problems and their causes, solutions to remedy the issues are constructed. Solution-Focused Therapy does not emphasize problems; rather, the emphasis is on identifying things within the helpee's life that are working well and using that as a basis to empower the helpee.

O'Connell and Palmer (2003) view this approach as a benefit to both the helper and helpee. They emphasize that this approach creates respect between the helpee and helper. They stated "one of the reported benefits of a more respectful working relationship is that practitioner's value and like their clients more! They see the client as a problem solver rather than as someone who is 'damaged,' 'ill,' 'inadequate,' or 'dysfunctional'" (p. 2).

Duncan, Miller, and Sparks (2003) list the three major concepts of this therapy: **If it ain't broke, don't fix it.** This relates to a rule that if the helpee is not complaining about something, do not delve into an issue. This is one of the major differentiations of Solution-Focused Therapy and some other family therapies. Other family therapies may seek issues family members are encountering and try to fix those issues, whereas Solution-Focused Therapy avoids involvement in identifying causes of problems, preferring to identify times when the helpee was able to overcome or minimize the problem. Thus, the helper highlights things that the helpee was doing correctly. This leads to the second concept–**once you know what works, do more of it**. Duncan and associates elaborate on this concept with the following remarks: "In practical terms, this rule means that therapeutic work should be focused on identifying times when the problem is not happening. Once found, all efforts should then be aimed at helping the client repeat and maintain these exceptional periods" (p. 107). The third concept is–**if it doesn't work, then don't do it again, do something different**. The general idea with this concept is to assist the helpee to discover what works well in her life and continue doing those things and also discover what does not work well and discontinue those activities and/or actions.

Goals

Nichols and Schwartz (2005) identify three major goals of Solution-Focused Therapy: (a) "Help resolve presenting complaints by helping clients do or think something different so as to become more satisfied with their lives" (p. 324). (b) Assist the helpee to change his thinking from problems to solutions. O'Connell and Palmer (2003) provide additional explanation of this goal with the following comments: "Solution-focused helpers believe in minimal intervention in clients' lives. They see the therapeutic task as raising clients' awareness of the constructive solutions already in their lives and to help them find ways to expand upon them" (p. 5). (c) Assist helpees to set clear and achievable goals.

Techniques

A solution-focused helper is free to use any techniques with which she feels comfortable as long as the techniques remain true to the basic concept of the therapy of concentrating on solutions, not problems. O'Connell and Palmer (2003) identify eight major techniques often used by solution-focused helpers: **problem-free talk, presession changes, goal setting, exception seeking, competence seeking, miracle questions, scaling,** and **between-session work**.

The technique of **problem-free talk** gets to the heart of Solution-Focused Therapy, in that the technique emphasizes the point that the helpees' life situation consists of more than problems. More important to the helpees' existence is the fact that, because they have arrived at this point in their lives, they have done some things that are positive. Therefore, the therapy talk should concentrate on the positive rather than the negative. Stated in other terms, this techniques zeroes on things that the family is doing right and uses this as motivation to continue doing those or similar actions or activities.

O'Connell and Palmer (2003) explains the technique and purpose of **presession change** with the following comments:

There is a core solution-focused belief that clients are already engaged in constructive action when they seek help. Some of these actions are positively helpful and others are preventing the situation from getting worse. Where practicable, clients are asked when they make an appointment to notice any changes that take place between then and the first session. Where that is not possible, the helper in the first session listens for evidence of what the client has already done that works for him or her. (p. 6)

The technique of **goal setting** is a collaborative effort between the helpee and the professional helper. As is the case in most, and should be in all professional helping relationships, the goals serve as directional signs for both the helpees and helper. Goals provide directions with regard to where the helping relationship is going and to some extent how the helpee and helper are going to get there. Thus, it is imperative that there is a meaningful collaborative relationship in the establishment of goals.

Exception-seeking technique realizes that for many families, when they come to counseling, they are and have been concentrating on the problem(s) that are impacting their lives. A technique that the solution-focused therapist uses is to get the family to focus on times when the problematic family life situation was either under control or being reasonably managed and use this information to help provide solutions to the issues being presented in therapy. Another part of this technique is to get the family to concentrate on areas of their lives where things are going well and see whether what is causing the positive life flow can be adapted to help deal with the problematic life situation.

The technique of **competence seeking** encourages the helpees to examine their resources, strengths, and adaptability and utilize these resources in improving their lives. According to O'Connell and Palmer (2003), an important aspect of this approach is the helper using "how" questions. O'Connell and Palmer say that how questions are much more productive than why questions. How questions tend to be more positive than why questions; also, how questions tend to aim toward solutions, whereas why questions often are examining problems.

The **miracle question** asks the helpees to imagine if a miracle happens and the life situation(s) in question were to go away, what would life be like? It appears that this type of exercise could have a beneficial result. To be more specific, as a result of the helpee's feelings at some level, the relief of not having the life issue(s) and knowing how life could be without the baggage of the issues, could serve as a motivator to seek positive solutions to those issues. This could cause the helpees to become creative in their thinking to reach resolutions to the issues.

Scaling technique is best explained by the following comments of O'Connell and Palmer (2003):

> Scaling can be used at any point in a session, but often supplements the miracle question. Normally the helper uses a scale of zero to ten, with ten representing no problem and zero representing the worst the problem has been, or perhaps how the client felt before contacting the helper. The purpose of scaling is to help clients set small identifiable goals; measure progress and establish priorities for action. (p. 9)

The **between-session work** technique is often used as the helper and helpees approach the end of the therapeutic sessions. According to O'Connell and Palmer (2003), the helper will provide a break in the closing sessions to compose his notes, which he will use to compliment the helpees on the progress they have made. In addition to the feedback, the helpees are given encouragement with regard to other things they could do to continue making progress.

Summary of Solution-Focused Therapy

Most of the other therapies are problem oriented; many of the other family therapies concentrate on problems that the helpee is experiencing. Through the identification of problems and their causes, solutions to remedy the issues are constructed. One of the uniqueness of solution-focused therapy is that it does not emphasize problems; rather, the emphasis is on identifying things within the helpee's life that are working well and using that as a basis to empower the helpee.

Conclusion of Family Therapy

Family therapy has become an integral part of the helping process when working with families and couples. Family counseling and therapy is so much a part of the psychological helping approaches that we may mistakenly think of it as having been a psychological tool as long as individual counseling and therapy. The fact is that family counseling and therapy emerged in the late 1940s and early 1950s. Although for young professional helpers this may seem like ancient times, the reality is that family counseling and therapy are relatively recent additions to the psychological helping family.

As is true with other forms of psychological and social helping professions, family helping approaches are in a state of evolving. The early family counseling and therapy approaches, generally speaking, based its work on analyzing families from a system and structural standpoint, as well as from patterns of family communication. Some of the earlier therapies, such as Bowen Family Systems Therapy and Structural Family Therapy, to mention only two, are good examples of these approaches. These and other therapies, such as Psychoanalytic Family Therapy and Cognitive Behavioral Family Therapy, are oriented toward viewing the problems of the family and the impact they are having. Narrative Therapy and Solution-Focused Therapy are perhaps models for twenty-first century therapies in that they take new approaches to assisting families deal with life situations.

As discussed in **Chapter 12's** summary of individual counseling, the previous discussion of selected family therapies is not presented as a comprehensive review of those therapies. The intent in the discussion is to provide basic information with regard to these family therapies. The reader is encouraged to conduct in-depth research of any of these therapies, as well as others not discussed in this chapter, to decide whether the basic concepts fit with the way he or she wants to conduct therapy.

Chapter Review Questions

1. What are the major concepts of Bowen Family Systems Therapy?
2. What are the major concepts of Psychoanalytic Family Therapy?
3. What are the major concepts of Structural Family Therapy?
4. What are the major concepts of Cognitive Behavioral Family Therapy?
5. What are the major concepts of Narrative Therapy?
6. What are the major concepts of Solution-Focused Therapy?

Mental Exercise

Instruction: Read the following case study and answer the questions listed at the end.

Calvin

Calvin is a 46-year-old White male successful businessman who has a yearly income of $146,000. Calvin graduated from both high school and undergraduate college in the top 10% of his classes. He continued his education by attending graduate school after marrying his wife, and completed a Master of Business Administration (M.B.A) degree.

Calvin is the youngest of three children born to very poor parents. He has an older brother and sister. His mother has a high school education and is a talented seamstress. However, because they live in an isolated area and the towns nearby are very small and basically economically depressed, she is only able to sew for neighbors, who often do not fully pay her for her work. Calvin's father is a farmer who graduated from the eighth grade. He is a good farmer, but has a small amount of land that is not very productive; therefore, he is barely able to provide a month-to-month living for him and his wife. This situation was true when the children were living at home with their parents. Calvin and his older brother, when they can, go to the farm to help their father, who lives 45 miles from where they live.

Calvin has been married for 22 years. He and his wife have four children, all girls. His wife has never worked outside the home since they have been married. Calvin has been fortunate to have always had a job, and through hard work and consistent saving, has been able to provide a comfortable living for his family.

Calvin and his wife have an active social life, belonging to several social clubs as well as being active in their church. Calvin and his wife have tried to provide their children with the many things they did not have as children, as both of them grew up poor. The children tend to take their standard of living for granted, and this is a source of frustration to Calvin because he believes the children should recognize how fortunate they are.

Calvin's siblings have not been as fortunate as he in that neither attended college. Calvin was fortunate to attend college on a football scholarship. Both his brother and sister are married, and neither of their spouses have good-paying jobs. Both his brother and sister and their spouses are hard-working honest people, but never seem to be able to "get ahead." They frequently ask Calvin for financial help, and this has created friction between him and his wife. Calvin's wife does not think it is fair for them to ask Calvin for help. She has stated many times, "It is not Calvin's fault they do not have better paying jobs." Although Calvin's parents never ask him for help, Calvin recognizes the fact that they have had and continue to have hard times, and he feels an obligation to help his parents. Calvin's wife is not pleased with him helping them, but rarely says anything as she does when he helps his brother and sister; however, her demeanor indicates to Calvin that she is not pleased. Calvin's wife has been fortunate in that her parents and siblings have not asked for financial help. It appears that they have reasonably paying jobs and/or they are good managers of their resources.

For the past two years, Calvin has had bouts of depression as he struggles with his feelings of guilt about his good fortune and the lack of fortune his parents and siblings have experienced. While he was attending undergraduate college, although he received a scholarship, his parents and siblings sent him money to help with his living expenses and tuition.

Because of depression, Calvin is seeking professional help.

Answer the following questions:

1. Which psychological therapy or therapies will you use in your helping relationship with this family? Explain why you have chosen this therapy or the therapies.
2. What are the major problems this family is encountering?
3. How will you handle Calvin's wife's feelings?
4. How will you attempt to establish rapport, trust, and so on?
5. Identify the crisis meeting resources (i.e., the resources the family has to help resolve their problems; e.g., good communication, money, strong family, and/or community support).
6. What is your perception of the family's definition of the event(s) (how does the family view the situation—do they consider it as one of the worst things that have or could happen to them, or do they consider it a problem but something that they can overcome)?

7. What will you do to get the family to acknowledge that there are problems?
8. How will you get all members of the family involved in the treatment?
9. What will be done to get the family reintegrated (i.e., functioning as a family unit)?
10. What type of behavioral changes will you attempt to get the family to work toward?
11. What are the goals you will encourage the family to establish for the helping relationship?
12. As you approach accomplishment of the agreed goals and objectives, what will you do to get the family to adapt to its new situation? (Remember that if you are successful in implementing behavioral changes as well as getting the family to accomplish their goals, the family structure, such as communication patterns, and other personal interactions among the family members will be different than what existed when they were having problems. This means that the family in some aspects has changed; therefore, the question is, how will you get them to adjust to these changes?)
13. How will you terminate the helping relationship?

References

Becvar, D. S. (2003). Eras of epistemology: A survey of family therapy thinking and theorizing. In M. P. Nichols, & R. C. Schwartz (Eds.), *Family therapy* (5th ed.). Boston: Allyn & Bacon.

Duncan, B. L., Miller, S. D., & Sparks, J. A. (2003). Interactional and solution-focused brief therapies: Evolving concepts of change. In T. L. Sexton, G. R. Weeks, & M. S. Robbins (Eds.), *Handbook of family therapy.* New York: BrunnerRoutledge.

Nichols, M. P. (2006). *Family therapy* (7th ed.). Boston: Pearson.

Nichols, M. P., & Schwartz, R. C. (2005). *Family therapy* (5th ed.). Boston: Allyn & Bacon.

O'Connell, B., & Palmer, S. (2003). Introduction to the solution-focused approach. In *Handbook of solution-focused therapy.* Thousand Oaks, CA: Sage.

Sexton, T. L., Weeks, G. R., & Robbins, M. S. (Eds.). (2003). *Handbook of family therapy.* New York: Brunner-Routledge.

Suggested Readings

Dent, A. (2004). *Sudden death in childhood: Support for the bereaved family.* New York: Butterworth-Heineman.

Helton, L. R., & Jackson, M. (1997). *Social work practice with families: A diverse model.* Boston: Allyn & Bacon.

Melzyer, L. (1988). *From denial to recovery: Counseling problem drinkers, alcoholics and their families.* San Francisco, CA: Jossey-Bass.

Nelson, T. S., & Thomas, F. N. (Eds.). (2007). *Handbook of solution-focused brief therapy: Clinical applications.* New York: Haworth Press.

Nichols, W. C., et al (Eds.). (2000). *Handbook of family development and intervention.* New York: Wiley.

Orton, G. L. (1997). *Strategies for counseling with children and their parents.* Pacific Grove, CA: Brooks/Cole.

Taylor, A. (2002). *The handbook of family dispute resolution: Mediation theory and practice.* San Francisco, CA: Jossey-Bass.

Wehrly, B., Kenney, K. R., & Kenney M. E. (1999). *Counseling multiracial families.* Thousand Oaks, CA: Sage.

Chapter 14

CONCLUSION

In this second edition of *The Professional Helper*, I have discussed some of the problems that inhabitants of the United States have experienced and what has been done to correct wrongs. Additionally, I have presented what I believe are some of the major issues that the United States of America will have to address and/or continue to address, and make significant decisions with regard to those issues. Stated in more succinct terms, what will the future of the United States look like as a result of the ways certain issues are addressed? Professional helpers are involved and will continue to be involved in analyzing issues and promoting responses as well as helping guide actions that will help provide solutions to those issues.

It is the contention of this author that there will be numerous professionals involved in helping evaluate and guide the nation through issues such as immigrations, women's rights, same-sex marriages, working with persons who have a disability, race relations, and a variety of other social issues, to mention only a few. Regardless of the educational background of the professional helper, all will have to be trained, educated and sensitive to the needs of those with whom they are attempting to help. While this edition has been primarily devoted to discussion of the roles of social and psychologically trained professional helpers, this author recognizes that many other types of professionally trained helpers will and must be involved in the helping process. As previously stated, this text has concentrated on professionally trained social and psychologically trained professionals; however, many of the characteristics discussed apply to other professionally trained persons. Additionally, while speaking of professionally trained persons, this does not mean the helper has to be trained at a master's and/or doctoral degree level. Advanced degrees do not guarantee competence; certainly, professional education is important and very helpful; however, certain other skills are equally important and several have been discussed. What has been discussed with regard to being an effective professional helper can apply to various levels of professional training.

As previously stated, helping is as old as human existence; everyone needs help, and, to some extent, everyone provides assistance to others. Therefore, there are various forms of helping, including informal and formal, as well as nonprofessional and professional. What has primarily been discussed in this text is professional helping.

As professional helpers, we have to be cognizant of the importance of our work and the impact our work can have on the lives of those whom for whatever reason engage us as helpers. Some helpees go to professional helpers because their situations, from their viewpoint, have gone beyond their abilities to control. They may have sought the advice of family and friends, but find that the situation has not significantly improved. They may have engaged in a variety of activities attempting to eliminate the worry involved in their life situation, but have not received the desired relief. Generally speaking, they are emotionally hurting and/or experiencing emotional stress and are expecting some relief. The point being made is that when helpees come to a professional helper, whether as self-referrals or otherwise, they need help.

As patients or clients seek help from a medical or legal professional, they look to him or her as professionals qualified to meet their needs. These types of expectations are no less true when a helpee seeks, or is referred to a professional helper. Therefore, it is incumbent on the professional helper to be prepared to meet the reasonable expectations of the helpee or those who have referred the person. This does not mean that the professional helper has to be a miracle worker and be able to solve any and all types of problems that helpees present. Obviously, this is unrealistic. However, the helper must be prepared to provide the best professional and ethical services possible. Consequently, this means that, as a professional helper, you must prepare yourself first by understanding yourself—understanding your emotions, your motivations, your attitudes and prejudices, and your attitudes about various life situations that helpees bring to the helping relationship. Second, as a helping professional, you must have a sound understanding of human behavior—to be more specific, you must have an understanding of the various ways that human behavior is motivated. Third, you must have some theoretical understanding of how to conduct the helping relationship from the standpoint of process, establishment of goals and objects, and implementation of the same. Finally, incorporated in all of the steps and process has to be adherence to ethical standards that protect the rights of the helpee.

The helper must prepare him or herself for this extremely important profession because a great deal is at stake. The results of most professional helping relationships go beyond easing or eliminating the emotional stress of the helpee—in many cases, the results impact family relationships and the ability to adequately interact with friends, coworkers, and other acquaintances. Certainly, the impacts go far beyond the immediate moments.

The helping professional has to view him or herself as one who is helping the helpee meet his or her potentials as a human being, thus being able to make positive contributions to the society in which he or she lives. There can be no more noble cause than this.

NAME INDEX

SUBJECT INDEX